ROUTLEDGE LIBRARY EDITIONS: THE ANGLO-SAXON WORLD

Volume 3

ANGLO-SAXON ENGLAND

ANGLO-SAXON ENGLAND

LLOYD AND JENNIFER LAING

LONDON AND NEW YORK

First published in 1979 by Routledge & Kegan Paul Ltd

This edition first published in 2023
by Routledge
4 Park Square, Milton Park, Abingdon, Oxon OX14 4RN

and by Routledge
605 Third Avenue, New York, NY 10158

Routledge is an imprint of the Taylor & Francis Group, an informa business

© 1979 Lloyd and Jennifer Laing

All rights reserved. No part of this book may be reprinted or reproduced or utilised in any form or by any electronic, mechanical, or other means, now known or hereafter invented, including photocopying and recording, or in any information storage or retrieval system, without permission in writing from the publishers.

Trademark notice: Product or corporate names may be trademarks or registered trademarks, and are used only for identification and explanation without intent to infringe.

British Library Cataloguing in Publication Data
A catalogue record for this book is available from the British Library

ISBN: 978-1-032-52976-9 (Set)
ISBN: 978-1-032-53420-6 (Volume 3) (hbk)
ISBN: 978-1-032-53421-3 (Volume 3) (pbk)
ISBN: 978-1-003-41195-6 (Volume 3) (ebk)

DOI: 10.4324/9781003411956

Publisher's Note
The publisher has gone to great lengths to ensure the quality of this reprint but points out that some imperfections in the original copies may be apparent.

Disclaimer
The publisher has made every effort to trace copyright holders and would welcome correspondence from those they have been unable to trace.

Anglo-Saxon England

Lloyd and Jennifer Laing

Routledge & Kegan Paul
London and Henley

*First published in 1979
by Routledge & Kegan Paul Ltd
39 Store Street, London WC1E 7DD and
Broadway House, Newtown Road,
Henley-on-Thames, Oxon RG9 1EN
Photoset in Palatino
and printed in Great Britain by
Lowe & Brydone Printers Ltd
Thetford, Norfolk
© Lloyd and Jennifer Laing 1979
No part of this book may be reproduced in
any form without permission from the
publisher, except for the quotation of brief
passages in criticism*

British Libary Cataloguing in Publication Data

Laing, Lloyd Robert

*Anglo-Saxon England.–(Britain before
the conquest).
1. Great Britain–History–Anglo-Saxon
period, 449–1066
I. Title II. Laing, Jennifer III. Series
942.01   DA152*

ISBN 0 7100 0113 4

Contents

	Acknowledgments	xi
one	**Introduction**	1
two	**Pagan Saxon England** c. AD 400–650	19
three	**Christian England** c. AD 600–800	88
four	**The Late Saxons** c. AD 800–1066	130
five	**Epilogue – The Normans and after**	183
	The best of Anglo-Saxon England	187
	Further reading	189
	Index	191

Illustrations

Photographs
1. Page from Gibson's edition of Camden's *Britannia*, 1695, illustrating Anglo-Saxon coins — 3
2. The Rev. Bryan Faussett (Liverpool City Museum) — 5
3. Page from *Inventorium Sepulchrale*, 1856 — 6
4. Page from *Remains of Pagan Saxondom*, 1855 — 7
5. The Kingston Brooch (Liverpool City Museum) — 19
6. Page from Faussett's diary, recording the discovery of the Kingston Brooch (Liverpool City Museum) — 20
7. The Monkton Brooch (Ashmolean Museum, Oxford) — 21
8. *Solidus* of Magnus Maximus (Heberden Coin Room, Ashmolean Museum, Oxford) — 30
9. *Solidus* of Constantine III (Heberden Coin Room, Ashmolean Museum, Oxford) — 31
10. Germanic belt-set, Dorchester-on-Thames (Ashmolean Museum, Oxford) — 34
11. Germanic style buckle, Colchester, Essex (Colchester and Essex Museum) — 35
12. Romano-Saxon pot (British Museum) — 36
13. Portchester, Hants, Saxon Shore fort — 38
14. Burgh Castle, Norfolk, Saxon Shore fort — 39
15. Pagan urn, Caistor-by-Norwich, R12 (Norwich Castle Museum. Photo: Hallam Ashley) — 41
16. Roman brooch, coin and mirror from Anglo-Saxon graves (Liverpool City Museum) — 42
17. Models of an Anglo-Saxon family (Leicester City Museum) — 45
18. Drawing of sunken-floor hut — 46
19. Sutton Hoo purse lid in gold and garnet (British Museum) — 49
20. Drinking cup, Sutton Hoo treasure (British Museum) — 50
21. The 'Anastasius Dish', Sutton Hoo treasure (British Museum) — 51
22. Benty Grange helmet, Derbyshire (Sheffield City Museum) — 51
23. The Sutton Hoo helmet (British Museum) — 52
24. The Sutton Hoo shield (British Museum) — 53
25. Inlaid *scramasax* from the Thames (British Museum) — 54
26. The Brighthampton sword: (a) scabbard mount; (b) chape (Ashmolean Museum, Oxford) — 55
27. Sutton Hoo lyre (British Museum) — 56
28. Quoit Brooch, Sarre, Kent (British Museum) — 58
29. Silver inlaid buckle plate, with Daniel in Lions' Den, Bifrons, Kent (Maidstone Museum) — 59
30. Mucking, Essex, belt-set (Mucking Post-Excavation. Photo: T. Jones) — 60

Illustrations

31	Cruciform brooch, Hockwold, Norfolk (Norwich Castle Museum)	61
32	Group of saucer brooches (Ashmolean Museum, Oxford)	62
33	Kentish square-headed brooch, Bifrons, Kent (Maidstone Museum)	63
34	East Anglian square-headed brooch, Kenninghall, Norfolk (Ashmolean Museum, Oxford)	64
35	Front (a) and back (b) of mould for square-headed, brooch, Mucking, Essex (Mucking Post-Excavation. Photo: T. Jones)	65
36	Jewellery from Mucking, Essex (Mucking Post-Excavation. Photo: T. Jones)	66
37	Rock crystal pendant, Kent (Royal Museum, Canterbury)	66
38	Cruciform long brooch (Leicester City Museum)	67
39	Small long brooch (Leicester City Museum)	67
40	Kentish disc brooches (Liverpool City Museum)	68
41	Kentish disc brooches and other jewels (British Museum)	70
42	Buckles with Style II filigree and other ornament (British Museum)	71
43	Crundale Down buckle (British Museum)	72
44	Drinking horn, Taplow (British Museum)	73
45	The Crundale sword pommel (British Museum)	74
46	The Caenby mounts (British Museum)	75
47	The Faversham phalerae (British Museum)	76
48	Bowl with faceted carination, Mucking (Mucking Post-Excavation. Photo: T. Jones)	77
49	Caistor-by-Norwich Urn E5 (Norwich Castle Museum)	77
50	*Stehende Bogen* urn (Norwich Castle Museum. Photo: Hallam Ashley)	78
51	Markshall Urn LXX (Norwich Castle Museum. Photo: Hallam Ashley)	78
52	*Buckelurne* (Norwich Castle Museum)	79
53	Body silhouetted in Saxon grave, Mucking (Mucking Post-Excavation. Photo: T. Jones)	80
54	Sewerby, Yorks, Anglo-Saxon 'live' burial (P. A. Rahtz. Photo: S. Hirst)	81
55	Anglian 'wrist clasps' from North Luffenham, Rutland (Leicester City Museum)	82
56	Bucket with human masks on vandykes, Mucking (Mucking Post-Excavation. Photo: T. Jones)	82
57	Glass 'claw' beaker, Mucking (Mucking Post-Excavation: Photo: T. Jones)	83
58	Byzantine buckle, Kent (British Museum)	84
59	Coptic bowl, Sutton Hoo (British Museum)	84
60	Reculver Church in 1816	88
61	The Devil's Ditch, near Newmarket, Cambs	94
62	Early foundations, Repton, Derbys	102
63	Brixworth, Northampton	103
64	The Durham Cathedral MS AII 10 (Dean and Chapter, Durham Cathedral)	105
65	The Book of Durrow (Trinity College Library, Dublin)	106
66	The Lindisfarne Gospels (British Library)	108

Illustrations

67	The Canterbury Psalter (British Library)	109
68	St Cuthbert's Coffin (Dean and Chapter, Durham Cathedral)	111
69	St Cuthbert's pectoral cross (Dean and Chapter, Durham Cathedral)	112
70	(a) and (b) Two views of the Bewcastle Cross (Photos: A. Crook)	113
71	The Witham Pins (British Museum)	114
72	Front (a) and back (b) of the Fetter Lane sword pommel (British Museum)	115
73	The Franks Casket (British Museum)	116
74	Aerial photograph of the Saxon palace complex at Yeavering, Northumberland (Photo: Dr J. K. St Joseph, Cambridge University Committee for Aerial Photography)	119
75	Tamworth Saxon water mill (Photo: P. A. Rahtz)	120
76	Merovingian tremisses, Sutton Hoo (British Museum)	122
77	*Thrymsa*, Crondall Hoard (Ashmolean Museum, Oxford)	123
78	*Sceattas* (Heberden Coin Room, Ashmolean Museum, Oxford)	123
79	Penny of Offa (Heberden Coin Room, Ashmolean Museum, Oxford)	124
80	Silver 'porcupine' *sceatta* and Northumbrian copper *sceatta*	125
81	Hereford defences (P. A. Rahtz. Photo: Hammond of Hereford)	128
82	Offa's Dyke from the air (Photo: Dr J. K. St Joseph, Cambridge University Committee for Aerial Photography)	129
83	The Alfred Jewel (Ashmolean Museum, Oxford)	130
84	Pennies of (a) Aethelred II and (b) Cnut	138
85	The Saxon *burh* of Cricklade, looking south (Photo: Dr J. K. St Joseph, Cambridge University Committee for Aerial Photography)	144
86	Coppergate, York (York Archaeological Trust. Photo: M. S. Duffy)	148
87	Late Saxon disc brooch, York (York Archaeological Trust. Photo: A. MacGregor)	148
88	Viking comb and comb case, York (York Archaeological Trust. Photo: A. MacGregor)	150
89	Wooden vessels, York (York Archaeological Trust. Photo: M. S. Duffy)	151
90	Pingsdorf Ware bowl (British Museum)	154
91	Thetford Ware bowl, Thetford (British Museum)	155
92	Winchester Ware vessel (Winchester Research Unit)	156
93	Coin of Alfred (Heberden Coin Room, Ashmolean Museum, Oxford)	157
94	Pennies of Burgred of Mercia and Edward the Confessor	158
95	Cheddar Palace after excavation (hall) (Photo: P. A. Rahtz)	159
96	Cheddar Palace – the fowl house (Photo: P. A. Rahtz)	160
97	Earl's Barton, Northants	163
98	Earl's Barton, detail	164
99	Haddiscoe Thorpe, Norfolk	165

Illustrations

100	St Cuthbert's stole (Dean and Chapter, Durham Cathedral)	169
101	Harleian Psalter (British Library)	170
102	Benedictional of St Aethelwold (British Library)	171
103	MS Harley 603 (British Library)	172
104	Winchester School Ivory of Nativity (Liverpool City Museum)	173
105	Book of Cerne (Cambridge University Library)	175
106	Jellinge sculpture, York (York Archaeological Trust. Photo: M. S. Duffy)	177
107	London ivory in Jellinge style (British Museum)	178
108	Gosforth Cross (Photo: A. Crook)	179
109	Cross head, Durham Cathedral (Dean and Chapter, Durham Cathedral)	180
110	Trewhiddle Hoard, Cornwall, horn mount (British Museum)	180
111	The Fuller Brooch (British Museum)	181

Maps

1	Germanic immigrants to Britain	xii
2	Britain in the early seventh century	92
3	England during the ninth century	134

Figure

1	The latest structures at Wroxeter, Salop (P. A. Barker)	37

Acknowledgments

We should like to thank the following individuals and institutions for providing illustrations for this book and allowing them to be reproduced: The Ashmolean Museum, Oxford, Plates 7, 8, 9, 10, 26, 32, 34, 77, 78, 79, 83, 93; Mr P. Barker, Figure 1; The Board of Trinity College, Dublin, Plate 65; The British Library Board, Plates 66, 67, 101, 102, 103; Cambridge University Library, Plate 105; Colchester and Essex Museum, Plate 11; Miss Andrea Crook, Plates 70, 108; The Dean and Chapter of Durham Cathedral, Plates 64, 68, 69, 100, 109; Mrs M. U. and Mr T. Jones, Mucking Excavation Committee, Plates 30, 35, 36, 48, 53, 56, 57; Kent Archaeological Society (Maidstone Museum), Plates 29, 33; Leicestershire Museums, Art Galleries and Records Service, Plates 17, 38, 39, 55; Arthur MacGregor and York Archaeological Trust, Plates 86, 87, 88, 89, 106; Merseyside County Museums (Liverpool City Museum), Plates 2, 5, 6, 16, 40, 104; Norfolk Museums Serice (Norwich Castle Museum), Plates 15, 31, 49, 50, 51, 52; Professor P. A. Rahtz, Plates 54, 75, 81, 95, 96; Royal Museum, Canterbury, Plate 37; Professor J. K. St Joseph, Cambridge University Committee for Aerial Photography, Plates 74, 82, 85; Sheffield City Museum, Plate 22; The Trustees of the British Museum, Plates 12, 19, 20, 21, 23, 24, 25, 27, 28, 41, 42, 43, 44, 45, 46, 47, 58, 59, 71, 72, 73, 76, 90, 91, 107, 110, 111; Winchester Research Unit, Plate 92. The remaining illustrations were either taken by the authors or, in the case of objects, taken for the authors by Liverpool University Joint Faculty Photographic Service, whose help with photographic problems has as always been invaluable.

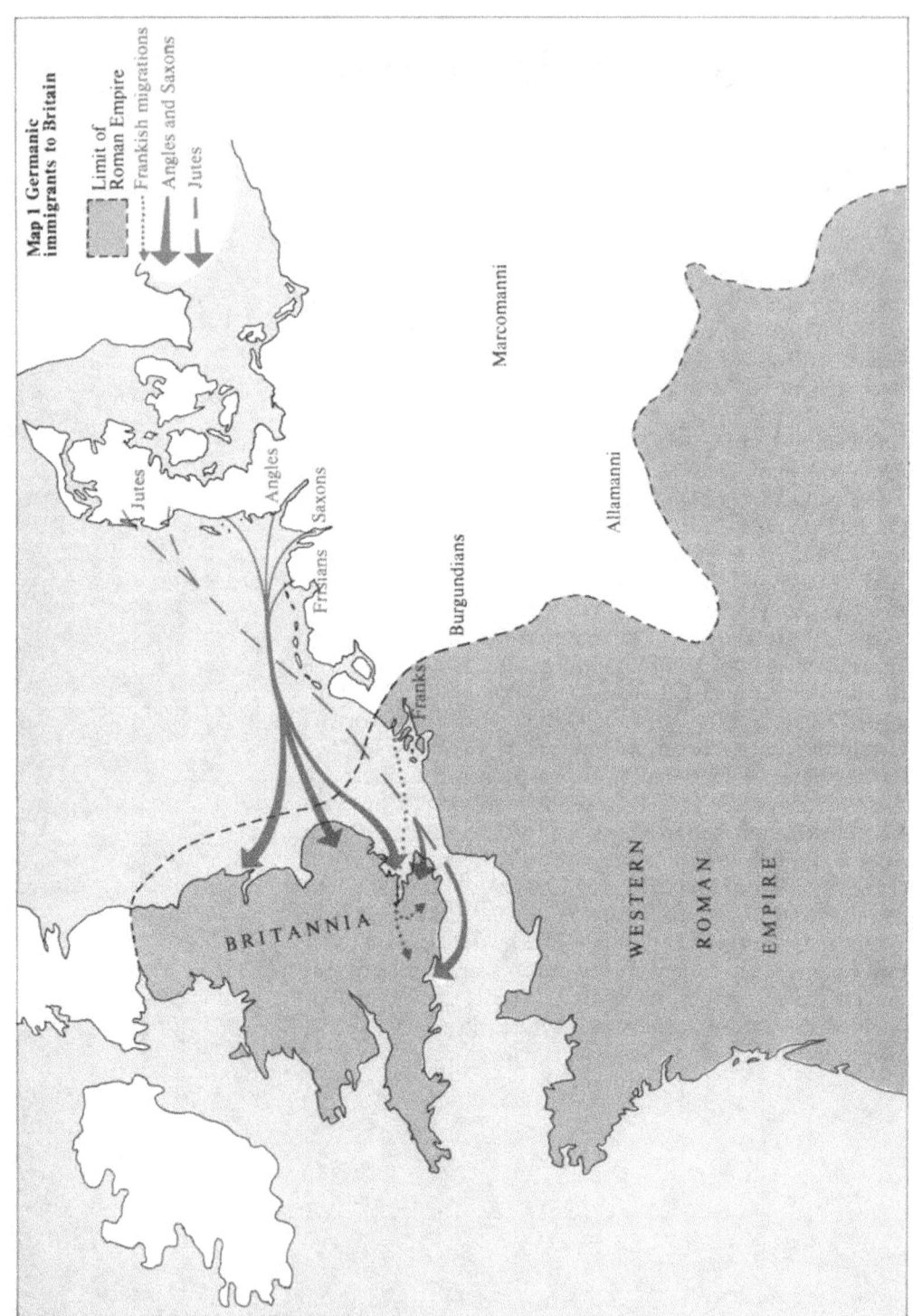

Introduction Chapter one

The 360 million English-speaking people in the world today owe their language in part to the adventures of an obscure Continental soldier of fortune called Hengist, who, in the fifth century AD, crossed the Channel with three shiploads of followers. The immigrants were pagan, non-literate and barbaric, heroes of a northern society so disorganized that they had little conception of national, racial or political loyalties. The Anglo-Saxons who made the land of England were a far cry from the peaceful farmers that the English people like to think of as the ancestors who gave them their culture, settlement pattern, many place- and personal names, some customs and above all their feeling of a common identity.

The story of the establishment of the Anglo-Saxons and their evolution into the English is of a flamboyant, dynamic barbarian culture, ultimately of Scandinavian origin, that between the fifth and the seventh centuries totally eclipsed the Roman civilization in Britain. In the seventh century the incomers were converted to Christianity and began to establish their own brand of civilized life. Within two centuries this new English society was itself fighting the greater barbarian and pagan threat of the Vikings. The Anglo-Saxons never did manage to totally subdue the Celts in Wales or Scotland.

In 1066 the Normans, the continental offshoot of the Vikings, arrived to dominate the land, and over the centuries the island has been host to Flemish, French, Scots, Welsh, Irish, Jews, Chinese, Pakistanis, Indians, West Indians, Poles and other small groups who have all added their share to English culture. Under the later veneers, however, the basis of everyday life even in the twentieth century owes much to the Anglo-Saxons.

The Anglo-Saxons have left some outstanding art treasures, from the barbaric splendour of a hero's funeral outfit to the subtle tones of Winchester School manuscript illumination. In late Saxon times the country led north-west Europe with her monetary system and her towns. Her legal institutions were advanced, her churches (many of which

Introduction

still stand at least in part) were fine architectural achievements and her churchmen were at the forefront of contemporary thought. Her art was the most mature in the west. The urbane, civilized Saxon of the eleventh century who rallied to resist William the Conqueror had little in common with his fifth-century ancestors.

The myth of the Anglo-Saxons
When asked, an old-fashioned Englishman might have been likely to say proudly that he was descended from the Anglo-Saxons. There his specific information would probably have ended: the only two memorable dates in early English history (as Sellar and Yeatman observed in their humorous book *1066 And All That*) are 55 BC when Caesar arrived and 1066 when William I did. Neither are of help in finding out who the Anglo-Saxons were. In fact, Anglo-Saxon history has until recently been largely disregarded educationally, dismissed (to quote the same jocular source) as a 'wave of Egg Kings', to be replaced by the more 'memorable' and comfortable myth.

The myth depended on a number of images of the Anglo-Saxon, some based on the stoical English virtues of 'fair play' and the 'stiff upper lip', others on an idea of agricultural primitivism – an impoverished but hard-working ploughman living in a bare wattle and daub hut in the midst of a luxuriant English landscape. Ascribing certain parts of our English vocabulary now regarded as 'crude' to an Anglo-Saxon origin added to this primitive impression. The image of the squalid-living Saxon was boosted by the sparsity of the archaeological remains. Slight marks in the soil were either undetectable or difficult to interpret with the techniques available until very recently, so that the excavated settlements seemed to have been appallingly primitive.

Like many myths, that of the Anglo-Saxon is fast becoming out of date, but it is curious and full of political and ideological undertones, not always in fashion. In the eighth century the Venerable Bede made the first attempt to discover the history of the English. His results perplexed him as well as later scholars and little further progress was made for eight centuries. The Normans were not anxious to further Anglo-Saxon nationalism, though it is fair to say that in the twelfth century there was great interest in England in Anglo-Saxon legal institutions which led to the transcription of Saxon legal documents – had it not been for this many texts would have been lost forever. The Anglo-Saxons were brought again to learned attention in

Introduction

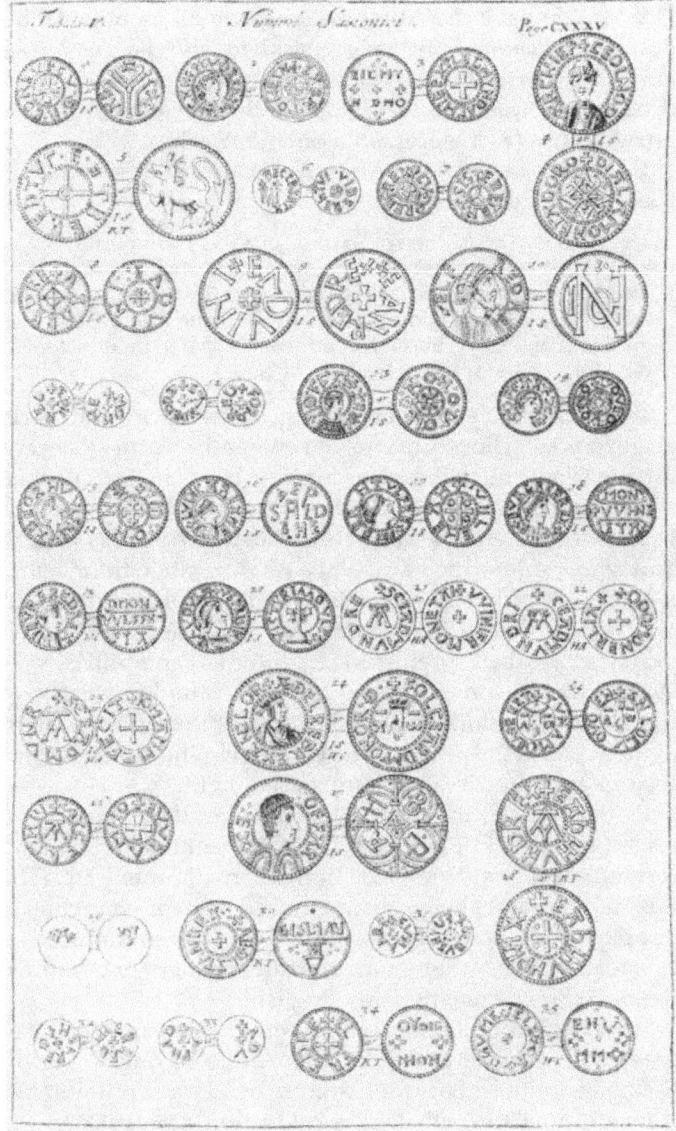

1 William Camden (1551–1623) was one of the first English antiquaries to take a serious interest in the Anglo-Saxons. His *Britannia* (first published in 1586) outlined their history. This engraving of Anglo-Saxon coins comes from Edmund Gibson's revised edition of 1695, which contained an extensive section on Anglo-Saxon coinage, the study of which Camden had himself pioneered. Compare no. 13 with Plate 79 and no. 10 with Plate 93 in this book

the sixteenth century by a combination of political and religious factors when Henry VIII founded the Church of England. A search for the cultural identity of the English nation ensued, and in the 1560s scholars were feverishly poring over old Anglo-Saxon documents. A Saxon dictionary appeared, and Old English place-names were used to plot the geography of Anglo-Saxon England. The earliest pagan settlers who followed Hengist, however,

Introduction

were still a total mystery. The antiquary William Camden (1551–1623) gave the Anglo-Saxons a small mention in his famous *Britannia*, and even studied the language: 'A language, then, which had lain dead for above Four hundred years, was to be reviv'd; the Books, wherein it was bury'd, to be (as it were) rak'd out of the ashes.'

Camden's view of the Anglo-Saxons was already cast in the mould of the myth:

> The Angles, Englishmen or Saxons, by God's wonderful providence were translated here out of *Germany*. . . . This warlike, victorious, stiff, stout and vigorous nation . . . spread its branches far and wide, being mellowed and mollified by the mildness of the soyl and sweet air, was prepared in fullness of time for the first spiritual blessing of God.

After this splendid beginning, interest in the early English was eclipsed by the seventeenth-century concern for the Classical civilization. John Aubrey (1626–97) spoke of the Anglo-Saxons as the 'Northern people who seemed to come to hasten time and precipitate the end of the world', and who 'declared so particular a war to written things, that it was not wanting in them that even the Alphabet had been abolished'. In that 'deluge of history', as the Anglo-Saxon period was called, prehistoric and Roman antiquities were said to have been destroyed and even the knowledge of them and their builders lost. Because of the lack of written evidence, and the primitive research techniques, the Anglo-Saxons appeared in a very unpleasant light.

By the eighteenth century the Saxons and Celts had been mixed together in one happy ancestral confusion by many romantic writers, who saw both as rustic intellects. The Saxons were not always distinguished from other medieval peoples, and one writer on architecture was so confused as to speak of 'Saxon' when he meant 'Norman' and 'Gothic Saxon' when he meant 'Early English'.

It was not until the nineteenth century that any headway was made in the study of the Anglo-Saxons. In 1819 Rickman noted that the church at Barton-on-Humber (Lincs.) must through logical deduction date back to the Anglo-Saxon period. It was not until 1834, however, that he felt confident enough to draw up a list of nineteen others which he supposed were as ancient. By 1846 little progress had been made. In that year a professor Henslow, discussing what are now known to have been Anglian pots, informed a learned society that he could 'see no reason for doubting their having been deposited by the aboriginal Britons'. In the same year some Anglo-Saxon ceramics from Kingston, Kent, were described typically vaguely and inaccurately as being of the 'Primeval Period'. The general unacademic approach to the study is demonstrated by the words of a barrow digger in 1874 who, on excavating in Cambridgeshire, noted with glee that he had found

> Three urns, the smallest very nice. . . . They were found in Stoney Hill with the skelitons and other things. I shall want ten shillings for the urns. I have got four heads two are Pretty good and two are Broaken and some Leg bones I have got a Bullick face with the horns on it Perfect.

In the interval, however, many finds had been proved to be Anglo-Saxon in date. In 1856 Charles Roach Smith published the diary of the eighteenth-century antiquary Bryan Faussett as *Inventorium Sepulchrale*, and the numismatist John Yonge Akerman brought out *Remains of Pagan Saxondom* the previous year. The latter publication inspired the historian John Kemble, who, whilst working in Hanover, noticed the similarity between urns there and in England. He published his discovery in 1856 and Anglo-Saxon archaeology had begun. It was not, however, a scientific study with the advantages that modern technology has brought. In 1857 the first recognized Anglo-Saxon hut was discovered in Oxfordshire, but the remains

Introduction

2 Portrait of the Rev. Bryan Faussett (1720–76). Faussett was one of the first antiquaries to excavate extensively the Anglo-Saxon burial mounds of Kent, and to record what he found. Like his near-contemporary James Douglas, who carried out similar investigations of Anglo-Saxon burial mounds, Faussett was a colourful character who narrowly escaped death as a child when thrown on the fire by the family's pet monkey. He built a famous folly in his garden at Heppington. He died believing the antiquities he had found and recorded so carefully were in fact Roman

Introduction

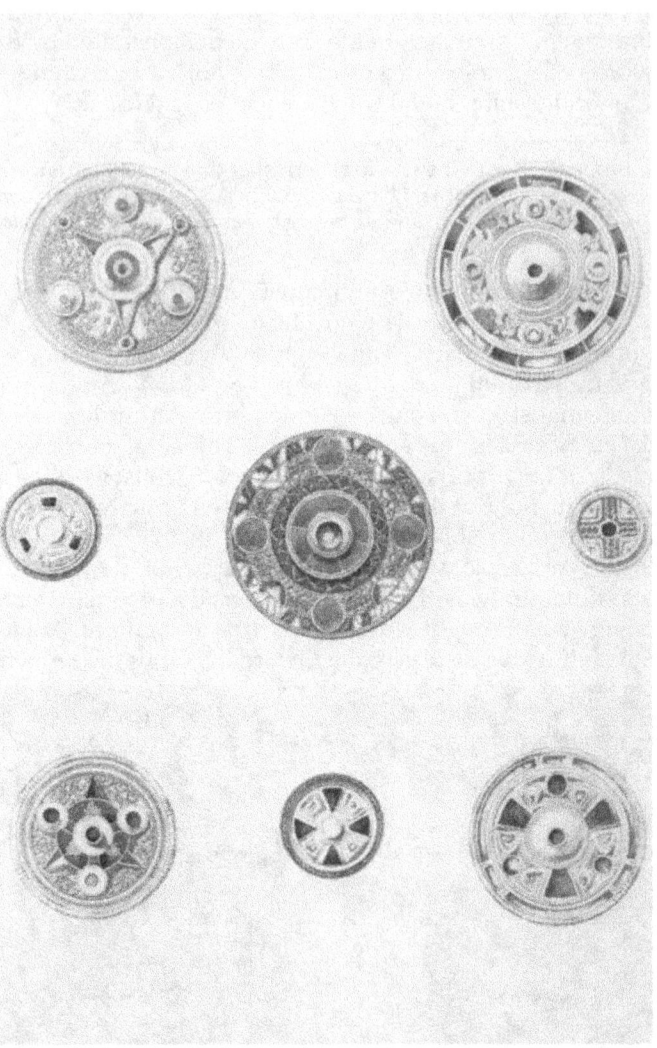

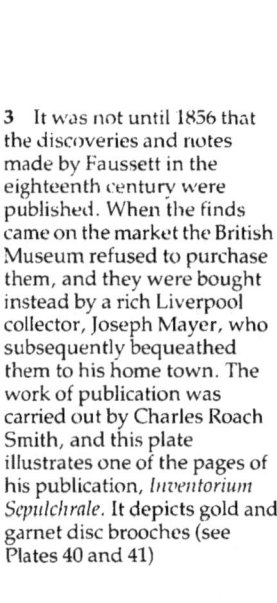

3 It was not until 1856 that the discoveries and notes made by Faussett in the eighteenth century were published. When the finds came on the market the British Museum refused to purchase them, and they were bought instead by a rich Liverpool collector, Joseph Mayer, who subsequently bequeathed them to his home town. The work of publication was carried out by Charles Roach Smith, and this plate illustrates one of the pages of his publication, *Inventorium Sepulchrale*. It depicts gold and garnet disc brooches (see Plates 40 and 41)

were so flimsy and apparently so squalid that the excavator interpreted them as being for industrial purposes. Progress was naturally slow, though for the rest of the century there was a gradual gathering together of facts from texts and badly recorded excavations. The pagan fifth and sixth centuries were still a mystery and only vaguely discussed.

The beginning of the twentieth century saw the publication in 1903 of the first of Baldwin Brown's monumental six-volume survey of the *Arts in Early England*, and in 1913 of E. T. Leeds's *Archaeology of the Anglo-Saxon Settlements*. The latter had chapters specifically dealing with the Angles, Saxons and Jutes whom Bede stated had invaded Britain,

Introduction

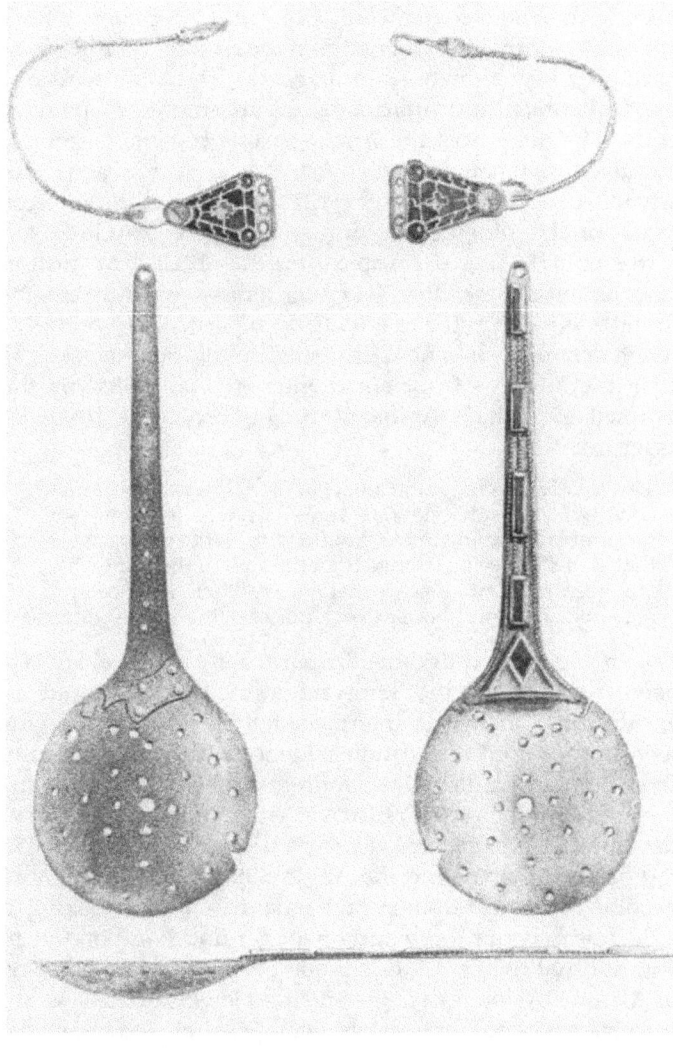

4 A year before *Inventorium Sepulchrale* was published, John Yonge Akerman published his *Remains of Pagan Saxondom*. Akerman was one of the first nineteenth-century antiquaries to consider Anglo-Saxon antiquities in their own right. Like many of his period, he was interested in all aspects of the past, and wrote several books on classical numismatics, publishing one of the first distribution maps in archaeological history. This plate from his book shows the gold and garnet clasps from the Crondall Hoard (for a coin from this hoard, see Plate 77) and a perforated spoon of the type found in Kentish cemeteries. Their function is uncertain

and it set the pattern for the next generation of scholarship. From then on archaeologists were determined to give the three groups of settlers material identity.

The myth prevailed despite these advances. It seems to have been felt in the early twentieth century that the English should not owe much to their Continental forebears. The view that the Saxons could have had any relationship with the Romano-British Celts they encountered that was not bloody, appears to have been untenable. Study was still permeated by the few historical sources which had led the antiquaries to their views. The situation was not aided by the First and Second World Wars, in which the English

Introduction

found themselves fighting the very peoples whose ancestors numbered among them the Saxons. The 1930s in particular saw a spate of propaganda which on occasions used historical and archaeological arguments to political ends. The subject of the Anglo-Saxons became extremely emotive. Archaeological techniques were still not advanced, and the results of excavations little different from those of the nineteenth century. The first Anglo-Saxon settlement to be excavated (in the 1920s) at Sutton Courtenay in Berkshire, had such flimsy ground remains that it was interpreted as having been particularly primitive when occupied. It is not surprising therefore that as late as 1948 the survey of ancient monuments compiled by the Council for British Archaeology reinforced the myth by asserting that

> The invaders were for the most part in a culturally primitive condition – their habitations were so wretchedly flimsy – a rectangular scraping in the ground with wattle walls and thatched roof seems to have been the limit of their known architectural competence – that traces of them have been recognized at only about a dozen places in the whole country.

In the past two decades in particular, archaeology has been using scientific knowledge increasingly both in excavation and in the interpretation of finds. Historians have reappraised the written evidence with a critical faculty that Camden would have admired and envied. There has, too, been an increase in discoveries as industry and urban developments expanded. An expansion of public interest in the past is notable, and the Anglo-Saxons have once more become of interest to their descendants who now belong to a European community and no longer find it imperative to suggest that their evolution is something special to the soil of Albion. No longer are the splendid jewels of the seventh century a phenomenon to be wondered at – they are the technological achievements to be expected from a people who far from being primitive, were culturally developed when they arrived on British shores. The growth of the English nation was not a miraculous flowering in the seventh century out of very unpromising material, but the natural development of a society whose barbarian ancestors had repeatedly wished to enjoy the benefits of Roman civilization on the Continent. Latest research suggests that the Anglo-Saxons did not massacre or drive out the native Romano-Celts as the ancient writers would have us believe, but that they took what they wanted from the dying civilization of Roman Britain, assimilated some ideas, rejected others, and modified yet more until they had

Introduction

produced their own brand of civilization, far removed from the myth that had grown up around them.

Nevertheless, although the time is probably becoming ripe for a reappraisal of the Anglo-Saxons, the state of knowledge is still fragmentary. There are still remarkably few settlements of the pagan Saxon period (c. AD 400–600), the middle Saxon period (c. AD 600–800) or even the late Saxon period (c. AD 800–1066) that have been found and excavated. Dating objects or buildings discovered is still extremely difficult and sometimes impossible. The written evidence does not always coincide with the archaeological results in general terms, much less in the details. The Anglo-Saxons tended to build in timber, and to make their possessions out of perishable materials such as wood, leather or cloth, so that those objects that do survive often give a distorted impression of the life of their owners. It therefore often becomes necessary to ask questions we know can be answered, rather than those we would like to have answered. It would be unreasonable to feed a computer with data about oranges and ask it questions about Nell Gwynn: yet only too often we look at the surviving pots and brooches of the Anglo-Saxons and expect them to tell us about the political affiliations or philosophy of, for instance, Hengist.

It is the period from the end of the Roman era in 410 to about 600 when such distortions are most evident. It was long known as the the Dark Ages since there were few written sources. Modern archaeological techniques in particular have managed to make out a few blurred shapes as though with an infra-red camera, but what William Camden said in the sixteenth century can still find some sympathy with modern readers:

> The origins and etymologie of the Saxons, like as of other nations, has been confounded with fabulous conjectures, not only by Monks, who understood nothing of Antiquity, but even by some modern men who pretend to an accuracy of judgement . . . . that they were one nation and called by one general name, sometimes *Saxons*, sometimes *Angles* or (to distinguish them from those left behind in Germany) Anglo-Saxons, is pretty plain . . . . what time soever they came over 'tis pretty plain they show'd a wonderful courage.

The people of early Europe

Around the time when the Star was guiding three wise men to a small town called Bethlehem, the Roman Empire, under its first and arguably most glorious emperor, Augustus, included most of what became Europe. The most northerly

Introduction

province at this time was Gaul. Here in 58–51 BC Augustus' adoptive father, Julius Caesar, campaigned against the Celtic peoples who made up the population of most of France, Britain and Central Europe. On the border of the civilized world were other barbarians, distinct from the Celts but ultimately of a common origin. These included the tribes known to the Romans as the Germani, who lived in Scandinavia and the North German Plain. From Classical sources, three main groups can be distinguished – the Scandinavians, a western group who included the Thuringians, Saxons, Angles, Frisians, Franks and Allamanni, and an eastern group who numbered amongst them the Vandals, Lombards, Burgundians and Goths (see Map 1). It was in particular the Angles, Saxons, Frisians and Franks, with the more enigmatic Jutes, who seem to have predominated in the making of England and who, with other groups, eventually gave rise to the modern Netherlands, Germany and Scandinavia.

The Germani were obscure until the second century BC when they came briefly into the spotlight of history, by amalgamating with some of the Celts, migrating south and threatening the Roman world. After several crushing defeats, the Roman army, under the command of the notable general Marius, met the invaders at modern Aix and diverted a probable invasion of Italy.

Julius Caesar encountered the Germani in the source of his Gallic Wars and set down information about them and their habits. To Caesar and to subsequent generations of Romans they were total savages – *feri*, wild things. Augustus refused to believe that the Germani could not be tamed. Between 12 BC and AD 9 a series of campaigns were devised to bring them into the Imperial fold. In AD 9, three legions under the generalship of Varus marched into the northern forests intent on conquest and never returned. This appalling dishonour was the largest single defeat in Roman history. Thenceforth the Romans were confined to the west bank of the Rhine where they traded with the barbarians with little hope of civilizing them. The Germani, however, were interested in gaining some of the benefits of civilized life for themselves and despite the strong frontier there was a great cross-current of goods and no doubt ideas between the two sides.

Roman historians were not particularly interested in recounting the exploits of the wild tribesmen who had caused them so many shaming defeats. Were it not for the *Germania* of Tacitus, written in about AD 98, the few remarks by Caesar, the *Geography* of Ptolemy (c. AD 140) and

Introduction

the fourth-century writings of Ammianus Marcellinus, we would be left with very few historical statements. The reluctance of Roman writers to mention the Germanic barbarians has not misled scholars, however, for there is ample material evidence.

Lifestyle

To gain an impression of the lifestyle of the barbarians who became the first English, the best place to search is Scandinavia, where the peat bogs have preserved otherwise delicate and perishable material including human bodies. Justifiably the most famous such burial is that of the Tollund man, who was found in a Jutland bog where he had been thrown after strangulation. His eyes are underlined, his forehead wrinkled and his skin tanned. On his head he wore a leather cap, and in his stomach remained the contents of his last meal. He had eaten a porage of barley, linseed, knot-weed and other weeds of cultivation. This unappetizing breakfast was matched by one consumed by a man buried at Grauballe, which had consisted of no fewer than sixty-three kinds of grain and weed seeds. There are 400 such burials from Scandinavia and northern Europe, spanning the period from 100 BC to AD 500, and they provide a reasonably accurate picture of the Germani and by extended inference of the Anglo-Saxons who came to Britain. Most seem to have been large-limbed, with the red or blond hair remarked on by Roman writers. The men were clean-shaven, though beards and moustaches are sometimes shown in sculptures. The fashionable man about to be thrown into a bog was happy to been seen dead in a short cloak of wool or a leather cape over trousers and tunic. The Thoresbjerg bog has produced examples of these clothes and one woollen garment which had been dyed a rich indigo. Iron Age and Migration period ladies were more modest than their Bronze Age predecessors (who are known to have worn see-through mini-skirts upon occasion). One Germanic lady's outfit from Huldremose, Denmark, consisted of a one-piece sack-like dress, somewhat reminiscent of a Greek peplos. Gathered elegantly at the waist and shoulder, a fold could be left behind the neck to provide a hood. Another had a woven woollen skirt in two shades of brown check which was fastened with a pin. For rougher weather this outfit seems to have been covered by two skin capes. In many ways the wrapped-up layered look of these ladies can have differed little from fashions in the 1970s.

Archaeologists have encountered a number of settlement

Introduction

types and burial customs. The Franks, for instance, inhumed their dead, the bodies being laid out in neat rows with pottery, weapons, jewellery and household items. The Angles practised cremation; the corpses were burned on pyres and the ashes interred in an urn. These burials seldom contain any grave goods of note, though sometimes a brooch or small personal possession was either added to the urn contents or burnt with the body. The Saxons for the most part favoured cremation: cemeteries of up to 2,000 urns have been found between the Weser and the Elbe. A few Saxon groups, however, preferred to inhume. The people of Jutland used both types of ritual. Horse sacrifices sometimes accompanied inhumations in central Germany, in the basin of the River Saale. In Sweden graves were marked by mounds of stone (barrows). Boats as receptacles for the dead were used in Sweden, Denmark and Norway upon occasion, a custom used for chiefs and their wives and which was of significance in Anglo-Saxon England later.

Habitation has been found in many forms, though no towns are encountered among the early northern barbarians. They lived both in villages and in single farmsteads, their houses being predominantly rectangular and built of timber. Along the north German coast villages have been found which were adapted to meet the problems of flooding in the low-lying lands. The village stood above the level of the surrounding countryside, the successive houses being built over the debris of the old rather in the manner of the *tells* of the Near East. Their occupants were mainly stock raisers, predominantly cattle men. Some villages were defended by a palisade, and a few, in central and southern Sweden, were more strongly fortified, rather like Celtic hillforts. The plans of some of these early settlements are echoed in later times – the radial layout of some modern villages in Holland and north Germany could be found 2,000 years ago.

Houses took a variety of forms. Vallhagar in Sweden, for instance, was occupied in the fifth and sixth centuries AD, and here the homes were of the type known prosaically as longhouses. These are houses in which the dwelling quarters for humans are under the same roof as, and in alignment with, those of the animals. Usually a cross-passage separated the two, but the general effect was to preserve warmth. At Vallhagar the entrances were at the ends rather than in the long sides, and the buildings, somewhat atypically, had stone walls.

Outside Scandinavia, any newly-wed groom might normally have expected to take his bride to a wooden aisled house. These were usually twice as long as they were broad, with wattle walls woven between a framework of stakes, the roof being supported by two rows of uprights perhaps tied by cross-beams. Sometimes added support was given to the walls by sloping exterior buttresses of timber. The floors were of beaten earth or clay and the roofs probably thatched. Such longhouses (which could be up to 24 or 27 m in length) have a long ancestry in prehistoric Europe.

Alongside the larger buildings were huts with sunken floors (*grubenhäuser*). These were frequently 3 m by 2 m or even smaller, and seem to have been put to a variety of uses – workshops, weaving sheds, bakeries and stores as well as dwellings. Some were relatively developed in plan, with a porch, and a plank floor covering the hollow. Similar buildings of plank and turf construction were to be found in Frisia in the eighteenth and nineteenth centuries and are also to be seen in the paintings of Van Gogh.

A few field systems have survived. Many seem to have been similar to the so-called 'Celtic fields' of Iron Age Britain; a patchwork of small rectilinear enclosures at odd angles, demarcated by stone or earth banks or palisades. There is no evidence for open-field agriculture until the Middle Ages.

Possessions were made of wood and have thus rarely survived except in waterlogged conditions. Trays, bowls, dishes and stave-built vessels such as buckets were used. Pottery was made locally, usually within the community, and both Celtic and Roman fashions are sometimes reflected. Glassware was first imported from the Roman factories in the Rhineland and later from their Frankish replacements. The most characteristic vessels to grace Germanic feasts were the drinking horns that were copied in glass from the real thing.

As was fitting for barbarians, the most common weapon was the sword. Made from iron it was frequently forged by pattern-welding, whereby bars of iron were twisted together and then hammered out to produce a patterned blade which was given a cutting edge with two further bars. The pattern was made prominent by filing, etching and polishing. Some swords had a ring attached to the hilt for magical purposes. Others had magical pendants of amber, crystal or meerschaum ornamenting the hilts or scabbards. Swords in general had a magical importance and were given names. They symbolized the fealty of the warrior to his leader, the duty of the king, the achieving of manhood and other facets of Germanic life.

Introduction

After the sword the most important weapon was the *angon* (barbed javelin), which was derived from the Roman throwing-spear, the *pilum*. The Franks favoured two other specialist weapons, the *francisca* or throwing-axe, which had a carefully weighted head, and the *sax*, a single-edged short-sword. Armour was rarely worn, though chiefs sometimes donned chain-mail and helmets. The main type of helmet was the conical iron *spangenhelm*. This was made up of leaf-shaped plates attached to a frame, the plates being coated with gilded bronze and the interior being lined comfortably with leather. Cheek-pieces were hinged to the cap, and chain-mail protected the neck. A fine example of such a helmet, datable to about AD 600, was found at Morken in the Rhineland.

Trade

Trade with Rome was common despite ups and downs. Caesar, for instance, records that entrepreneurs were operating a trade across the Rhine with tribes that included the warlike Suebi. These tribesmen, unlike other north-west European barbarians, refused wine on the grounds that it rendered men too soft and like women to be able to endure hardship.

By the late first century AD the trade was flourishing, having been fostered in the early part of the century by an opportunistic businessman, Maroboduus, chief of the Marcomanni (see Map 1, p. xii). He correctly sized up the Rome market as being eager for amber and set about satisfying the demand. Meanwhile, some Romans tried to by-pass the middlemen and go straight to the source, while barbarian tribesmen brought their wares to market places on the edges of the Empire. The trade flow was augmented by diplomatic gifts, of which a probable example is the hoard of silverwork from Hildesheim. Discovered in 1868, amounting to seventy pieces, it is one of the finest collections of silver from the Roman world.

Until the middle of the second century trade prospered, but in 173 trouble in Marcomanni country finished them in their role as middlemen. In the late Roman period, however, trade picked up, along somewhat different routes, including an eastern one along Russian and Polish rivers. This was probably controlled in some measure by the Goths, the group of northern barbarians who established themselves on the Black Sea. Along this route flowed gold, in the shape of Imperial coinage, and the collapse of the Roman Empire did nothing to stop the tidal flow, though now it came from the 'new Rome' of Byzantium. Much seems to have wound up in the islands of Bornholm, Oland and Gotland – a hoard from Broholm on the island of Fyn, for example, yielded 4,153 g of the precious metal.

It was not merely the chieftains who benefited from the trade. Even minor settlements have produced their quota of Roman coins and pottery. By the fourth century, Classical influence was prevalent throughout the lands of the Germanic tribes: it extended to the types of brooches, armlets and pendants worn, to the forms of pottery used and to the type of decoration employed on possessions. A leather belt from the bog at Vimose is decorated with a design based on a Roman dolphin. Roman influence permeated to the most mundane level, as exemplified by the querns for grinding grain that were imported from the lava quarries of the Eiffel.

Along the frontiers too barbarians learned the Roman way of life by being employed to police the no-man's land. Their graveyards have been found to contain merchandise produced in Roman workshops in northern Gaul. The orientation of their graves (to the south instead of the west) betrays their Germanic origin. The men were buried with heavy iron swords, and the women with bow and other brooches in pairs. The barbarian attitude to Rome is summed up by the fourth-century burials at Furfooz in Belgium. Here the dead were laid to rest between the pillars of a still usable Roman bath block but in accordance with Germanic custom; paying lip-service to Roman civilization even as it was disregarded.

Like most barbarians, the Germani were organized into tribes. The basis was kinship, and blood ties united warrior bands within the larger tribal group. In the absence of a formal legal system, blood-feud was an important factor in the carrying out of justice. The kin of the wronged man sought retribution by avenging themselves on the entire kin of the offender, though vendetta could in many cases be avoided by payment, a system no doubt devised by some Germanic 'Godfather'! Matters which required more formal trial went before the leading man of the community. Chastity was highly regarded and adultery (which could only be committed by women!) seems to have been, on some occasions at least, punishable by death. Women were the property of their husbands, and could thus be bought and sold. Sometimes widows of important men were sacrificed, and some males of high birth enjoyed polygamy. Notwithstanding their lowly and, by modern standards, unliberated status, some women managed to attain positions of power and respect in the community.

Introduction

Government was generally controlled by the tribal chief, the council of the elders, and the general assembly of all the warriors. Chiefs were sometimes elected for military campaigns, but others held their position due to royal birth and were, in effect, kings. Kings could not however command implicit obedience, nor were they necessarily succeeded by their sons.

Apart from the freeborn, there were also slaves. Unlike their Roman counterparts enslaved people lived in their own homes and paid their masters grain, cloth or cattle at regular intervals.

The great migrations

From the third century AD onwards there were changes. First there was a growing awareness that perhaps the impregnability of the Roman Empire was a myth and that once the frontiers had been breached there was nothing to stop settlement within its bounds. Events within the Empire did little to contradict this impression. Pirates found life increasingly easy and there was civil unrest. In Gaul dissatisfied peasants made guerrilla attacks on the provincial administration, while in Persia, Roman forces were hammered and the Emperor Valerian was taken prisoner by Shapur I in 260, from which captivity he never escaped. In the 260s Roman Dacia (present-day Romania) was overrun by Goths and the province had to be abandoned. In the later years of the third century there were widespread rebellions in Gaul, Roman Britain temporarily broke away under the leadership of an ex-Channel pirate called Carausius, and there were uprisings in Spain. The barbarians had been set on the move and it was only a matter of time before they breached the Imperial frontiers for good.

It seems that the immediate cause of the movements was the aggression of the Huns, whose very name has come to be used as a symbol of barbarism. These nomads have obscure origins: they seem from descriptions to be of Mongolian stock and to have come from Asia. It is possible that feuds with the Chinese started their motion westwards. Certainly nomad Mongols were raiding the Great Wall in the second century BC. By the late fourth century AD the Huns raided in Mesopotamia and Syria and in about 372 they came into Europe, settling in Hungary where they terrorized the Ostrogoths. By 440 their leader was the terrible and by now semi-legendary Attila, who, it is recorded, walked haughtily, rolling his eyes from side to side. A war-lover of restrained action and great counsel, he was apparently gracious to suppliants and lenient to those he protected.

This short, stocky individual, with his small head and eyes, flat nose and grey beard, advanced to Constantinople in 447 where he defeated the imperial armies, forcing the Emperor to submit and make payment of territory on the Danube and hard cash. Attila then turned his ambitions to western Europe and his followers swarmed into Gaul, ostensibly to drive out the Visigoths. Near Troyes they were defeated but, after a brief respite, Attila led his men towards Italy. His campaign was successful, but for some reason that has long aroused curiosity he withdrew to Hungary and from then on the Huns were of little importance in Europe. They had, however, made an impact that Western Europe was never to forget.

Their enemies the Goths had a longer career in Europe. Moving ahead of the Huns, they pressed ever westwards. They had divided into the Ostrogoths and the Visigoths. The latter defeated the Roman forces at the battle of Adrianople in 378 and then made Constantinople their target. Finding this hurdle too great they turned their attentions west and the eventual result was the sack of Rome in 410, under the leadership of Alaric. In the long run the sack of Rome was of minimal significance, for Alaric was a Christian and looted only the houses of the rich rather than devastating the entire city. For contemporary Romans, however, it had a profound importance; to them the fall of the Imperial city symbolized the end of the old order and the collapse of all worthwhile values. The Visigoths subsequently settled in Gaul and Spain, staying in power in the latter area until 711 when it was conquered by the Moors.

In contrast, the Ostrogoths found it more difficult to escape and from about 370 were under Hunnish domination. In 454 they managed to throw off their oppressors and turned their thoughts to following the route taken earlier by their cousins. They moved into Italy in 488 and under Theoderic established a new Ostrogothic kingdom which copied the Roman Empire in its administration. Ostrogothic art and coinage too followed Imperial models as far as possible. As an entity the Ostrogoths were finished when the Emperor Justinian reconquered Italy in 535–55.

The other great barbarians who had an important impact on late Roman civilization, and thereby indirectly affected smaller groups of Germanic tribes, were the Vandals. In 406 they walked across the frozen frontier of the Rhine and began a career of raiding in Gaul: Mainz, Trier, Rheims,

Introduction

Amiens, Boulogne and Tournai were among the first cities to understand the meaning of the word 'Vandal'. It was recorded at the time that priests were burned alive, nuns raped and vineyards and olive groves devastated. After two years or so without any real opposition the Vandals moved into Spain where a further two years of pillaging ended only when a Visigothic army was put in the field by the Romans. By this time the branch of Vandals known as the Asdings had adapted themselves to a life at sea and successfully seized the coast of Spain ('Andalusia' comes from the word 'Vandalitia'). Under their leader Gaiseric they aimed to possess the cornfields of north Africa. In 439 the Romans had to abandon their African lands whereupon the Vandals set up their own king. In the sixth century, however, the Vandals once more acknowledged Roman overlords.

The success of the great migrations would not have been possible without the other problems that were besetting the Roman Empire, not the least of which was inflation. By the mid-fifth century, however, the pattern of civilized life in the west was at an end. Constantinople, the capital of the Eastern Empire, flourished for another thousand years until its fall, as Byzantium, in 1453. Rome itself, still within the Eastern Empire's protection, kept its influence through the Christian Church.

In place of the western provinces of the Roman Empire barbarian-based societies grew up. In many cases the old way of life was not smashed: barbarians billeted themselves on the estates, taking a proportion of the lands but leaving the landowner largely to his own business. As a result written sources did not end on the Continent, and the two cultures interacted with one another. Of the new forces, the Franks grew to power. This led to the establishment in 800 of the Holy Roman Empire (the Carolingian Empire) by Charles the Great, which was to have an important influence on the rest of European culture and development.

In this manner the barbarians took advantage of the Empire's weaknesses and managed to disrupt Classical ways of life on the Continent. It was this break-up of power that led to the abandonment of the most northerly Roman province, Britain, in 410, and which gave the Anglo-Saxon barbarians their chance of colonization. The reasons for their willingness to cross the Channel are obscure, but various geographical factors such as rises in sea level as well as the pressures of the other barbarian groups, may have contributed.

Pagan Saxon England
c. AD 400–650

Chapter two

A spectacularly golden reminder of a barbarian past glinted in the August sunshine of 1771. Eleven centuries before the brooch had adorned the shoulder of an Anglo-Saxon lady of substantial means; now it sparkles under the lights of Liverpool Museum. The blaze of gold was enriched by the dark blood-red of garnet, the caerulean blue of glass and the clear white of shell. In one instant, four years' hard digging did not seem a day too long to the Rev. Bryan Faussett. He had investigated over 200 grave-mounds on the gentle hillside overlooking the picturesque village of Kingston. It had not all been pleasant work, as his meticulous diary shows. Speaking of one grave he reports that

> This grave had a remarkably fetid smell, as had all the articles taken out of it. We observed on this day, but never before, that some of the others which we opened had an unusual smell, but none of them anything like so strong as this. It thundered and lightened very much all the while we were digging, but at a distance: but about four o'clock, there came on so violent a storm of it, attended with excessive heavy rain, that we were obliged to decamp as fast as we could.

5 The Kingston Brooch. This is the finest of all the seventh-century Kentish composite gold and garnet disc brooches so far found. Discovered by Faussett in grave 205 at Kingston Down, Kent, on 5 August 1771, it measures 8.4 cm in diameter and weighs 2.2 g. The slightly convex front plate was devised to prevent loss of perspective when viewing its concentric design, which is relieved by the cruciform pattern and arrangement of boss and roundels. The overall effect of the gold and garnet is relieved by the use of blue glass and white shell. The panels of gold filigree work are very stylized animals which have lost their heads and become ribbons. Notice too the 'paillons' – pieces of gold foil with a trellis pattern set behind the garnets in each cell or 'cloison' of the jewel, to bring out the 'life' in the garnets. Even the back is ornamented – the head of the pin is inlaid with garnets, and the catch-plate, pin-head and pin-head surround are all ornamented with gold filigree. Like 'modern' brooches it has a safety loop

Pagan Saxon England

The Kingston Brooch, as Faussett's discovery is called, is one of the greatest archaeological treasures to be found in British soil. Nearly 8.75 cm across it consists of two gold plates bound by a strip of beaded gold wire and secured by three gold clasps on the rim. The surface is slightly convex so that the circular concentric pattern of inlays does not lose its perspective, and the pattern is further enlivened by the ingenious use of a cruciform pattern, roundels and a central boss. The design shows total mastery of the medium, and the skill displayed in the manufacture shows that the craftsman was not only a designer of exceptional talent, but a skilled smith who knew how to intertwine gold filigree and cut and set the delicate inlays in their gold scrolls. This represents a year's work.

The rest of the finds from the grave bear witness to the high status of the woman buried there. The burial mound in which she had been laid was unusually large, and her grave was found to be 3 m long and 2.5 m wide. She had been laid in a solid wooden coffin, bound with metal clamps and accompanied by a pottery beaker, a glass drinking cup, two gold-lined bronze-handled bowls (one possibly a hanging bowl) with their trivet stand, a gold pendant and chatelaine and two safety-pin style brooches of silver.

Credit for rescuing the brooch must be given to the nineteenth-century antiquary, Charles Roach Smith, who on the spur of the moment decided to call at a house where he had been told some antiquities were kept. Being a gentleman in the true English tradition, he hesitated before

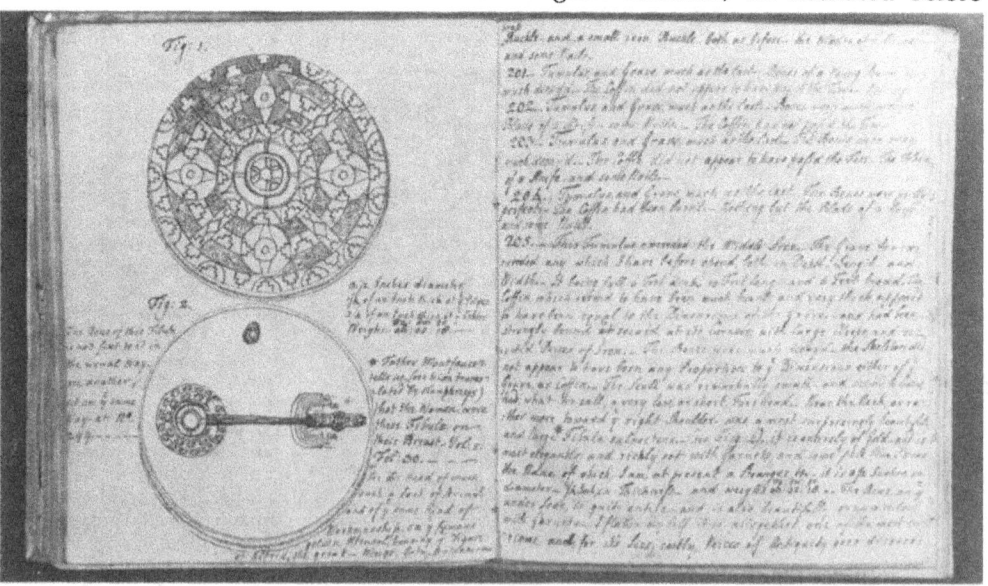

6 Page from Faussett's diary, recording the discovery of the Kingston Brooch. At the bottom of the right-hand page can be read 'I flatter myself it is, altogether, one of the most curious, and, for its size, costly, pieces of Antiquity ever discover'd.'

Pagan Saxon England

knocking on the door, since he had not made an appointment. However, his boldness paid off, for it led not only to his discovery of a precious collection of Kentish Anglo-Saxon treasures, but to the diary of the Rev. Bryan Faussett who had kept as detailed an account of his diggings as had ever been made in the eighteenth century. Subsequently the Faussett collection was placed on the market, and pressure was brought to bear on the British Museum to buy it, but the museum would not oblige, and had it not been for the intervention of the Liverpool collector Joseph Mayer the entire assemblage might have been lost. Mayer kept the notebook and made it available to scholars. He bequeathed the collection to Liverpool at his death, and the treasures are the finest from the period outside the British Museum.

Similarly beautiful finds still emerge from the soil. As recently as 1971, workers laying a pipe to carry natural gas to Ramsgate noticed some bones at Monkton, which eventually proved to be the remains of twenty-two Anglo-Saxon graves. Among the finds was a large composite disc brooch of electrum and silver, very similar to that from Kingston but less accomplished. It was inlaid with garnet, blue glass and shell, the latter originating in the Orient. Two years later another of these sumptuous jewels was found at Gilton, Kent.

These fine treasures epitomize the early Saxons in their brash, garish flamboyance. Yet they also show the early English to be capable of exquisite workmanship quite at variance to the myth of their squalor.

7   The Monkton Brooch. New discoveries of Kentish jewellery are frequently coming to light. This brooch was unearthed in 1971, during the laying of the Thanet section of the North Sea Gas pipeline. Compared to the Kingston Brooch, however, it is an inferior object. It appears to have been 'cannibalized' from at least one other brooch. The silver back-plate is engraved with the design for another composite brooch, the gold filigree is clumsy and the quality of the gold is poor. The garnets and glass are also set in cloisons of bronze, not gold

The sources

If some of the early ancestors of the English left splendid evidence of their lives, sadly for those of us who are excited by the thought of gold treasures, they were in the minority. The study of the early settlers is fraught with difficulties and disputes because they were non-literate, they used buildings and everyday objects that were mostly of perishable material, and their settlements and cemeteries have usually left no mark above ground. However, the very large number of English place-names with origins ultimately among the Anglo-Saxons is testimony to the former existence of such settlements.

The historical sources for the fifth and sixth centuries are very sparse, and written by non-Saxon observers. They are the same as those available for the Celts at this time. The most useful are Gildas, Nennius and Bede, amplified by a few remarks by Classical authors or others. The Anglo-Saxons were rarely mentioned among other Dark Age peoples. The sources which seem most promising at first were usually written long after the events they describe, and some, like the *Anglo-Saxon Chronicle,* rely heavily on the earlier writings still available to us. Interpretation of the sources is difficult – all are spectacularly biassed and in some cases can be proved incorrect.

Gildas was a British monk who died in about 572: he was therefore alive when the Anglo-Saxons were consolidating their conquests, but he viewed the break-up of the Roman civilization and the incoming pagans with horror. He was a persuasive writer simply because of his passions: he saw the Anglo-Saxons as a pestilence, and in the very title of his work, *Concerning the Ruin and Conquest of Britain,* shows that he is neither mincing his words nor aiming for impartiality. He was certainly familiar with some Classical authors, and had obviously received a semi-classical education. This factor is in itself illuminative of the state of the western British community during the early sixth century: evidently Anglo-Saxon culture was not predominant. For all that, his account of the history of the Romans is sparse and distorted, and he can be used as a source for the events of the period only with great caution. This for instance is how he describes the *adventus*:

> The fierce Saxons, of ever execrable memory, [were] admitted into the Island, like so many wolves into a sheep fold, to defend them from the northern Nations. A thing more destructive and pernicious than ever was done to this Kingdom. O the mist and grossness of this sense and apprehension! O the dullness and blockishness of these souls!

Yet, with the help of other sources, at least some of

Pagan Saxon England

Gildas' narrative has been pieced together into a fairly coherent form. One of the most important is a collection of writings that used to be ascribed to a ninth-century Welsh monk, Nennius, but is now demonstrated to have been the compilation of several hands. 'Nennius' is famous for having stated that he had made a heap of all that he could find, fact and fiction. Since he does not distinguish between the two, the result, which was called the *History of the Britons,* is confusing.

In 731 the Venerable Bede, writing from the northern monastery of Jarrow, published his *Ecclesiastical History of England.* When he came to tackle the history of the fifth and sixth centuries he was as far removed from the events he described as we are from Charles II's reign. Whereas there is a wealth of documents from which to reconstruct Restoration England, Bede had available primarily the polemic of Gildas and no doubt a series of other writings now lost. In short, like Nennius, Bede had a jumble of information which he tried to organize long after the event. His main concern was to explain the origins of the kingdoms that had emerged by his own day and he therefore found it helpful to project backwards the political situation of his own time. In doing so he inevitably simplified the story. Bede's narrative has given rise to another semi-myth, that of three clear-cut groups of invaders in fifth-century Britain, each with distinct homelands and areas of settlement.

Bede stated that the settlers who came to Britain were of the three most powerful nations in Germany, the Saxons, Angles and Jutes. He explained that the Jutes were the ancestors of the people of Kent, the Isle of Wight and the people among the West Saxons who were in Bede's own day still called Jutes, in Hampshire. The East Saxons, he asserted, came from Old Saxony, as did the South Saxons and West Saxons. Fron the country called Anglia 'which is said from that time, to remain deserted to this day, between the territories of the Jutes and Saxons', were descended the East Angles, Midland Angles, Mercians, Northumbrians (whom he designated as living on the north side of the Humber), and the rest of the English.

Bede's story sounds complicated enough, but the facts are more tangled still. The sixth-century Roman historian Procopius provides one clue to the complexity when he fails to mention the Jutes, but substitutes instead the Frisians in his narrative of the conquest, while another clue is provided by evidence such as the place-name Swaffham in Norfolk which suggests that at least one group of Suebians arrived. Archaeology also attests the Franks.

Pagan Saxon England

In some measure Bede's assertion that Anglia had remained deserted since the time of the Anglo-Saxon settlements is borne out by the evidence of Continental archaeology. At the beginning of the fifth century many settlements on the North Sea coast were deserted – this is true of sites such as Wijister, Feddersen Wierde or Gristede. Whereas there are thousands of fourth-century cremation urns from the cemeteries on the Elbe and the Weser, there are very few of the fifth century. Votive offerings were no longer made in the Danish bogs, except sporadically. There are hints at this time too that Frisia was being settled by incomers, probably Anglo-Saxons.

Other useful sources of information are a few saints' *Lives*, poems, annals, law codes, letters and the occasional Classical reference to events in Britain. They are fragmentary and in general merely hint that the main sources might be right or wrong on particular points. Also, obviously, they give the opposition's view, and therefore the picture is that viewed through Celtic or Roman eyes.

If historical sources are unsatisfactory, how accurate is the surviving material evidence as it appears from under the archaeologist's spade? The archaeological evidence comprises almost entirely the finds from graves – there are over 50,000 of them from over 1,500 burial grounds. These graves of the early Anglo-Saxon settlers were furnished with objects for the after-life and the inventory of goods recovered runs to tens of thousands. Useful and informative though these graves are, they pose problems of their own when it comes to interpretation. Not only have the goods been naturally selected by time (which has chosen to destroy certain materials by the actions of soil and weather and by the random chance of discovery) but they have been selected in the first place by the bereaved themselves. Objects deemed suitable for use after death are not necessarily those indispensable during life. Many may be heirlooms, over a century or more old when deposited in the soil, while others seem to have been made specially for interment. Then, as now, people were sometimes canny, putting old objects of little use to the living to the service of the dead. Many of the artefacts, too, may have been in traditional forms, no longer current in everyday use. The dating of individual graves therefore can often be difficult and the interpretation of the finds even more so. What is to be made of a few Saxon brooches in an Anglian area? Were they brought there by Saxons in the incoming population? Were they brought in by a trader? Did they arrive at the place where they were found soon after manufacture, or did they reach their final resting place a century or so later?

These problems are at their most tangled in the study of pottery which, because it is generally well preserved and undergoes changes of fashion fairly predictably, is usually the archaeologist's standby. However, the pagan settlers made their pots by hand and decorated them very simply, so no two pots are likely to be exactly the same. Some changes of fashion on the Continent are readily reflected in pottery in Britain but the scholar cannot be certain that some styles did not remain in vogue longer in the colonies than in the homeland, particularly if a close match is not possible. Pagan period pottery, too, is particularly friable and survives less well than most.

Given such difficulties it might well be wondered how any dates can be put with confidence to any pagan artefacts. For the Roman period coins can be used to give dates to objects associated with them and mass-produced artefacts such as pots were widely traded and often subject to short-lived but traceable fashions. Dating is also provided by documentary sources and inscriptions. In the fifth century, however, Roman pottery and coinage disappeared from use and inscriptions ceased except in the extreme west. The archaeologist must therefore turn to the Continent for helpful evidence. Here, Roman objects continued in use and have often been found in association with barbarian artefacts. Frankish history, too, is well known and thus Frankish objects can be dated readily. When barbarian objects are found in Britain that are similar or identical to objects found in datable contexts abroad, a network of dates can be built up. The premises behind such dating methods are that artefacts found on the Continent must pre-date the settlement of Britain, objects found in Britain and the Continent must relate to the period of migration in the fifth century, and objects found only on the British side of the Channel must belong to the period when the settlements had been accomplished and the Anglo-Saxons were already establishing an English culture. It will be readily understood that such methods of dating are very hazardous and only very general date brackets can often be reached.

During this century much time and effort has been spent in trying to distinguish the Angles, Saxons and Jutes from the material goods they left behind. Material has been found for instance that is similar in 'Anglian' areas on the Continent and in Britain. The same goes for 'Saxon' goods. When the question of the Jutes was tackled, however, confusion set in. Although material was found that was common to the traditional areas of the Jutes, it was later found too in other areas. The conclusions must be that the incomers arrived from a number of areas on the Continent and quickly interacted with each other and the British population to produce a new culture. It will, nevertheless, be seen during the discussions of pottery and art in particular that very close links have been proved between certain areas of the Continent and Britain, and that the terms Angle, Saxon and Jute have a very specific significance in terms of material culture, even if this cannot be extended to the political cohesion implied by Bede.

The terminological situation is further complicated by the use of the words 'Angle' and 'Saxon' by the people themselves. It seems that the incomers regarded themselves as Angles the minute they set foot on British soil, despite their origins. The Celts and Romano-Britons on the other hand used the word 'Saxon' to refer to the incomers. This term survives to this day in fairly common use as 'sassenach' in Scottish parlance, which has come to be a relatively derogatory title for those British people who are not Celts. A similar term is used in Welsh and Irish.

The term 'Welsh' was used to mean the native British, both those still in the old province of Britannia and those beyond. The modern nation of this name simply carries on this tradition, though the Britons of the time seem to have described themselves as 'Cumbri' (from *combrogi*, fellow-countrymen). A survival of this can be seen in the place-names Comberbach, Comberton or Cumbria. Thus it was that the seventh-century king Ine called himself king of the Saxons and described his subjects as English (Angles) or Welshmen. Recently some scholars have favoured referring to the newcomers as English from the moment they arrived, and to their forefathers on the Continent as the ancestral English. The present authors do not favour this terminology on the ground that it suggests too direct a cultural link between the barbarians of northern Europe and what in the Middle Ages and beyond became England. At the risk of sounding over-conservative or retrogressive therefore, in this book the term 'English' will be confined to the period after the fifth and sixth century, and the terms Saxon or Anglo-Saxon used before this period and as general appellations.

The last main type of evidence for the pagan period is that of place-names. Dating the names of individual places is difficult since there were rapid linguistic developments in the period of the settlements and it is impossible to know how long any one form was in use. On the other hand, place-name study can indicate the spread and extent of settlement. It can suggest what relationships the newcomers might have had with their native neighbours, and in some cases give hints of the original homelands of the villagers. It can, too, point towards those places where other types of fieldwork might usefully be carried out.

Roman Britain and the Anglo-Saxons

The Romans occupied Britain between AD 43 and 410, and during that period the people enjoyed such benefits that civilized life, a strong centralized government and the strength of four legions could provide. After initial rebellions, notably and most famously by Boudicca and Caratacus, the area south of Hadrian's Wall (see Map 1, p. xii) settled down and adopted Roman life with enthusiasm. By the second century AD, towns were being redeveloped, villa estates grew up in the countryside and the province was indoctrinated with the ways of Rome. After about 214 all those within the bounds of the Empire were citizens, and after 313 the Empire adopted Christianity. The Celts, who had been developing their own distinctive culture and political life on the eve of conquest, started to be influenced very strongly by Classical culture. In Wales and Cornwall this was relatively less than in England, and the inhabitants remained more Celtic and less Romano-British.

The safety of the province was threatened from outside even before the British Celts had themselves stopped rebellion against the invaders. In 122 or thereabouts, Hadrian's Wall was built to sever the northern tribes from their allies. The frontier was extended northwards for a few decades with the building of the Antonine Wall, but by 180 or thereabouts, those tribes north of the line from Carlisle to Newcastle were effectively free from Roman rule. It was these tribes who continued to be antagonistic to Rome. Their forefathers had little chance when the Romans marched into Scotland, but as time went on, the Picts in particular grew strong and clever at taking advantage of Rome's problems elsewhere. In addition to these border skirmishes, the Scotti from Ireland were forced out of their homelands from the third century on, and found themselves with no way to sail but east, bringing them to the west coast of Scotland. Archaeological and historical evidence shows that they constantly raided the west coast of Lancashire and Wales. Place-names show that they made early settlements despite the line of forts built by the Romans in the fourth century. The Scotti eventually obtained a foothold in the north and established the kingdom of Dalriada in the fifth century, and went on to bequeath their name to Scotland. In the later fourth century they allied with the Picts several times in order to overrun Hadrian's Wall. By a quirk of fate, when the Romans were forced to abandon Britannia, the Picts and Scotti became absorbed by their own affairs, and turned to fighting each other until they amalgamated in the ninth century.

It was therefore not the Picts or the Scotti who featured in Gildas' terrible description of the end of Roman Britain, but their barbarian cousins and sometime allies, recorded loosely as the Saxons, who were part of the Germani.

The Germani were no strangers to Roman Britain. Roman policy had led to large numbers of barbarians from newly conquered lands being drafted into the auxiliary units of the army. Since Rome depended on her aggressive policy for existence, there were plenty of recruits. By the second century, however, the auxiliary regiments had started to become far more 'establishment' than had been intended – the difference between them and the cream of the army, the legions, was diminishing. This left the necessity of finding a new type of army unit in which to place the raw barbarians who wished to fight in the name of Rome. The problem was solved by the creation of a new type of force – the *numeri*, or light-armed fighters from barbarian lands. From the second century on the numbers of *numeri* used became larger, and it was through these in the third century that Britain became accustomed to barbarians from Germanic lands. During the third century the *numeri* in Britain came exclusively from the Germanic lands, as if in response to Britain sending her own recruits from the borders to Upper Germany in the reign of Trajan (AD 98–117) and later.

In 277 or perhaps a year later either Burgundian or Vandal tribesmen were sent to Britain, possibly as *numeri*. A century later in 372 there was a transference to the province of Allamanni under king Fraomar. This might have been a settlement of the tribe, but is more likely to have been the granting of special powers to Fraomar over an already existing *numerus* of his own people.

Barbarians also found their way into provinces by the establishment of *laeti*. These were resettled barbarians with hereditary obligation of military service who were allowed to live in depopulated areas. In Britannia, however, the historical records do no more than hint that there may have been a few *laeti* in the late fourth century. Nevertheless the sound of Germanic dialects, the idea of worshipping Woden, and other facets of Germanic life must have been fairly familiar to the Romano-Britons by the late fourth and early fifth centuries. But it is of paramount importance to note that these tribesmen, although of Germanic origins, were eager to adopt Roman ways, and were quite willing, when it became expedient, to slaughter other Germanic peoples who were trying to enter the province illegally.

It was therefore not these barbarians who were the threat to Romano-British safety; it was rather their untamed kinsfolk who, from the third century on, increased their pressures on the province, just as their cousins on the Continent harassed Rome. A series of forts was built along the south and east coasts of Britannia, and others were added in the following century. An official known as the Count of the Saxon Shore was created, with responsibilities for the shores of Gaul and Britannia. There is no doubt that the Saxons were enjoying successful careers as pirates in Channel waters, and to judge from the siting of the forts, they were sailing and rowing up the rivers to the heartland of the province. Saxon incursions increased and Roman forces found it impossible to keep up their obligations in the province. With the successes of the barbarians on the Continent, troops were withdrawn in the late fourth century to fight abroad. The Saxons allied with the Picts and Scotti in 367 and Hadrian's Wall was overrun. After the 380s the Wall was virtually unoccupied by troops. It was a time of civil unrest. Between 383 and 388 a local usurper, Magnus Maximus, took control in Britain and made a spectacular attempt to gain control of the Empire before being defeated. He took with him large numbers of troops and never returned. By the early fifth century Rome's control of Britannia was slipping and the defences deteriorated. The British started electing their own emperors. The last and most important from the Saxon standpoint was Constantine III. Understandably but misguidedly he decided that the defence of the Empire as a whole depended upon the safety of Gaul. He may also have had some idea of pleasing the legitimate emperor. Constantine mustered what troops he could: few could have been willing to leave their lands and families open to attack. Thus did Constantine III sail for the Continent. His mission failed and in 410 the Britons threw out his officials and apparently asked the emperor Honorius for help. They were told that they were on their own, and must look to their own defences.

Now that the Britons had no chance of short-term (and, as it turned out, long-term) help from Rome, they set about organizing their protection. They seem to have elected leaders, of whom we have the names of a few, among them Vortigern (not a personal name but a word meaning over-

Pagan Saxon England

king or tyrant), and Ambrosius (senior) who may have been the father of Ambrosius Aurelianus. The latter was apparently replaced by Arthur, who is possibly the most famous figure in British history and mythology.

Many forts were totally abandoned by this time but others had increasingly civilian occupants in small numbers. A few villas certainly flourished into the fifth century, as did towns. Nevertheless, it must be assumed that infiltration into the countryside was increasingly easy for any barbarian band, and indeed several settlements of the Anglo-Saxons have been proved to have started in the Roman period. Archaeology shows that the immigrants were managing to set up home either with or without official permission even before the turn of the fourth century.

8 Gold *solidus* of Magnus Maximus (reigned AD 383–8). Maximus, who figures in medieval Welsh legend as Maxen Wledig, was a Spanish usurper who took control of Britain then made a bid to gain control of the Empire, before being defeated at the Battle of Poetovio in Italy in 388 by Theodosius. The reverse shows two emperors enthroned with Victory personified in the background. The mint signature (AVGOB) indicates the coin was struck at 'Augusta'. As London was renamed Augusta in the fourth century, it has been claimed this was a product of a mint there. The OB stands for *obryziacum* (pure gold). (Enlarged)

It seems clear that Vortigern, though in supreme power, was not unopposed, for the elder Ambrosius seems to have been his enemy. The historical sources hint that any disputes in Britain were certainly not confined to Anglo-Saxons and Britons, but that the Britons themselves disagreed over the best way to safeguard their future.

Despite opposition, Vortigern invited Hengist and Horsa into Britain in about 428, as paid soldiers to help safeguard the province. They duly arrived with three shiploads of followers as mercenaries in place of the legionaries, who in happier times had been in military occupation. That it should have been necessary to pay alien warriors suggests strongly that there were not enough men of the right age or ability left in Britain to be trained as soldiers. There must, too, have been few capable of giving the training, for those retired legionaries who had served in the regular armies must have been quite elderly by 428. Whatever the reasoning of the moment, the invitation was a departure from previous actions. This time the men employed were true barbarians, who kept their way of life and their customs. In the past the barbarians recruited into the

Roman army had been highly Romanized and propaganda had been firmly in favour of their adopting Roman ways and thought. It was this difference that was vital to the subsequent history of Britain.

The records relate that the Britons eventually tired of, or possibly became unable to pay, the mercenaries and told them to leave. Hengist retaliated by sending for more of his kinfolk from the Continent. Presumably he was confident that they would be able to deal with opposition. By about 441-2 the Anglo-Saxons had accumulated in number. Gildas graphically describes the countryside after their attacks. The intruders apparently used battering rams to demolish town defences; they slaughtered both churchmen and laymen. Swords flashed and flames crackled, and altars were encrusted with purple dried blood as though from some fabulous wine press. Dramatic though this sounds, archaeology has produced little evidence to support it and none that can definitely be dated to the time.

The historical sources relate that everything did not go well for Hengist and Horsa, however, and the British rallied with such success that Hengist was forced to resort to devious means. He organized an early 'St Bartholomew's Eve' massacre that would have made Catherine de' Medici envious. A peace conference was arranged to which Vortigern and 300 'top people' in Britain were invited. Hengist thereupon had the entire company killed with the exception of Vortigern, who was allowed to live, but spent the rest of his miserable life wandering from place to place, broken, despised and hated by both his own people and his enemies. If this event did happen (which is far from certain) it must be assumed that British resistance was at a low ebb around this time and that very few survivors would have been capable of organizing realistic war efforts. It is certainly true that barbarians entered the country in larger numbers after the middle of the fifth century, and that many

Pagan Saxon England

9 *Solidus* of Constantine III (reigned AD 407–11). Having been proclaimed emperor by his troops in Britain, Constantine crossed over to Gaul and allied with the barbarians. He briefly captured Spain, but due to the treachery of Gerontius, one of his generals, the province was overrun by Vandals and others in 409. He was captured by the general of Honorius, the official Roman emperor, and executed in Italy. The reverse shows the emperor holding a figure of Victory and a standard, his foot on a captive. The mintmark denotes that the coin was struck in Arles in France (Constantia). Constantine III figures in medieval romance as Bendigeit Custennin. (Enlarged)

of the estates that had survived until this time declined and ceased functioning.

The Anglo-Saxons had not overcome all the resistance, for between c. 460–500 they had to contend with the organized attacks of Ambrosius Aurelianus and Arthur. Ambrosius is described as being the son of parents who were the last to have worn the purple and to perish in the storm, i.e. they were of Imperial status. The 'storm' presumably refers to the general unrest of the fifth century. Arthur was the last named champion of Roman Britain. In about 495 he won a decisive battle against the Saxons, for which he has been awarded a place in legend. The incomers were certainly held back for a period of decades, but the result was that they consolidated their successes in the east before moving west again. There was a military reversal in 515 when Arthur was killed at the battle of Camlann, and thereafter a curious lull occurs in the historical account of the Saxon offensive. Whatever the reason for this (and it might simply be a gap in the account), the Saxons are recorded as actively aggressive towards the west after the mid-sixth century. A certain Cynric took Salisbury in 552 and began building what eventually became the kingdom of Wessex. Cynric is notable for being one of several leaders whose names are not Saxon but British. The only sensible explanation for this would be that in the preceding century of conquest those British who came under Saxon influence were not wiped out. It suggests that intermarriage must have been common enough for men of mixed blood to become leaders. Gildas does not mention such a phenomenon, but he would not be expected to discuss people whom he would consider collaborators. With the large-scale withdrawal of troops from Roman Britain, the loss of the men who followed Constantine III, the massacre of the Romano-British leaders by Hengist and the blood shed by the Ambrosian and Arthurian campaigns, it is not difficult to assume that a large proportion of the remaining British population must have been female. Any intermarriage would necessarily leave little archaeological evidence if this were the case, for a woman in both Germanic and Roman traditions adopted her husband's way of life. It is notable that the modern tradition of hanging old shoes on wedding cars stems from the Anglo-Saxon custom of the father taking one of the bride's shoes and giving it to the groom as a symbol of the changeover of authority. The groom established his male superiority by striking his spouse with it.

Whatever his origins, Cynric was an important figure in

the conquest and by 568 a young king, Aethelbert, ruled a newly developed kingdom of Kent. In this year Aethelbert advanced on the town of London, which still managed to retain some semblance of Roman civilized life. He was turned back not by a British force but by the combined efforts of the Anglo-Saxons Ceawlin and Cuthwulf. The latter then subdued Bedford, which appears to have continued to be a British stronghold up to this time, and marched west. Finally in 577 Bath, Cirencester and Gloucester were taken by the Saxons at the battle of Dyrham.

During these skirmishes and fluctuating fortunes of war and peace the Saxons had been busy establishing their own strength in embryonic kingdoms. The first to develop was Kent, and undoubtedly the most influential and important figure from c. 555 to 616 was king Aethelbert. His kingdom was well developed, as the archaeological discoveries show, and kept up its contacts with the Continent. By this time the kingdom of the Franks was well established. King Clovis (465–511) had defeated both the Gallo-Romans at Soissons and the Allamanni near Cologne. He had become Christian and had established a capital at Paris, and from these beginnings the French nation eventually developed. Aethelbert was favoured enough by the Franks to be allowed to marry their princess Bertha. She was a Christian and her own priest was already in Kent in 597. This illustrates the degree of civilization that must have been attained by the Kentish people. It can be argued that this would have been most easily achieved if the old Roman way of life had not been totally obliterated as Gildas suggests, and certainly the archaeological evidence hints at the receptivity of the Anglo-Saxons to civilization.

This, then, is the picture gained primarily from the historical sources, much of which is not in conflict with the testimony of the material remains. The artefacts unearthed in excavation and by chance nevertheless have a more detailed story to tell, a narrative that would have made uneasy reading for Gildas and a surprise for Bede.

Archaeology and the relations between Romano-Britons and Anglo-Saxons

The archaeological evidence relating to the end of Roman Britain and the first Germanic incursions, is being increased each year. Yet it is naturally fragmentary, and cannot be used, for instance, to corroborate the historical account of battles and spreading settlement or to give concrete dates and routes of invading armies.

Pagan Saxon England

10 Germanic belt-set, Dorchester-on-Thames, Oxfordshire. This belt-set, seen here restored, came from a grave which has figured prominently in the discussion of early Germanic soldiers in Britain. The grave was one of a series in the Dyke Hills, a late Roman cemetery outside the town, investigated in 1874. The belt fittings are characteristic of a group produced in Continental workshops in the late Roman Empire (note the characteristic confronted animal heads on the buckle loop), and in 1961 it was suggested that the burial was that of a Germanic federate soldier serving in a garrison in late Roman Dorchester. Two other, female, graves in Dorchester were contemporary, and the objects accompanying them probably came from Frisia. It is now realized that such belt fittings were not necessarily 'military' in character

The claim by the documentary sources that Vortigern invited mercenaries into Britain has long been of interest to archaeologists, who have looked for the evidence among the material remains. In this context the various categories of chip-carved and animal-ornamented belt fittings that have been found in fourth- and early fifth-century contexts have assumed considerable prominence. They have been found in Germanic federate graves on the Continent, for example at Vermand in France, in military-looking graves in Romano-British cemeteries at Winchester and Gloucester, in an apparently military burial at Dorchester-on-Thames, and isolated in Richborough. Such belt fittings, however, have also been found in a variety of other contexts, including Roman towns, villas and Saxon Shore forts, as well as early Anglo-Saxon cemeteries. Recent reappraisal of these fittings has led to the conclusion that although they were certainly produced for Germanic taste, they were probably used widely both by barbarians in the Roman army, and by civilians, including Romano-Britons. It is not impossible, of course, that many of the fittings discovered in Britain in apparently civilian contexts were indeed worn by mercenaries, but it cannot be proved. By the same token, the Germanic types of spearheads sometimes found in Roman forts, such as Carvoran on Hadrian's Wall, are not necessarily evidence for mercenaries rather than for Germani in the regular Roman army.

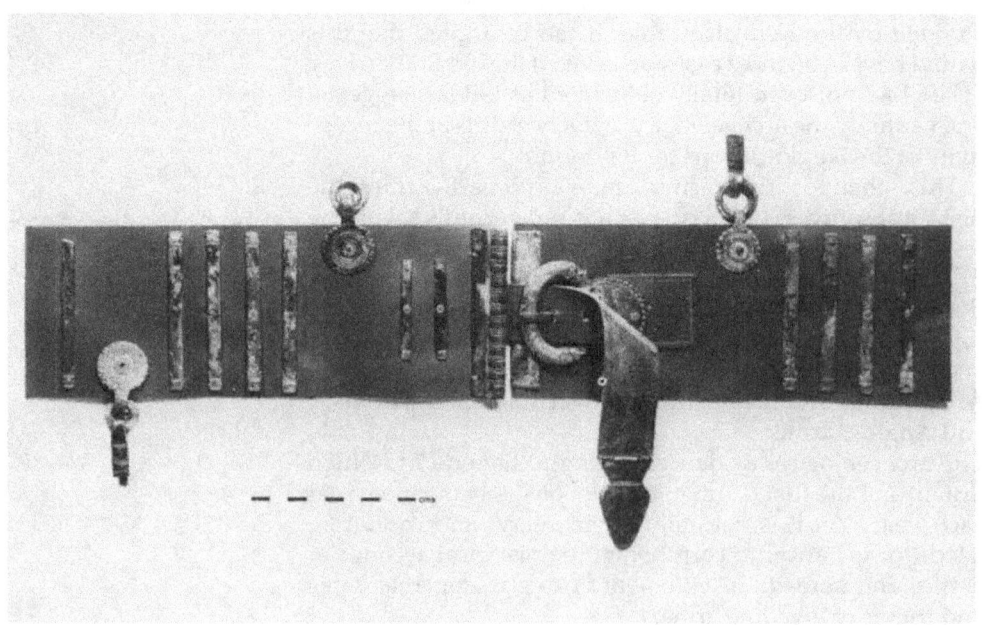

That Romano-Britons developed a Saxonized taste is also reflected by late Roman pottery. Roman factories started to produce pots with definite Germanic decorations in the fourth century. These pots have been named Romano-Saxon, and indicate a degree of cultural exchange between the two peoples in the later fourth and early fifth century. They are matched by what have been rather confusingly called Saxo-Roman pots, which are Roman in style and decoration but made in the coarse wares favoured by the Germanic barbarians. These hybrid pottery styles died out in favour of true Anglo-Saxon pottery when the Romano-British pottery industry ceased to function properly in the 430s.

Whilst such finds do not substantiate the story of Vortigern's invitation, they do not contradict it, and they do point to growing Germanic taste in late Roman Britain, quite at variance to Gildas' assertion that the Anglo-Saxons and Britons were in violent conflict.

The mainstay of Roman civilization had been the towns – places such as Londinium (London) with its 330 acres of ordered urban life, or Corinium (Cirencester), one of the most splendid regional capitals, or the tiny 13-acre Petuaria (Brough-on-Humber) with its flourishing theatre and school of mosaic artists. The towns were defended from attack, from civil unrest and from incoming barbarians and kept themselves intact well into the fifth century, and some

11 Openwork buckle from Colchester, Essex. Length: 6 cm. It was made on the Continent to suit Germanic taste, and imported to Britain in the late fourth century, perhaps on the belt of a Germanic soldier

Pagan Saxon England

even into the sixth. One Germanic chief on the Continent is noted for asserting that he had no quarrel with walls, and though this was not true of some of the Anglo-Saxons, who certainly did attack towns and even settled within them, it seems to have held good for others.

Until recently it was thought from the historical sources that the Romano-British eked out a miserable existence in their towns, increasingly impoverished and struggling, with a sea of Anglo-Saxons camped outside in some grand siege lasting many decades. Apart from the physical impossibility of such a situation, archaeology is constantly bringing forth evidence that the Romano-British exploited the outsiders, by using them as an outlet for what Roman goods were still being produced (see Figure 1 for a description of post-Roman town development). If friendly enough relations could be established, the Saxons would have been just the people to defend the townsfolk from other barbarian marauders. The Saxons on the Continent had proved time and time again that they wanted not to massacre and annihilate, but to eat of the fruits of civilization: we have no reason to suppose it was otherwise in Britain.

The archaeologist's trowel has uncovered many exhibits to demonstrate that some Anglo-Saxons entered into friendly (or at least mutually tolerant) arrangements with the local townsfolk. Anglo-Saxon huts of the type built by the pagans have been found inside the town walls, at

12 Romano-Saxon pot, from Faversham, Kent. Made in Roman ware and in a Roman kiln, this pot with its shoulder bosses, narrow neck and flaring rim was intended to cater for Germanic taste. Such pots (and pots made in Germanic fabric but in Roman shapes) are evidence for the presence of Germanic people in Britain before the end of the fourth century

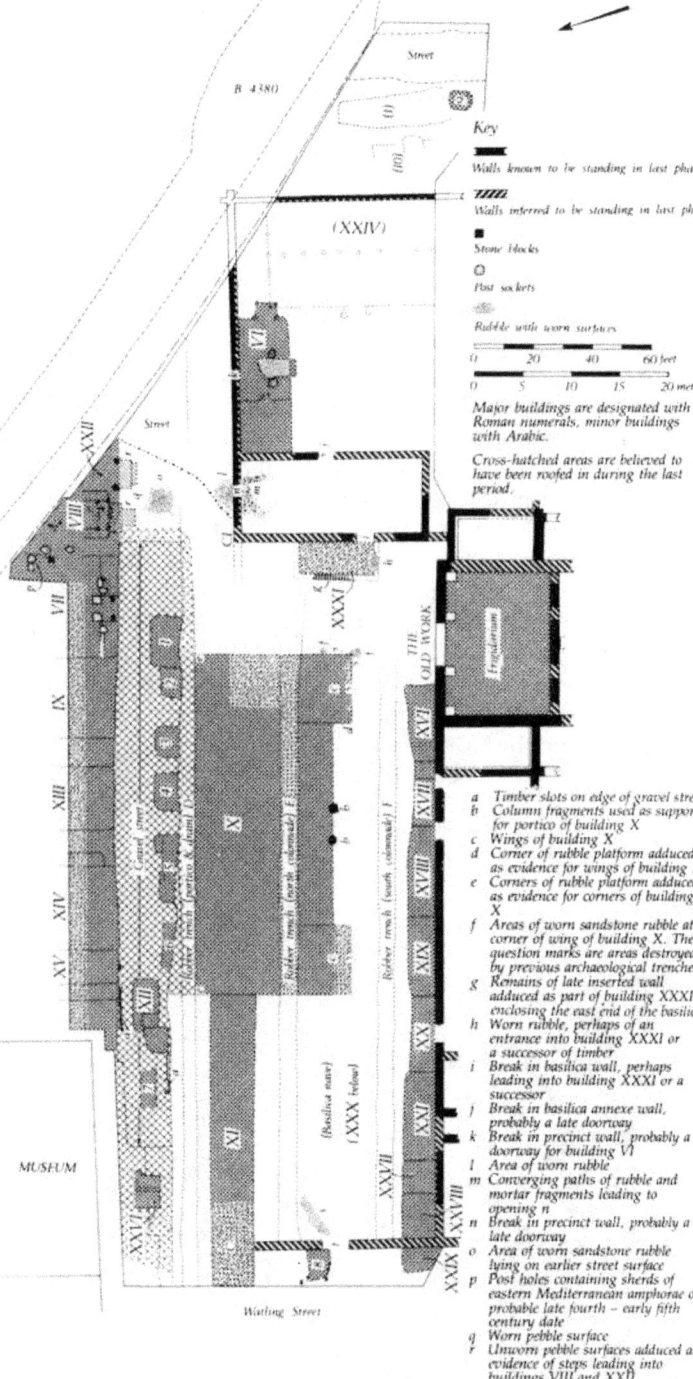

Figure 1 A plan of the last structures built on the site of the basilica adjacent to the public baths in the centre of *Viroconium Cornoviorum*, present-day Wroxeter, near Shrewsbury.

Although excavation is still in progress, the final sequence of events is becoming clear. After the destruction of the basilica, probably during the early part of the fourth century, the area was occupied by timber buildings. The impression is one of decay and squalor, with meat bones strewn among the rubble and fires lit on the pebble floors. At first sight this seems to support the generally accepted view of the end of many Roman towns – a steady decline leading to eventual abandonment. However, the evidence from the very latest period of occupation of the basilican area shows that it was completely redeveloped with a planned complex of timber-framed buildings, shown in this figure, some of them very large and looking back to Classical models.

This drastic reorganization of the city centre needed wealth and organization. This is not the work of peasant villagers, nor can it be attributed to incoming Irish or Saxon colonizers. It has all the hallmarks of Roman public works translated into timber, and is very probably a complex of religious or public buildings, or the demesne of a great man.

The date of this last rebuilding is at present quite uncertain, and could lie at any time between the later fourth and mid-fifth century, though a date early within this period seems increasingly likely.

Pagan Saxon England

Canterbury, Dorchester-on-Thames and London, for instance. At York legionary fortress the headquarters building continued in use in the fifth century, perhaps at first by the Romano-British but later by the Anglo-Saxons. We are left to guess at the relationship of the two peoples. In London the palace of the Anglo-Saxon kings is believed to have been sited inside the military fort in Cripplegate, while at Winchester the site of the Anglo-Saxon royal palace coincided with that of the Roman forum, and may have overlain the old basilica or town hall. At Gloucester the palace at Kingsholm was likewise built within the Roman fort. When in later times the Anglo-Saxons began developing towns, they often chose the old Roman sites. Their town layouts were in some measure dictated by those of the Roman predecessors, though the choice of site might have been governed by the geographical and other factors that led to the original growth of the site.

Romano-British and Anglo-Saxon had a period of overlap in some forts, as can be seen most readily on the site of Portchester. Here a Saxon Shore fort had been garrisoned quite normally into the fourth century. However, throughout this century and into the fifth, the units became less regular. The rather forbidding 6 m high walls that now draw visitors by the thousand, and which were walked in the Middle Ages by Norman sentries, rang in the fourth and fifth centuries with the cries of children. The units which

13 The walls of the Roman fort at Portchester, Hants, still stand about 6 m high, furnished with impressive bastions. The fort is one of those built on the 'Saxon Shore' to protect Britannia from invaders from the Continent. Built in the late third century, it is one of the most impressive Roman ruins in Britain. Recent excavations have shown that it was probably partly defended by a Germanic garrison, with their families, in the fourth century. In the fifth the original occupants were augmented by Anglo-Saxon newcomers, who continued to live within the fort in huts of Anglo-Saxon type

garrisoned the fort enjoyed the company of their families, and it is this that led to the interpretation of the archaeological evidence as being of the remains of a group of *laeti* (see p. 28) and their dependants. As time wore on, the inhabitants became culturally more Germanic and less Roman. During the sixth and seventh centuries the main settlement moved out of the fort though the finds show that the fort was still used and the land within the walls was still cultivated. The Roman fort walls and gates remained in use in the Anglo-Saxon period and at some indeterminable date before the Middle Ages, the fort was of enough importance for the landgate to be reconstructed.

It was probably more in the countryside than in the towns that the Romano-British population had to adjust themselves to a new way of life. Here it was not possible to defend settlements with strong walls, or to find the manpower to repel an attack. In the Roman period, the countryside had been covered with large or small estates, each with its 'villa'. The term is a portmanteau one, covering a variety of structures from modest bailiff-run farms to the sumptuous mansions of the Cotswolds. All, however, had a definite economic basis and were supported by farming or by the forests, potteries or mines, for example. Many had therefore fallen into decay well before the end of the fourth century as the economic life of the Empire had been disrupted. Others managed to stay in operation into the

14 Burgh Castle, Norfolk. This Saxon Shore fort was built in the late third century AD. In the seventh century king Sigeberht of East Anglia gave the site to an Irish monk, Fursa, to found a monastery. Traces of this were found in excavation in 1960–1, when oval huts (possibly used as cells or workshops) and a cemetery were investigated

fifth century and during the Anglo-Saxon incursions.

The Anglo-Saxons were primarily farmers, and, arriving in the countryside with few possessions but the clothes they stood up in, and clutching a few family heirlooms, they would have realized the sense in farming the old estates. Recent evidence suggests that there was little break in land-use.

Shakenoak in Oxfordshire is the site of a recently excavated villa, where evidence to corroborate this continuity has come to light. The farm was inhabited in the mid-fifth century by people of mixed origins (both Anglo-Saxon and Romano-British), though their life style was still materially Roman. Other sites too have produced evidence of the proximity of Romano-British and Anglo-Saxon communities. The Continental situation in which barbarians billeted themselves on landowners, might well be reflected in these British contexts. The Gallic writer Sidonius Apollinaris describes such a situation on his own estate; the barbarians took a proportion of the lands for themselves, leaving the owner to his own work, and referring to themselves as guests and the landowner as host. Although there is no direct written evidence to support this hypothesis in Britain, some early Anglo-Saxon legal terms have been shown to be derived from the language of the Roman estates.

In some cases the Anglo-Saxons can be proved to have taken over existing farms that were in partial or total decay. They did not, however, move into the Roman house itself. This sometimes causes surprise to modern minds used to the concept of 'doing up' old properties. However, Roman villas needed many slaves and servants to run, and know-how to work things like the underfloor heating systems. There could be little to be said in favour of arriving home after a hard day's marauding (as Gildas would have us believe) or tilling the fields (as archaeologists would prefer), to an overworked wife, a squalling baby and a masterpiece of mosaic art depicting Neptune on a stormy sea, the details of which were obscured by the smoke from a makeshift brazier. It was therefore arguably not because the Saxons had primitive tastes that they preferred to erect their own warm, comfortable, easily run timber-and-thatch homes.

The picture of a mixing of the Romano-British and Anglo-Saxon populations is echoed by the siting and sequence of certain early Anglo-Saxon cemeteries, many of which are located outside Roman towns, for instance Caistor-by-Norwich, Ancaster and Casterton. A surprising number of early cemeteries are, furthermore, in close proximity to major Roman settlements. Thus the cemetery at Thurmaston is near Roman Leicester, while that at Heworth is not far from Roman York. Some pagan Anglo-Saxon burials have even been found within Roman settlements, for example at York, Catterick, Aldborough and Cambridge. Indeed a surprising percentage of pagan Anglo-Saxon cemeteries are on sites which have produced Roman finds, implying that there was a Roman settlement underlying them or adjacent to them. Not a few seem to have started as Roman cemeteries and then been used later for Anglo-Saxon burials. Over thirty examples of this type of burial ground have been discovered, though of course it cannot normally be proved that the use of the site was unbroken or that the continuity was deliberate. It is, however, noteworthy that several of the cemeteries that include Roman burials have produced some of the earliest Anglo-Saxon finds in England, and a recent study of the orientation of early Anglo-Saxon burials in Northumbria shows some to have retained the local Romano-British orientation. Such willingness to share final resting places argues eloquently for friendship between the two elements in the population.

To judge from cemetery finds, the early Anglo-Saxons found Roman objects attractive. The artefacts were not merely rubbish survivals, perhaps contained in the soil used to backfill the graves, or even curiosities picked up on abandoned Roman forts or settlements. Amongst the most

Pagan Saxon England

15 Pagan Anglian urn, R12, from Caistor-by-Norwich. This pot, with its finger-tip rosettes and *stehende Bogen* arched ornament, can be matched almost exactly on the Continent – there is a fourth-century urn which is almost identical from Midlaren. It belongs to a group known as the Cuxhaven/Galgenberg Type. This, and other stylistically 'early' urns from the site, have led some experts to suggest that the cemetery at Caistor was first used in the third or fourth century by Germanic settlers in the town of Caistor (see also Plate 49)

Pagan Saxon England

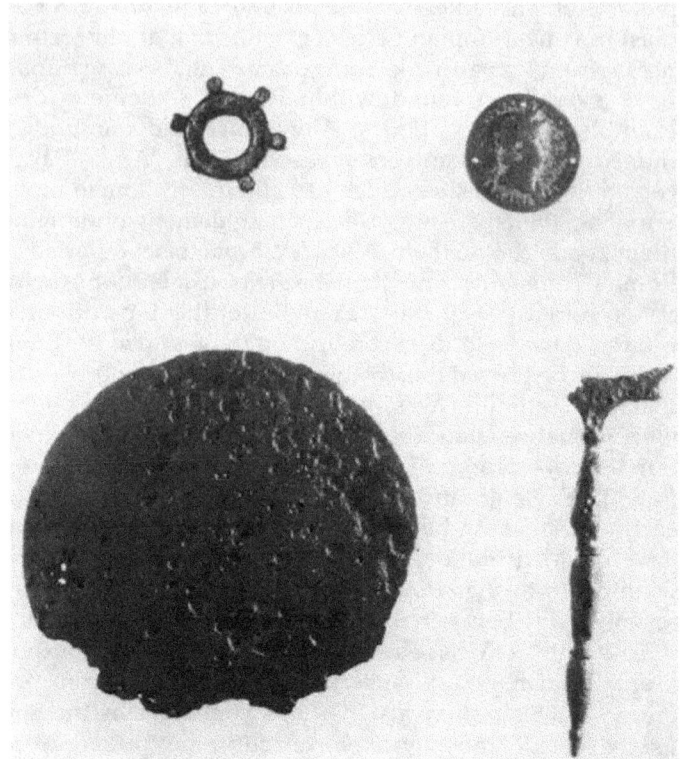

16 Roman objects from Anglo-Saxon graves. The mirror and its handle (*bottom*) are from grave 12, Gilton, Kent. The sestertius of Nero (*top right*) was gilded and found attached to what was identified as a bridle-bit from grave 83 in the same cemetery. The remaining object (*top left*) is a Roman enamelled brooch from Gilton Grave 67

common are glass vessels and complete Roman pots. The chances of unbroken glass or ceramic vessels 'lying around' on abandoned sites to be picked up by the passing Saxons is extremely remote; they are more likely to have been acquired directly from their original owners. Most of the objects are for adorning the person – brooches, pins, beads, bracelets and toilet articles. There are, too, objects which are extremely rare on Roman settlements, such as mirrors, *paterae* (bronze saucepans) and ornamental bronzes. There are three Roman mirrors from Anglo-Saxon sites, which were clearly buried as part of the grave furniture, and occasional finds are the fine enamelled hanging bowls of Roman origin.

From this, certain possibilities emerge in the mind of the curious scholar. With a few notable exceptions, all the objects are exactly the sort of thing people call heirlooms. Jewellery and other forms of adornment are always favoured because of their personal associations, and bronze, pottery and glass vessels have similar sentimental value. If these objects are heirlooms, they could well be objects acquired by predecessors of the deceased through marriage or trade, when they first settled in Britain, or alternatively they could be reminders of their Romanized past for Britons who had otherwise embraced Anglo-Saxon culture.

Roman coins are particularly common finds in Anglo-Saxon graves, despite the fact that they had ceased coming in to Britain around 400 and by around 430 were no longer in use as currency. Something in the region of 500 have been found, all of different dates. Whether these were found by chance or kept as heirlooms cannot be ascertained. Many were pierced as ornaments and one Saxon had a coin gilded to mount on a horse harness which was found at Gilton, Kent. A clue to the meaning of this phenomenon is provided by the Scandinavian bracteates – gold pendants made in imitation of Roman coins. Like the coins, they symbolized all things Roman, and they bore Imperial portraits. By retaining Roman coins the Anglo-Saxons imply that they were indulging in a nostalgia for the Roman past from which their ancestors had hoped to forge both their present and their future. Such aspirations must account for the popularity of Roman coin designs as models for the first Anglo-Saxon coinage types of the seventh century. Some aspects of Romano-British technology seem to have been taken over by the Anglo-Saxons from their neighbours, for example the use of enamelling and perhaps the use of millefiori glass.

How many Anglo-Saxons came to Britain to achieve this historical cataclysm? One estimate of the new population in the sixth century has put the total at not more than 50,000–100,000. If we wish to juggle with figures, we can note that the Romano-British population of the second century has been calculated as at least one million. Even allowing for a population decline in the late Roman period, this still suggests that only a tenth of the population of the sixth century could have been Anglo-Saxon.

Place-names provide the last category of clues to Romano-Saxon relations. The names people call their settlements and landmarks change drastically over the ages, and it is only by tracing the changes in the names over the years (by studying the earliest forms as they appear in charters or other early manuscripts) that the exact derivation can be discovered. Place-names are indeed notoriously difficult to study and evaluate. Nevertheless, they have some information for us to do with what we will. It is notable for instance, that the Anglo-Saxon name element *-wicham* in some cases is derived from the latin *vicus* meaning a settlement. This suggests that it was used by the

Anglo-Saxons to denote an already existing settlement. Examples of such places seem to be Wycomb, Leicestershire, West Wickham, Kent, and Wickham St Paul's in Essex. Nevertheless a very large number of place-names are Anglo-Saxon in origin or were Saxonized from their British originals. A large number seem to have been formed of the names of the original inhabitants – Essex (the East Saxons), Sussex (the South Saxons) are typical of such words. Villages too were named in like fashion – those with *inga* in their composition often have been proved to refer to the original settlers from the Continent. Thus Hastings refers to the early Anglo-Saxon settlers who followed a certain and otherwise unknown worthy called Hasta. The *Hestingorum gens* are a tribe referred to in the eighth century by Symeon of Durham. However, how such names related to the make-up of the population is uncertain, for the Anglo-Saxon place-name need not denote either the absence of the British in the community, nor their subservience. But there are some place-names which refer to the 'welsh' or native Britons, which does suggest that there were enclaves of the original inhabitants who congregated together.

Hearth and home
Despite the picture that is emerging of considerable cultural fusion between the Romano-British and the Anglo-Saxons, the majority of the incomers settled down to live a life very similar to that of their cousins on the Continent. The few Anglo-Saxon settlements that have been excavated point to an entirely barbarian way of life, with only a few borrowings from the nearby Roman settlements. The small number of villages that have been discovered from the pagan period (there were no Anglo-Saxon towns at all during this time) were probably abnormal examples which did not endure – it may be inferred that successful hamlets must lie hidden under modern villages with Saxon names.

One conclusion readily drawn from the excavations of pagan Anglo-Saxon villages is that the early Englishman's home was emphatically not his castle. It is also true that those Englishmen who nowadays complain about new homes simply being so many little square boxes can have no conception of how their ancestors lived – in little square boxes scattered more or less at random with the intervening areas filled in with little round boxes.

Travellers crossing the Thames at Gravesend on their way to Tilbury in Essex, and turning north along the A128, will be unaware that within a mile and a half to the east of the road lies one of the most remarkable places in the history

17 Model figures of an Anglo-Saxon family, made for the Festival of Britain Exhibition in 1951

of the Anglo-Saxons. The village is Mucking, of which even the name preserves the memory of Mucca's people who, according to the results of recent excavations, presumably arrived at the beginning of the fifth century and built several hundred huts in the following two centuries.

The site of Mucking is typical of what used to be thought the favourite terrain of the Anglo-Saxon settlers – on a river bank, on open land. Today, especially after research done at places such as Chalton, Hants, it is recognized that the early Saxons also built on hilltops. However, research is still too much in its infancy for us to be certain whether such sites are aberrations from the normal pattern.

The lifestyle in an early settlement can be pieced together from the meagre traces of buildings, the finds in the houses and their rubbish heaps, and from their cemeteries. Only a few objects are generally found on village sites, for only rubbish was discarded, and the more valued possessions were handed down to offspring or buried with the dead.

The most common type of building is the 'sunken hut' (*grubenhaus*), a term that has come to cover a large number of buildings. They have little in common except that they all

Pagan Saxon England

leave some depression below ground level. Excavators have usually been faced with a welter of holes and depressions that in no way resemble the remains of any modern structure. Accordingly a number of reconstructions have been tried, to persuade their readers how the Anglo-Saxons lived. A large number of the structures appear to have been made by the digging out of a shallow pit and the erection of roof supports, equally disposed. This suggests that the walls were very flimsy, that there were no adequate floors

18 Excavators working on pagan Anglo-Saxon village sites in England often encounter shallow oblong hollows, perhaps up to 1 m deep and some 2 or 3 m by over 2 m in extent. These seem to have been the below-ground elements of small huts, which may have looked like this. The hollow in some cases may have been for a suspended floor, and not all were the mean hovels early investigators imagined. This drawing is based on discoveries at West Stow, Suffolk

and that life was lived on the very primitive level assumed in the nineteenth century.

An interesting experiment has been carried out after the extensive excavations at West Stow, Suffolk, where a large number of early Anglo-Saxon houses have been found. Instead of contenting themselves with reconstructions of the buildings that made the Anglo-Saxons live literally in pits with flimsy thatched roofs, the excavators considered other constructional possibilities. It became immediately apparent that the huts here (and therefore possibly elsewhere too) could have been substantial and comfortable homes, with wooden suspended floors instead of dug-out earthen ones. The site was originally to be used as a rubbish tip by Bury St Edmund's Council, but has now been reprieved and life-size reconstructions of the houses have been erected. By building the walls on the cross-planks for the floor, it has proved possible to provide a splendid hut that would leave no traces of walls for posterity. Such wooden floors would naturally have rotted unless they had been suspended – thus accounting for the 'scraping' out of the ground that has perplexed so many antiquarians. It was possible to construct the houses using only two or six posts driven into the soil, just as the excavations had uncovered. Other reconstructions have been tried, on the lines of the traditional 'sunken' hut, notably in the Open Air Museum of West Dean, Sussex.

The great diversity of construction and function of 'sunken-floor' huts is readily apparent at Chalton, Hants, where one sunken floor hut measured 8.6 m by 5.4 m, with four massive posts down the centre to support the ridge. This hut did not have a suspended floor, but was clearly no mean hovel, and finds from it suggested it was in use in the seventh century. In the same village another *grubenhaus* was positively minute, a mere 2.4 m by 1.4 m, and hollowed no more than 10 cm into the chalk, its light roof supported by two external posts. Such a structure could never have been inhabited. Many of them were almost certainly industrial – weaving sheds, workshops, stores and the like.

Although *grubenhäuser* are in the majority on many sites, they are in a minority on others. At Chalton there were only four out of sixty-one buildings excavated, the others being rectangular post-built structures. The largest of these were 9 m or more in length, with opposed doorways in the middle of the long sides and an internal partition wall cutting off a fifth of the total area. Smaller buildings lacked the partition wall, while those which were smaller still had a single doorway in the middle of one side. One building found in 1976 was 24.4 m long by 5.1 m wide, composed of four separate units with a central line of posts, more or less in an alignment but slightly out of true, suggesting that the original nucleus had been extended. At Chalton, some buildings were set within rectangular fenced enclosures. Here is the heroic picture found in *Beowulf*, the Anglo-Saxon epic poem, in which the hero and his followers feast in halls round which were distributed 'bower houses'.

This picture is reinforced at Catholme, a recently excavated site in the middle Trent valley, where there were only seven *grubenhäuser* among the sixty-five buildings. Catholme's history spans many centuries. The earliest occupation can be traced back to the late fifth century, and it continued seemingly unbroken until the arrival of the Danes in the tenth. The buildings other than sunken-floor huts were rectangular and post built, the posts sometimes being set in trenches. The largest buildings were up to 20 m long, and there was evidence for internal partitions dividing them into rooms, as well as for verandahs in a few cases. Alongside the buildings, which seem to have been roughly arranged in groups, were what may have been barns.

Pagan Saxon England

The occupations followed in Saxon villages vary from settlement to settlement. Weaving was certainly important, and the largest *grubenhaus* at Chalton contained a pile of clay loom-weights. Two lines of weights were found in a house at Grimston End, Pakenham, Suffolk, where they had fallen from the loom. At Chalton there was evidence for iron-forging and bronze-working, while at Mucking there was also some indication that lead – possibly looted from a nearby Roman villa – had been worked.

Some trade as well as home production figured in the economy. The people at Chalton had a passion for oysters, perhaps learned from their Roman neighbours in the early days of the settlement, and probably imported them from Portsmouth harbour. Imported glass and ceramics included some wheel-turned pots manufactured in northern France, as well as more local products.

Pottery was manufactured and traded from the village of West Stow. Here archaeology has been fortunate enough to bring to light the workshop of a potter whose products were already well known from the cemeteries that have given him his name in archaeological literature – the Illington-Lackford potter. His richly ornamented pots, which may have been at first inspired by late Roman pottery, have been found on a variety of sites. As at Chalton, over 300 Roman coins and pieces of Roman pottery from the site demonstrate Roman contacts in the early days of the settlement.

No ploughs have been found from the fifth century to the tenth, presumably because iron was too valuable to be discarded without being reworked from scrap. Shears, however, show that sheep were kept for wool as well as meat, and indeed sheep farming was England's main industry by the late Saxon period.

The Anglo-Saxon as hero

The street was paved with variously coloured stones, and the road kept the fighting men in a group. The war-corselet shone, firmly hand-locked, the flashing iron rings sang in the armour as they came on their way even to the great hall in their war-gear. Tired from the sea, they laid down their broad shields, their strong bucklers against the building's wall; they then sat down on the bench. The body-armour rang out, the warrior's armour. The spears, the weapons of seamen, of grey-tipped ash wood, stood all together. The armed band was furbished with war-gear. Then a haughty hero asked the fighting men about their lineage: 'From where have you brought plated shields, grey corselets and masking helmets, this pile of spears? . . . I have not seen so many men of strange race more brave in bearing.'

Thus the seventh-century poet of the epic *Beowulf*

described Anglo-Saxon warriors. Archaeology supports the picture provided by the poem, though the hero and his war band in the poem were kitted out more in the manner distinctive of seventh-century East Anglia than the rest of pagan Saxon England.

The poem is often quoted in conjunction with the results of the excavation of a unique warrior's burial, to give an idea of the world of the Anglo-Saxon heroes. The burial was at Sutton Hoo in Suffolk, excavated first under threat of the Second World War and then re-excavated and reappraised in 1967. It was certainly not the only grave of its kind, but is the sole example to have survived intact into the twentieth century, and to have been examined scientifically from the start. The grave shows many features that point to links with Sweden and it is now thought to be the interment of king Raedwald of East Anglia who died in 625. The absence of a body among the contents has long perplexed scholars, but the acid conditions of the sandy soil near the river Deben are now thought to be sufficient explanation for this.

The burial certainly seems to be dedicated to the precept that you can take it with you when you go. Despite the conversion of king Raedwald to Christianity (there are two baptismal spoons in the grave), his followers sent him to the after-life with the full honours of a pagan hero, in his ship. The vessel was filled with gold, silver and garnet, jewellery and all the necessary accoutrements of a royal warrior. The

Pagan Saxon England

19 Purse lid with gold and garnet mounts, Sutton Hoo, Suffolk. The Sutton Hoo treasure shows Anglo-Saxon artistry at its best. The finds came from a royal ship burial, probably that of king Raedwald of East Anglia (d. AD 624 or 625). The purse lid was found associated with a small hoard of Merovingian coins (see Plate 76). The ornament includes pairs of interlocked boars (*top centre*), hook-beaked birds (*bottom centre*) and what have been termed 'Daniel in the Lions' Den' compositions which in fact are taken from pagan Northern mythology. The ground of the lid was originally of ivory or bone. The purse itself would have been of leather. The 'Man and Monster' plaques show Swedish connections. Length: 18.8 cm

Pagan Saxon England

20 Drinking vessel, Sutton Hoo. Originally restored as a drinking horn, recent study has shown it to have been a cup. The body is a modern restoration, but the mounts of silver gilt are original. The interlaced animal ornament has been stamped on the thin metal. Notice the human masks at the points of the vandykes. Early seventh century

dead hero was laid to rest with his helmet, sword and shield. A whetstone or sceptre and a standard proclaim his royalty. His entertainment was to be provided by a lyre (now reconstructed by the British Museum), and he would have been able to eat from a variety of silver bowls and quaff from one of seven silver-decorated drinking vessels. There was a magnificent silver dish with stamps of the emperor Anastasius of Byzantium (491–518) underneath, and at the east end of the burial chamber were bronze cauldrons and a mass of chainwork. It is the jewellery that excites the imagination and the splendidly decorated gear of the hero that brings the world of the Anglo-Saxons nearer. A simple list of the grave goods is eloquent testimony to the lifestyle of a royal hero.

This burial is unusually rich, and also late in the pagan period, but the other evidence for warrior equipment underlines the fact that the early Saxons were a warrior-based society. If Hengist did not have the ornate armour of the legendary Beowulf or the historical Raedwald, he would certainly have been well equipped with weaponry.

Helmets are rare finds in any period and only a couple of examples have survived from Anglo-Saxon England. The simpler of the two is probably the more typical, and was found in a seventh-century barrow at Benty Grange in Derbyshire in the nineteenth century. It had a domed frame composed of iron bands radiating from the centre of the

Pagan Saxon England

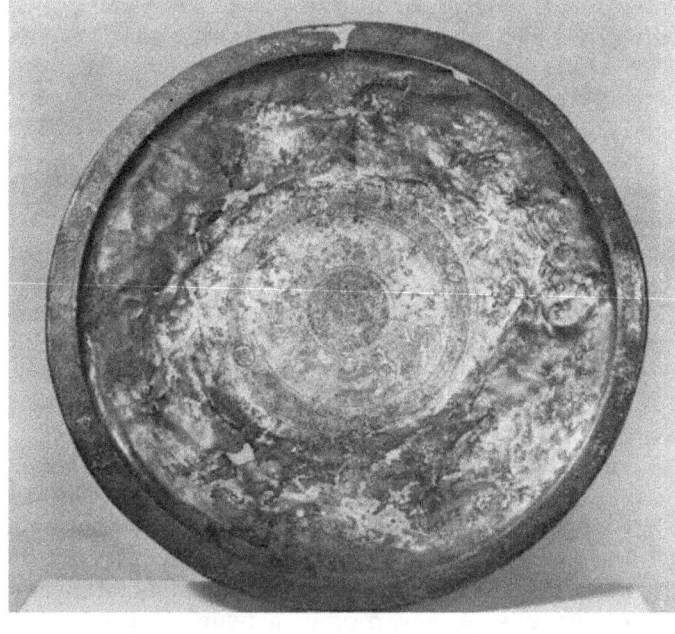

21 The 'Anastasius Dish', Sutton Hoo. This huge silver dish (diameter 72.4 cm) was made in Byzantium and carries four impressions from two control stamps in the workshop of the emperor Anastasius I (491–518). The style of the dish, however, would have been old-fashioned by the time of Anastasius – its fussy ornament went out of vogue around AD 400

22 Helmet frame with boar's crest, Benty Grange, Derbyshire. One of two helmets from Anglo-Saxon burials (the other is from Sutton Hoo, Plate 23). The helmet was composed of plates of horn, attached to the frame with silver rivets. The crest is Celtic rather than Anglo-Saxon in character, and is inlaid with silver. Its eyes are garnet. The boar was a symbol of strength, associated with the god Freyr

Pagan Saxon England

crown and riveted to an iron headband. The spaces between the bands were filled with horn plates, fastened with ornamental silver rivets, and the medial band extended to the nose where it was decorated with a silver cross. For a crest it bore the free-standing figure of a boar, originally iron-plated and inlaid with silver. Its eyes were staring red garnets. In style it is Celtic rather than Anglo-Saxon, though both Celts and Saxons regarded the boar as a symbol of strength and ferocity, and it was associated with the god Freyr. In *Beowulf* such helmets are described: 'The blood-stained sword with its mighty blade cuts off the boar-images of enemies' helmets', or: 'Figures of boars, gold adorned, shining, fire-hardened, glittered over the cheek-pieces. The warlike beast guarded the lives of fierce warriors.'

Helmets are frequently depicted in art, and are generally of this bowl-shaped form with a projecting nose-guard. They appear worn by the little figures that adorn the mounts of the Taplow drinking horns (see p. 72), and by the men of the Franks Casket (see p. 116). One of the best representations of a warrior in a helmet, again of the

23 Helmet from Sutton Hoo, as recently reconstructed. A ceremonial object, probably never worn in battle, this helmet has close counterparts in the Vendel and Valsgärde cemeteries in Sweden. It is ornamented with repoussé plates, and was either made in Sweden or in East Anglia by Swedish craftsmen using Swedish dies

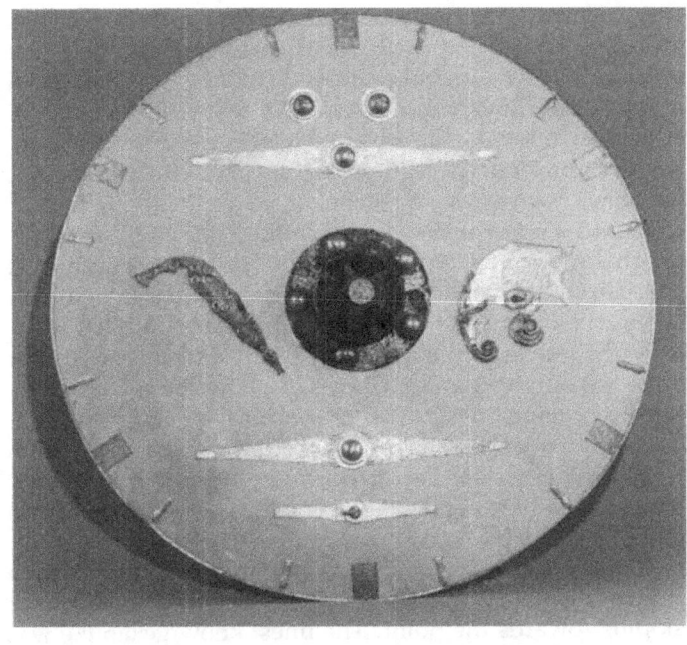

24 The Sutton Hoo shield, restored. This recent reconstruction shows the domed central *umbo* or boss, designed to protect the hand, and the various mounts. The body of the shield was of wood (mostly perished), and it originally measured about 83.8 cm in diameter. Rampant horses adorn the flange of the shield boss, and the whole again has counterparts at Vendel in Sweden

seventh-century appears on a gilded bronze buckle found at Finglesham, Kent, in 1964. The hero is naked apart from his belt, and his helmet is bowl-shaped and crowned by huge horns ending in what appear to be birds' heads. This type of helmet seems to be Swedish, though it may have an Iron Age Celtic ancestry, and may also have been, by the sixth or seventh century, out of regular use in fighting. Warriors wearing similar helmets appear on the stamped plates that decorate a late sixth-century helmet of Swedish manufacture found in the royal ship burial at Sutton Hoo. This superb helmet has a vizor which covers the face, and eyebrows ending in boars' heads. Like much in the Sutton Hoo burial (see p. 49), it was a ceremonial object, probably never worn in the heat of real battle, and it can be assumed that helmets were rarely worn by the ordinary Anglo-Saxon warrior.

Nor was body armour often worn, though once again Sutton Hoo and Benty Grange have provided examples of chain-mail, and there is one further example from Kent. Chain-mail is shown on the Franks Casket (see p. 116).

All warriors, however, carried shields. They were normally made of limewood, and were circular, up to 1 m across, with a central hole which was covered by the boss and took behind it the grip, so that the boss is in effect protecting the fist. Usually only the iron fittings survive – central *umbo* or boss and the shield grip. Part of the wood

Pagan Saxon England

survived in a grave at Petersfinger in Wiltshire, where it was found to have been made of sheets fixed together like plywood. It was probably curved like a watchglass, and would often have been covered in leather. Ornamental attachments for shields are known, the best example being from Sutton Hoo. All-leather shields without any ornament may have been carried by some.

Socketed spearheads are common grave finds, suggesting that most men carried them for hunting or warfare. A specialized type of thrusting spear, descended from Roman types and known as the *angon*, is also found in what seem to be the graves of the rich. Bows were certainly used, but none has survived intact. Traces of a bow about 1.5 m long were discovered at Chessel Down on the Isle of Wight, a cemetery which has also produced arrowheads. Archers with small bows are depicted in Anglo-Saxon art – it may have been a hunting weapon. The throwing-axe (*francisca*) of the Franks was also used in battle.

The most characteristic weapon was the *scramasax*, a single-edged iron hacking sword, with an angled back sloping towards the point. The finest known example was

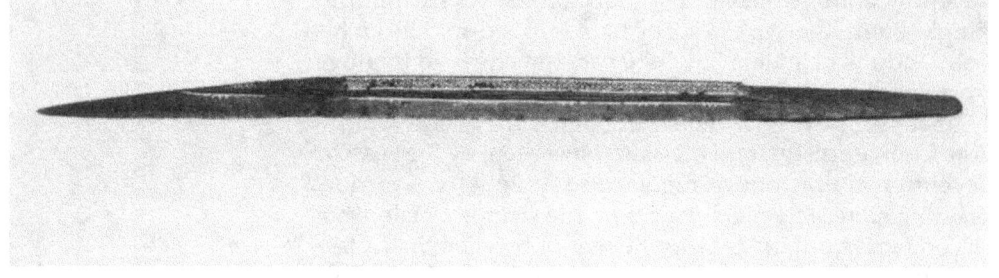

25 Iron *scramasax*, inlaid with bronze, copper and silver. Length: 81.1 cm. Dating from the late ninth century, it was found in the river Thames. It is a characteristic type of single-edged Anglo-Saxon sword. The other side carries an inlaid magical formula in runes

found in the Thames. It was inlaid with silver and bronze along the back of the blade, and had the runic alphabet inlaid in silver. It dates from around 800. Beowulf carried a similar weapon in a sheath suspended from his mail-coat, and so did his monster adversary Grendel. The sixteenth-century antiquary William Camden, in recounting the suggested origin of the term Saxon, noted of antiquarians that:

> One will have them deriv'd from *Saxo*, son of Negnon, and brother of Vandalus: another from their *stony* temper: a third from the remains of the Macedonian army: a fourth from certain knives: which gave occasion to that rhime in Engelhusius,
>
> > The Saxon people did as most believe,
> > Their name from *Saxa*, a short sword, receive.

The most treasured possession of the pagan Saxon warrior was his sword. In modern times, they would have cost as much as a television set. Few have survived as they were handed down from father to son. They appear to have been given names occasionally, like king Arthur's legendary sword Excalibur. They were also believed to possess magical powers. They were double-edged, cutting rather than thrusting weapons, about 90 cm long, and were kept in a scabbard (usually of wood and sometimes fleece-lined), suspended from a belt. The hilts were often elaborate – a horn example survives from Cumberland, decorated with filigree gold insets – but many hilts were of wood. Typical of the pagan period are three-cornered pommels with slightly curved-in sides. A fine example with bronze and silver mounts was found at Brighthampton, Oxford, and is ornamented in the late Roman style. It is a Continental piece of the fifth century and has a rivet in the form of a cross on it. In Kent a distinctive type of sword with a ring on the hilt developed – such ring swords are mentioned in *Beowulf*. The ring could sometimes be replaced by a bead of amber or rock crystal and seems to have had a magical significance. A ring-sword was found at Sutton Hoo with a skeuomorphic ring (that is, made for ornamental purposes). Some sword

Pagan Saxon England

 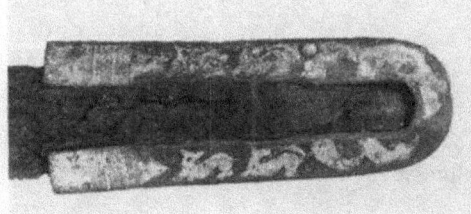

hilts are very elaborate, such as the gold and garnet ornamented example from Sutton Hoo or that decorated in gold from Coombe in Kent, which dates from the sixth century. A sixth-century sword pommel from Faversham has a nielloed rune *tir*, and a later Norse poem says, 'if you want victory, learn victory runes and cut them on to your sword hilt . . . and name Tyr twice'. This *tir* rune suggests an invocation of Tiw, the god of war and death.

Thus equipped the hero went into battle. Fighting forces were probably numerically small. In the late seventh century the Laws of Ine of Wessex announce that 'up to seven men' were thieves, 'from seven to thirty-five a band and above three dozen an army'. In 786 Cynheard's army amounted to eighty-five men, which was nearly sufficient to capture Wessex from king Cynewulf. Hengist and Horsa are described as having come over in three ships, while

26 The Brighthampton sword, Oxfordshire. The mounts are of (a) the scabbard mouth and (b) the chape. The sword was found in grave 31 of the Anglo-Saxon cemetery. The mount for the scabbard mouth is in typical late Roman style, with running scrolls in chip carving. The chape is inlaid with crouching animals in gold. Dating from the first half of the fifth century, it is probably an import from the Meuse area, though a British origin has also been suggested for it

Pagan Saxon England

Cerdic and Cynric came over in five. In other words, war bands coming to England were of the order of 100–250 men, which helps to account for the considerable mix-up of peoples in the population of early Anglo-Saxon England. Such armies were organized on a basis of personal loyalty, with as its nucleus the war band of the chief. In return for their loyalty, the chief rewarded his followers with weapons, gold rings, feasts and drink.

The strongest image of the hero that spans the centuries is that of him among the war band in the feasting hall, where he would be listening to songs and poems glorifying heroic adventures. A lyre measuring about 74 cm long was found at Sutton Hoo, with sound-box and frame of maple and pegs of poplar. Other lyres were found at Taplow and Abingdon, and one is illustrated being played by David in an early Canterbury manuscript. Harps are mentioned in *Beowulf*, where it is reported that the troll Grendel woke when he heard 'loud merriment in the hall, the music of the harp and the clear sound of the minstrel'. Other musical instruments known from Anglo-Saxon manuscripts are the horn, trumpet, pipe, shawm, rebec and probably the bagpipes. A Danish-period flute has been found at York.

The feasting hero was also entertained by dice and board games, and gaming pieces are fairly common finds in graves. At Caistor-by-Norwich an urn was found to contain thirty-three pieces, a third black (of ivory), the rest white (of

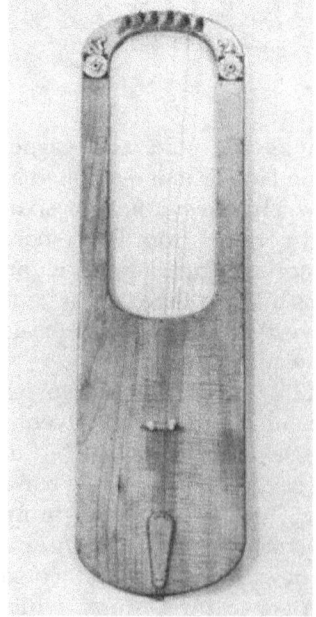

27 Reconstruction of lyre, Sutton Hoo. The stringed instrument from the ship burial was originally reconstructed as a harp, but this reconstruction is more probable. A similar lyre is illustrated in a Canterbury manuscript showing David as Harpist, dating from the mid-eighth century (see Plate 67)

bone). The same cemetery produced a set of thirty-one knuckle-bones of sheep, used in a game similar to jacks. The largest was engraved with a runic inscription which has not been deciphered. Decorated bone playing pieces have been found at Taplow, Sarre, Faversham and elsewhere. One from Witchampton Manor has two horses' heads on it, rather like a chess knight, though there is little evidence for chess-playing in England before the Norman Conquest. Not all players were honest – two loaded dice were found at North Elmham, Norfolk, in the Bishop's Palace, contrived so that they always came up with a six.

Other pastimes were hunting, falconry, bear-baiting, bull-baiting, athletics, horse-racing, horse-fighting, swimming and weapon sports.

Anglo-Saxon literature abounds with tales of brawls resulting from drunkenness at the feast, caused by mead, wine or beer. In *Beowulf*, after the defeat of Grendel, the hall was adorned with gold wall hangings, and the men on benches round their king quaffed mead while the king presented gifts to the hero and his followers. The court minstrel played and sang, and the cupbearers served wine. The queen offered wine to the king and his guests, and at the end of the feast the benches were cleared away and the beds (which were pallets) laid out. At such a feast the lord's retainers were expected to make promises or boasts about their loyalty. In the story of the *Battle of Maldon* one hero urges his companions to remember their mead speeches, 'when we warriors in hall raised our boasts at the bench about harsh battle. Now we can test who is brave.'

Such, then, was the Anglo-Saxon hero, drunk, boastful, brave, a barbarian in a mould made centuries before in the flamboyance of late prehistoric Europe, and not so very different from his Celtic counterpart.

The pagan Saxon as artist
The brooch that the Rev. Bryan Faussett found in his explorations at Kingston Down (see p. 19) is among the greatest treasures of Dark Age barbarian Europe. Before the Kingston brooch, however, lay two centuries of developing art, an area of human endeavour that is essentially abstract and from which it is therefore difficult to make historical inferences. Almost all our knowledge of pagan Saxon art comes from metalwork. No doubt the Anglo-Saxons in the fifth and sixth centuries impressed their friends and neighbours with decorated leather, wood, cloth and other perishable possessions, but these have not survived, except for a few patterned braids. The earliest sculptures were not

Pagan Saxon England

carved until the coming of Christianity, and the earliest paintings similarly have an origin in religious manuscripts. It is on the jewellery that the mastery of the pagan Saxon artist can be seen at its best, and it is through this medium that its development can be followed.

It comes as a delight to the scholar therefore that pagan Saxon jewellery is not only of great archaeological importance but is pleasing aesthetically. Anglo-Saxons tired of old fashions almost as quickly as modern people and their jewels are therefore often more readily datable than other types of archaeological find. To judge from the discoveries in graves, many Anglo-Saxons seem to have owned at least one simple brooch. Fashions in jewellery too are distinctive of the different Continental homelands of the Anglo-Saxon settlers; they can hint at family connections or trading links across the Channel, between specific regions.

Of the many jewels found in Anglo-Saxon graves, the most rewarding both aesthetically and archaeologically are brooches. In the late Roman period many Roman safety-pin brooches were taken north into barbarian homelands where they were copied and developed. Many of these were then

28 Quoit Brooch, Sarre, Kent. This is the finest of a series of pieces of metalwork from south-east England that have been the subject of considerable debate. The style of ornament, named, after the characteristic product, the 'Quoit Brooch Style' is quite unlike later Anglo-Saxon ornamental work. It has been claimed as Frankish or Scandinavian (Jutish), but Continental parallels are not very convincing and it should probably be seen as a native style derived from late Roman which was current in England around the middle of the fifth century. The brooch has two elements, a penannular brooch (which itself is a Romano-British type of dress fastener) and a quoit, decorated with fairly naturalistic animals in zones. It is of parcel-gilt silver, 7.8 cm in diameter. Note the three-dimensional birds on both quoit and pin imported to Britain, where Anglo-Saxon versions were produced.

The inhabitants of England developed their own types of brooches, drawing upon late Roman art as the source of their inspiration for the ornamentation. The finest are known as *quoit brooches*, and display a distinctive art which can also be seen on buckles, strap-ends, pendants and other objects, notably those of Roman Derivation. The Quoit Brooch style is highly individualistic, unlike anything Continental, and almost certainly represents a Romano-British response to Anglo-Saxon stimulus around the middle of the fifth century. As the name indicates it is found at its best on the quoit-shaped plates that were added to native-style penannular brooches. The finest example was found in the Anglo-Saxon cemetery at Sarre. The brooch has characteristic concentric rings of crouching animals. Made of silver, it has a pair of confronted birds in relief on the quoit, and another on the pin. A feature of this art style is that the animals have a double outline and hatched fur. Quadrupeds abound, but there are also sea horses and facing human (?) masks.

Pagan Saxon England

29 Silver inlaid buckle, Bifrons, Kent, depicting Daniel in the Lions' Den. Made of iron, it carries an inscription VIVAT Q . . . VI FECIT (Long Live the Man who Made [Me]). The central figure of a man with uplifted hands is an *Orans* (an Early Christian at prayer), while the flanking lions are surmounted by peacocks and beneath them are lambs, both Christian symbols. The *Orans* (i.e. Daniel) has the long hair associated with Frankish kings. It was made probably in a Frankish workshop in North Gaul, and brought to Britain in the early fifth century probably by a Christian Frank. It was found in 1867 by a gamekeeper, and 'restored' by his daughter. Length: 9 cm

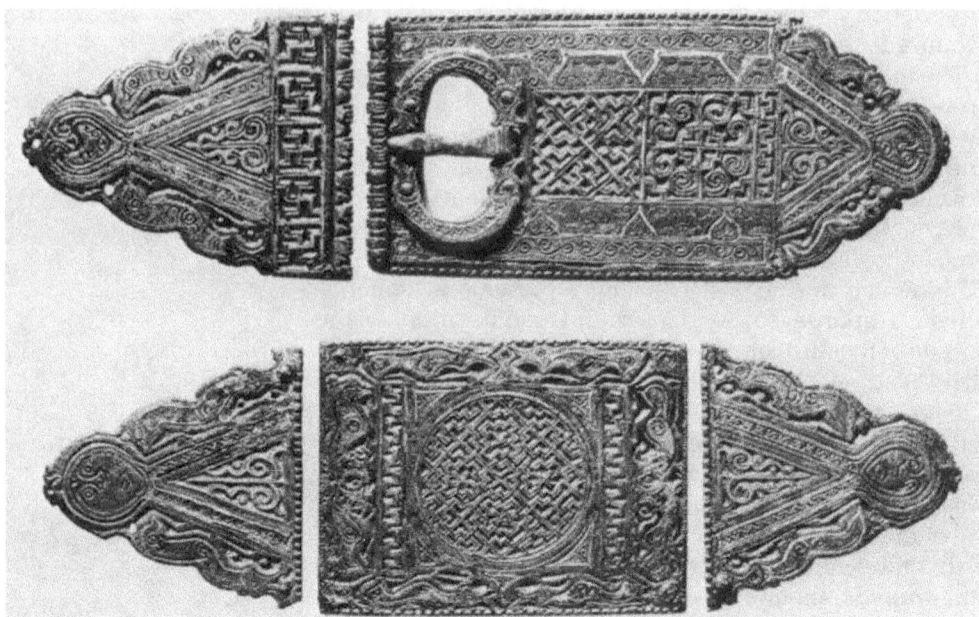

30 Belt-set from Anglo-Saxon grave 117, Mucking, Essex. Overall length: 16 cm. Bronze with silver inlay. This is a classic example of 'Quoit Brooch Style' ornament. Notice the animals bordering the triangular plates, the human masks and the Roman fret, scroll and meander patterns. The buckle element itself has characteristic confronted animal heads. Length: 16 cm

The quoit brooch metalworkers took up the ornamental device of using silver inlays which had been pioneered on the Continent and which first reached Britain on imported buckles. Inlaying can be seen at its best on an imported buckle from northern Gaul which was found at Bifrons in Kent and which depicts Daniel in the Lions' Den. Among the British manifestations of the technique is a disc brooch from Faversham ornamented with quoit brooch animals.

Quoit brooch style metalwork was fashionable in Kent around the mid-fifth century. Around the same time, and slightly earlier, imitations were being made in Kent and elsewhere of the late Roman belt fittings of the type found at Vermand in France and at Richborough and Dorchester-on-Thames in England.

While such insular developments flourished on British soil, other brooches were being devised on the Continent and imported by the incoming Anglo-Saxons. One of the earliest types is that known as the *cruciform brooch*, the prototypes of which barbarian craftsmen put on the market in Anglian and adjacent areas abroad in the 390s and which, in various guises, remained popular in England into the sixth century.

Once introduced to Britain, cruciform brooches were developed to cater for Anglo-Saxon taste, and, although their evolution is complex, it has been well studied. The earliest have a head plate with projecting round knobs

Pagan Saxon England

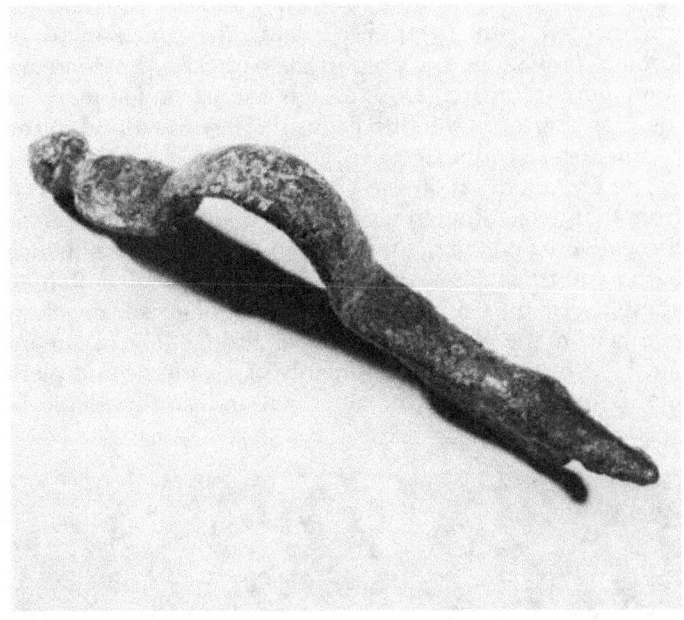

31 Cruciform brooch, Hockwold-cum-Wilton, Norfolk. Ultimately inspired by Roman bow brooches, cruciform brooches are among the earliest in Anglo-Saxon England. This example is particularly early, and lacks the two side knobs on the head that on later examples have given rise to the name 'cruciform'. In England cruciform brooches were soon elaborated with animal heads on the feet. The majority of the early cruciform brooches have been found in East Anglia, but there is another fairly early group in Kent. First half of fifth century

which give them a roughly cruciform shape, and they have been found in Kent, Suffolk and Cambridgeshire with outliers as far north as Yorkshire. Very early on smiths elaborated the brooch foot into an animal head, probably after having seen similar motifs in Roman metalwork.

Like the cruciform brooches, the *saucer brooch* was popular for a long time and underwent many modifications and developments. Its vogue was roughly contemporary with that of cruciform brooches, but its greatest successes came slightly later. The first smiths to start the fashion piloted the idea with a gilt bronze saucer-shaped roundel with a pin on the back, decorated with either five running scrolls or an equal-armed cross with scroll ends – both designs being adopted from Roman metalwork. Saucer brooches are found in the Continental homelands of the Saxons.

Equal-armed brooches are among the most attractive possessions of the early settlers. A small central bow with wide, equally balanced head and foot plate forms the shape of an H turned on its side. They are decorated in late Roman provincial styles, and thus in many way resemble the buckles and strap-tags of 'Vermand' type. Only a few are known in England, concentrated north of the Thames. These too were popular with the Saxons on the Continent.

Last among the types of brooches introduced to England by the early fifth-century settlers are *applied plate brooches*.

Pagan Saxon England

These are related to saucer brooches and are simple discs ornamented with an applied plate. The ornament is of Roman derivation, and among the earliest in England are some with a floriated cross design popular in Germany in the first quarter of the fifth century. They are found in the south-eastern counties.

The ornament on all these types of brooches is derived from that of late Roman provincial workshops. But even as these were enjoying fashion in England, distinctive barbarian art styles were evolving out of similar Roman stimulus, on the Continent. The trigger for artistic developments were the 'Vermand' style belt fittings. The ornament on these bronzes consisted mainly of geometric and plant motifs, alongside which were naturalistically depicted

32   Group of saucer brooches, fifth to sixth centuries. Of gilt bronze and of dished shape, these brooches were popular among the Saxons. The earliest are those with geometric ornament, and have either five scrolls or a floriated cross design. The geometric ones shown here belong to the late fifth century, and are of types found particularly in the south Midlands. The two in the bottom left of the picture are decorated with Style I ornament, and date from the sixth century

animals in crouching positions. These, despite the realism of their portrayal, are mythological and include considerable numbers of sea monsters. The ornament on some equal-armed brooches is almost identical to that on the Roman chip-carved fittings, so it is not impossible that the careers of craftsmen took them out of Roman pay and into the lands of the Germans in the early fifth century.

The artistic developments of the pagan period have been well studied and analysed. The first style that was of significance to Anglo-Saxon art in Britain is known after its most famous student as Salin's Style I. In this, Roman-inspired animals were found in the design. They were executed in chip carving and are less naturalistic than in earlier styles. The sea creatures formerly favoured also

Pagan Saxon England

33 Square-headed brooch, grave 41, Bifrons, Kent. Square-headed brooches are among the most characteristic of Anglo-Saxon jewels, and were made in a bewildering variety of forms. Two main groups can be distinguished, one characterized (as here) by a foot plate without a medial rib, the other by a divided foot plate. Note the facing mask on the bow and the confronted animal heads on either side of the foot plate. Brooches of this type with undivided feet are found only in Kent, and this example should probably be dated to the period AD 500–20. Although it has been suggested that it was made locally, it was more probably an import from Jutland. It shows a relatively early version of Style I ornament

Pagan Saxon England

disappeared to be replaced by quadrupeds, the animals being surrounded by contour lines. The animals in this style are purely Germanic, no doubt with meanings drawn from German mythology, now lost.

On the Continent, Style I underwent several phases of development, having been created sometime around 475. It was introduced to England almost immediately. It seems that Kent was the first area to import what are known as *square-headed brooches*. These were decorated with Style I ornament, and had been developed from Roman bow brooches, and had a large square plate head, bow and plate foot coming to a point. The earliest can be dated to around 480–500 and they are recognizable from the characteristic ornamental device of a crouching animal with human head.

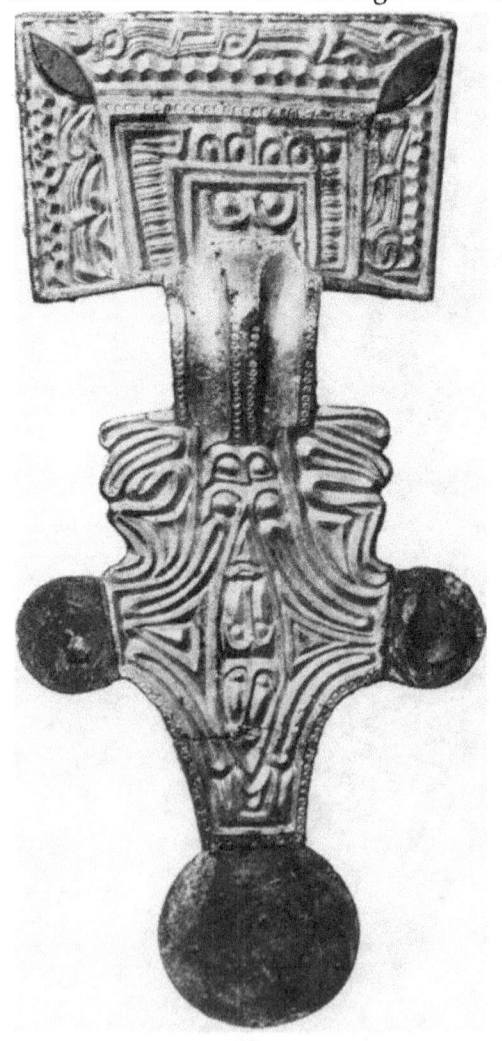

34 Square-headed brooch of East Anglian type, with the foot divided by a medial rib (ornamented with facing human masks). From Kenninghall, Norfolk. This example is not one of the first in the series, and can be assigned to the sixth century

Later variants had longer bows. Since the earliest show signs of wear, it can be inferred that they were brought across the Channel by immigrants. Some scholars have regarded their owners as the Jutes, since this type of brooch is found in traditionally Jutish areas. At about the same time other square-headed brooches were being imported into East Anglia. They can be distinguished from those of Kent by having the ornament on the plate divided by a midrib or bar. These have little animal ornament, the decoration being entirely based on Roman-derived geometric patterns.

Dedicated followers of fashion in early sixth-century Kent had a number of square-headed brooches from which to choose, all displaying versions of the popular Style I ornament. Little is known about their manufacture, though a 'factory' for their production has been discovered at Helgö, Sweden, and part of the mould for casting one was unearthed at Mucking.

From the end of the fifth century Kent holds the stage in pagan Saxon artistic and archaeological studies. For a long time the archaeology of early Kent has been haunted by the ghosts of Bede's Jutes, and various attempts have been made to recognize distinctively 'Jutish' objects, cruciform brooches and the square-headed brooches mentioned above being early contenders for the title. Such objects could be Jutish, but they need not be. The fact is that the Jutes, as a distinctive entity, are somewhat elusive archaeologically. One category of object, however, certainly points to strong connections between 'Jutish' Denmark and Kent in the period after 480 – *bracteates*.

Bracteates are round pendants of hammered gold, the name coming from the Latin *bractea*, meaning a thin piece of metal. They were made in Denmark initially in imitation of imported Roman gold coins in the late fourth and early fifth century. Except for a few stray finds, for example at Bifrons in Kent and from Oxford, which belong to the early days of

(a)

(b)

35 Front (a) and back (b) of a clay mould for casting a square-headed brooch, from Mucking, Essex. This is the only known example of a pagan Saxon brooch mould from England, though a considerable number have come to light at Helgö in Sweden. From hut 109

36 Group of jewellery from Mucking, Essex. The necklace includes characteristic blue-and-white 'eye' beads of glass. Inside can be seen a button brooch with facing human mask and a small long brooch of panelled type. Button brooches are related to saucer brooches, and date from the sixth century. The small long brooch is of a type current in East Anglia around the same time. Apart from the two saucer brooches and glass bead the other objects are two disc brooches with ring-and-dot ornament (*bottom left*) and a rare Frankish imported brooch (*bottom right*).

37 Rock crystal pendant in silver sling, from Kent. Rock crystal appears to have had special properties in the eyes of the pagan Saxons, and such pendants are not uncommon finds. Length: 6 cm

settlement, nearly all the examples found in England are of the most advanced type, datable to the sixth century. They are ornamented with abstract linear patterns, descended from the Roman coin designs.

There is therefore a limited amount of evidence that people who might be identified with Bede's Jutes were

dominant in the fifth and sixth century in Kent. From around 525 however, Frankish influence is more apparent in the selection of grave goods. There can be little doubt that there always had been Franks in Kent since the early days of settlement. Contact with Frankish lands is clearly attested by various imports and by characteristic graves. Typical of the grave-finds are throwing axes – *franciscas.* Frankish influence in sixth-century Kent can account for a variety of charming objects that have been unearthed. They include brooches with radiate heads and tiny brooches made in the shape of birds. In the meantime, Frankish workshops had discovered in England a market for their fine wheel-made pottery, and in reciprocation Kentish square-headed brooches were traded to Gaul.

The Franks, however, lost their domination of the markets in the middle of the sixth century, when the kingdoms saw an artistic flowering in Kent. This was a peculiarly Kentish distillation, and its culmination was achievements like the Kingston Brooch.

The *disc brooch* is perhaps the finest achievement of the Kentish artist. Long before such masterpieces as that from

38 (*Left*) Cruciform long brooch. This example, from Westcotes near Leicester, is typical of a large series of evolved cruciform brooches of the mid-sixth century. The decoration is mainly of punched dots, and the foot has lost nearly all resemblance to an animal. Length: 12.5 cm

39 (*Right*) Small long brooch, Market Overton, Rutland. Small long brooches are to be found in a bewildering variety of shapes which span the sixth century

40 Group of gold and garnet disc brooches, from Kent. The earliest, perhaps of the second quarter of the sixth century, are the two smaller examples on the bottom right. The others are of the early seventh century

Kingston had been perfected, Kentish artists had been experimenting with simpler disc brooches and with the use of gold and garnet. Disc brooches were first copied from Frankish originals around AD 525. On these early examples inlay was confined to three or more rarely four wedge-shaped garnets alternating with panels of recumbent Style I animals. In the centre of the brooch nestled a round inlay. As time wore on such simple brooches were elaborated with further inlays, which took on a stepped form. Inlays appeared on the border, and filigree made its appearance.

By the seventh century Kentish taste ran to more elaborate brooches, and the central inlay was surrounded by a gold plate with filigree and with garnets set in cloisons round it. Stepped cloisons were very popular on these brooches, some of which are superb examples of restrained craftsmanship. There are about 150 surviving examples of disc brooches of non-composite type, and their distribution seems to suggest that their creators worked in the vicinity of Faversham in Kent.

Finally, composite brooches like the Kingston example were evolved, with a front and back plate filled in to give a massive effect. Of these composite brooches less than a dozen survive – the brooch known as Sarre I, the Amherst Brooch (Sarre II), the Dover Brooch and the recently discovered Monkton Brooch (see p. 21) are typical. The success of the brooches led to their being copied in their Frankish homelands, but without the same verve.

Composite disc brooches mark the peak of the Kentish craftsman's skill, but the same expertise was used in the production of a variety of other objects, such as pins and pendants.

The seventh-century Kentish smith employed a variety of different techniques. The polychrome work of the disc brooches was done in cloisonné, whereby cells were made and soldered on to a base plate to take the inlay, which was then held in place by turning over the tops of the cloisons. The technique originated in the East, and had been developed by the Goths round the Black Sea. It then spread through Europe. Twisted gold wire (filigree) and droplets of gold (granular work) were also used, sometimes combined with cloisonné. Filigree and granular work were first developed in Roman workshops in the late Empire, and were also employed by Byzantine smiths, who may have passed on some taste for filigree to the Lombards. On early metalwork, such as the quoit brooch products, chip carving was popular. This technique was based on woodcarving, and again developed in Roman provincial workshops

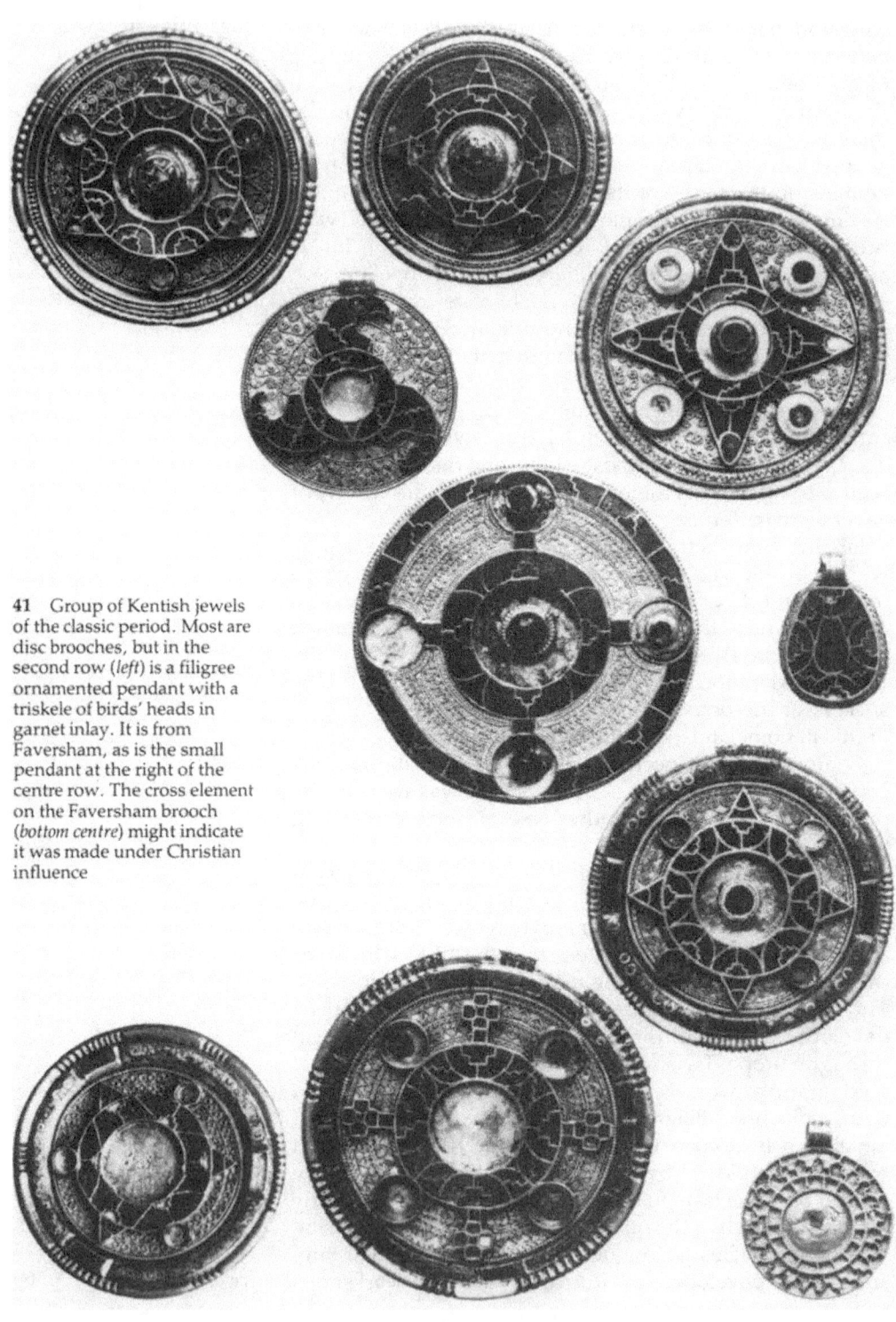

41 Group of Kentish jewels of the classic period. Most are disc brooches, but in the second row (*left*) is a filigree ornamented pendant with a triskele of birds' heads in garnet inlay. It is from Faversham, as is the small pendant at the right of the centre row. The cross element on the Faversham brooch (*bottom centre*) might indicate it was made under Christian influence

where it was designed to provide a reflecting surface. Both chip carving effects and cloisonné work were also produced by solid casting.

Gold was the primary material used, and the inlaid garnets may originally have come from India. Other substances favoured by the early jewellers were amethysts (originally from the east Mediterranean), rock crystal, agate, onyx, amber, ivory and blue glass.

While Kentish jewellery was developing, a new style of ornament was evolving in Scandinavia. This is known as Salin's Style II, also an animal ornament style, but one in which the bodies have been stretched out into intertwining ribbons of interlace known as lacertines.

In later periods, the names of individual artists exist, but art historians are still able to disagree over the evolution of particular styles or schools. In the Dark Ages, only the objects themselves can point to cultural changes, or the innovations or inspirations, of their creators. It is not surprising therefore that as with Style I, the origins of Style II have been much debated. Current opinion, however, holds that interlaced patterns seem to have developed independently of one another in many different areas, and that the beginnings of Scandinavian Style II were already apparent in some of the later Style I products, and in some other objects such as the latest of the bracteates. The

42 Group of three buckles. The first and third have Style II animals executed in gold filigree, and come from Faversham, Kent. The central buckle is typical of the less ornate examples found in Kent. The ornate examples date from the seventh century

43 Richly decorated buckle from a seventh-century grave at Crundale Down, Kent. The fish forming the central rib may be a Christian symbol. Filigree interlace borders the buckle, which has a restricted amount of cloisonné inlay on the pin plate

stimulus behind the sudden emergence of the new art trend was probably the adoption of geometric interlace by artists outside the Mediterranean, where it had long been fashionable. Interlace ornaments are found among Frankish grave goods from the tomb of Queen Arnegunde at St Denis, datable to around 570. In view of the close tie between Kent and this area at this period, it is likely that the art style spread to Kent by the end of the sixth century. It is arguable that interlace might already have been in use in Kent before the fully developed Style II was transmitted from Scandinavia sometime at the end of the sixth century: interlace can be seen on a sword from Coombe, which may be datable to the late sixth century.

Interlacing animals appear on a wide variety of objects, and the style is well exemplified by a series of buckles on which the interlacing figures are executed in filigree. These buckles, of roughly triangular shape, are elaborated with bosses at the angles, and often with cloisonné work too. Some of the finest come from Faversham, the centre of Kentish jewellery production. A slightly unusual example from Crundale has a border of interlace and a central midrib in the form of a fish. A particularly fine buckle with cloisonné inlay on the loop as well as the main boss was among the finds from a Kentish-type chieftain's burial at Taplow, Buckinghamshire. The objects unearthed from it

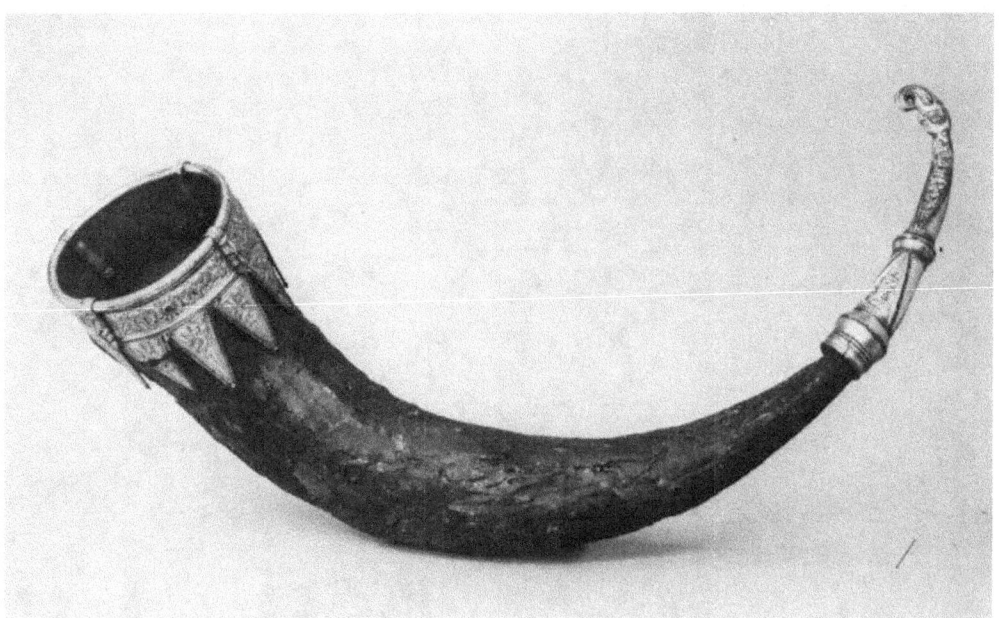

include drinking horn mounts which show both Styles I and II and another style which combines elements of both and is consequently known as the Fusion Style.

The Kentish version of Style II is characterized by double outlined ribbon animals with bodies infilled with dots. This feature can be seen on the mount for a similar goblet from Farthingdown in Surrey. It was also a feature of the type of Style II used in East Anglia, and was employed in the Sutton Hoo treasure. Some of the finest examples of Style II ornament are to be seen on distinctively Kentish bracteates, some of which seem to lose their animal character in a tangled mass of line. As the seventh century wore on interlace became less and less zoomorphic, though careful study under a magnifying glass reveals the rudimentary heads and tails of the snakes that adorn such superb later seventh-century pieces as the mounts from Faversham and the roundel from Hardingstone, Northants.

Some time in the seventh century a new type of animal was introduced in art. The descendant of earlier Anglo-Saxon beasts, but less attenuated and more aggressive, it bites its own body. It appears on a mount from Caenby, in Lincolnshire, and on the back of a gold and garnet composite disc brooch from Faversham, for instance. An even finer example adorns the silver gilt pommel of a sword from Crundale, on which two beasts gnaw one another. The

44 Drinking horn, Taplow, Buckinghamshire, with silver gilt mounts. Note human masks on the clips for the rim mount, bird's head terminal, and helmeted figures on the vandykes of the rim mount. The rim mount is in an English version of Style I. The terminal mount is decorated with what has been termed 'Fusion Style' ornament, combining elements of both Style I and the more evolved Style II ribbon ornament. Style II decoration also appears on the Taplow horn, thus providing the art historian with a 'museum' of pagan Saxon art styles on one object. The find came from a barrow which was no doubt the grave of Taeppa who is commemorated in the place-name (the *low* element means a mound). The barrow, which was opened in 1883, produced in addition a Coptic bowl, four glass vessels, a gold buckle with Style II ornament, thirty bone counters, an embroidered garment, and the mounts for another similar drinking horn, among other objects

Pagan Saxon England

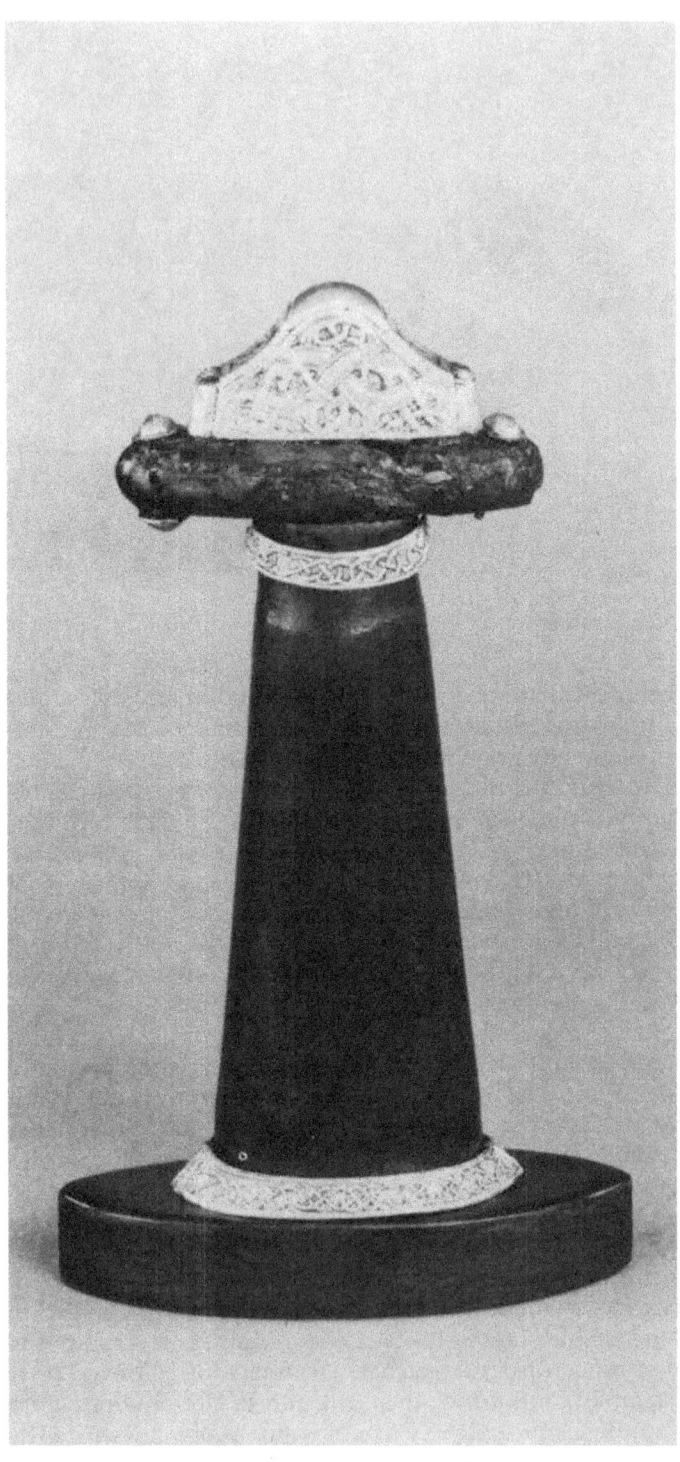

45 The Crundale sword pommel, Kent (restored). This seventh-century sword is ornamented with two mounts with simple interlace and, on the pommel, a pair of biting animals gripping each other's bodies. It is of silver gilt, and dates from the seventh century. The type of animal which appears here and on a few other pieces represents a development from those of the earlier pagan period. Its immediate predecessor adorns the Sutton Hoo purse mount (Plate 19, centre top of purse) and it cavorts across the pages of the Book of Durrow, an early Northumbrian manuscript, in more evolved form. Length of pommel: 4.4 cm

Pagan Saxon England

46 Series of bronze mounts, possibly for a shield, from Caenby, Lincolnshire. At first sight there is no sign of any animal in the ornament of these mounts, but careful scrutiny reveals 'heads' and 'tails' on the interlace. Birds' heads with hooked beaks terminate the 'mushroom'-shaped mounts. They represent the last flickers of Style II in England. In the same burial was a silver mount with 'Crundale' style animals

engraved creatures process on the back of the Faversham disc brooch. These beasts lend themselves to line drawing, and were taken up in the late seventh century in Northumbria, where their jaws snap away in the Book of Durrow (see p. 106). They also reached East Anglia, where they were used to enliven the Sutton Hoo treasure.

The religious Saxon

> Then the Geats prepared for him a pyre firm on the earth, hung around with helmets, battle-shields, bright body armour, as he had craved: then the mourning men laid in the midst the famous chief, their loved lord. The warriors began to heap up on the barrow the greatest of funeral pyres: the wood-smell rose up dark above the smoking glow, the crackling flame, mixed with the cry of weeping – the threnody of the winds stopped – until it had consumed the body, hot to the heart. Sorrowful of heart, they lamented the sadness in their souls, the killing of their chief: likewise the woman with bound hair sang a dirge . . . the sky swallowed up the smoke.

This description of an Anglo-Saxon chieftain's burial comes from the epic poem *Beowulf*. It continues by explaining how a barrow was built on the edge of a headland, visible far and wide to people at sea, and how the mourners left various objects on the mound as a parting gesture to the dead hero.

Such a description, all too rare, helps to bring an

47 Elaborately ornamented phalerae, perhaps for horse harness, from the King's Field, Faversham, Kent. These are ornamented with degenerate animal interlace similar to that on the Caenby mounts. Seventh century

immediacy to the cinerary urns which stand in row after dreary row in museum cases, and to the rusty iron swords and spears beside them. For all these dull objects do have their own tale to tell about the pagan Saxon's belief in the hereafter, if they can be interpreted correctly.

The early English practised a variety of burial customs. North of the Thames (traditionally Anglian areas) burial usually meant cremation, the ashes being interred in specially made urns. Sometimes small personal items were

48 Bowl with faceted carination, Mucking, Essex. Such vessels are characteristic of the Saxon areas on the Continent, and can be dated to the first half of the fifth century

49 Cremation urn from Caistor-by-Norwich (Urn E5), decorated with incised pendant triangles and finger-tipping. Comparable pots (known as Plettke A3 type) have been dated on the Continent to before AD 300, but this example is unlikely to be as early

added, either burnt or intact, such as knives, combs or pieces of jewellery. Miniature implements such as tweezers (which may have been used for embroidery) were sometimes made specially for the grave. The cremations were usually placed directly in holes in the ground accumulating into large cemeteries which were sometimes laid out into rows.

The pots used for cremations were usually made specially for the occasion and their decoration can be matched with

Pagan Saxon England

50 Urn with *stehende Bogen* (arch) decoration, from Caistor-by-Norwich. Such urns are characteristic of the period of settlement around the middle of the fifth century, and have their counterparts in the 'Saxon' areas of the Continent

51 Fragments of a cremation urn from Markshall, Norfolk (Urn LXX), ornamented with a human face. The exact counterpart for this urn can be found at Wehden in Germany (now in Hanover). Both pots must have been the work of the same potter – did he cross over to Britain in the later fifth century?

Continental pottery designs. They can thus shed some light on the homelands of their owners, and also on the dates of the migrations. Broadly speaking, in the period before 450 there were three main styles of urn ornament prevalent in England. The first favoured massed lines or corrugated grooves (horizontal on the neck, vertical on the body) producing rectangular effects. These have been found in Anglian areas on the Continent, but similar pottery is also found in the areas traditionally associated with the Jutes where chevron and diagonal linear designs and curvilinear patterns were popular. The close similarities in the pots from both areas show great similarities between 'Jutes' and 'Angles'. In the area occupied by the Saxons on the Continent, elegant bowls, some with pedestal feet or faceted carinations have been found. Here too, large urns with narrow necks were popular, decorated with curvilinear patterns, of which standing arches and finger-tipped rosettes were the most characteristic.

Around the middle of the fifth century when the Germanic settlements in England increased there was, coincidentally, the introduction of a new style of pottery to the Continental homelands. This was characterized by the widespread use of knobs and bosses to produce three-dimensional effects, and the pots are therefore known as *Buckelurnen* (i.e. bossed pots). Every stage of their fifth-

52 *Buckelurne* from Spong Hill Anglo-Saxon cemetery, North Elmham, Norfolk. Cremation urns with prominent bosses became fashionable from the mid-fifth century onwards. Later examples were decorated with a variety of stamps, some of which (for example rosettes) recall those on late Romano-British pottery

century development on the Continent is matched in England. In some cases it is even possible to point to urns on both sides of the Channel made by the same potter. It is either to be inferred that the pots were brought over by colonists, or, more likely, that the potter himself was one of the travellers. A particular urn from Markshall in Norfolk was given a unique decorative scheme with circular bosses modelled into human faces. Such an unusual design could only have been created by the same potter who created a

Pagan Saxon England

similar pot, found at Wehden, Germany, and now kept in Hanover.

Sixth-century Anglo-Saxons began to find bosses unattractive or old-fashioned, so potters created a new look by using stamps (sometimes combined with bosses) which they arranged into triangular or rectangular patterns. Some information is available about the manufacture of these cremation ceramics from the handiwork of the Illington-Lackford potter (see p. 48) whose workshop at West Stow has already been mentioned.

Some of the later pagan period pots were decorated with magical designs including runes, swasticas and the symbol of Thor. The *wyrm*, a serpent or legless dragon, also features on ceramics, symbolizing the destruction wrought by death and also perhaps the dragon that protected the treasures in burial mounds from looting. In this aim he was, over the centuries, singularly unsuccessful.

Inhumation was particularly popular south of the Thames (Saxon areas) and the body was accompanied by various personal articles necessary for a comfortable life after death. Although the advent of Christianity discouraged furnished graves (material possessions being quite irrelevant in the Kingdom of Heaven) some people hedged their bets by adding a few goods to burials for a century after St Augustine's conversion mission. As late as the tenth or eleventh century some people were still being laid to rest at Saffron Walden with a few of life's comforts.

53 The silhouette of a long-vanished body in a pagan grave at Mucking, Essex

Some burials were distinguished by a barrow or mound. Sometimes the mourners saved energy (or possibly cashed in on the additional sanctity) by using existing prehistoric mounds, but in the seventh century the barrows were custom-made, as, for example, at Kingston Down or Taplow. Burial in a ship was extremely rare and is only known at Sutton Hoo and Snape in East Anglia.

The purpose behind cremation was probably to release the soul from the body. The Anglo-Saxons were very worried about hauntings, and some cremation urns have little glass windows in the sides to allow the soul to come and go. In some instances the body was decapitated to prevent the dead walking, as at Chadlington, Oxfordshire. Corn was sometimes burned to keep the ghosts at bay; this happened at Marston, Northants, for example, but was one of the customs expressly forbidden later by Theodore in his *Penitentials*.

A few graves, particularly in Surrey, have a second skull which may reflect the Anglo-Saxons' belief in the sancity of the head and could be the trophies of head hunting. Such a bizarre note is often struck, to modern ears, with Anglo-Saxon burials. Women were not infrequently killed to accompany a man to the after-life. At Finglesham, Fathingdown and Mitcham (the first in Kent, the latter two in Surrey) women's bodies have been discovered contorted as though buried alive. The same fate may have befallen the unfortunate female whose remains were found at Sewerby,

Pagan Saxon England

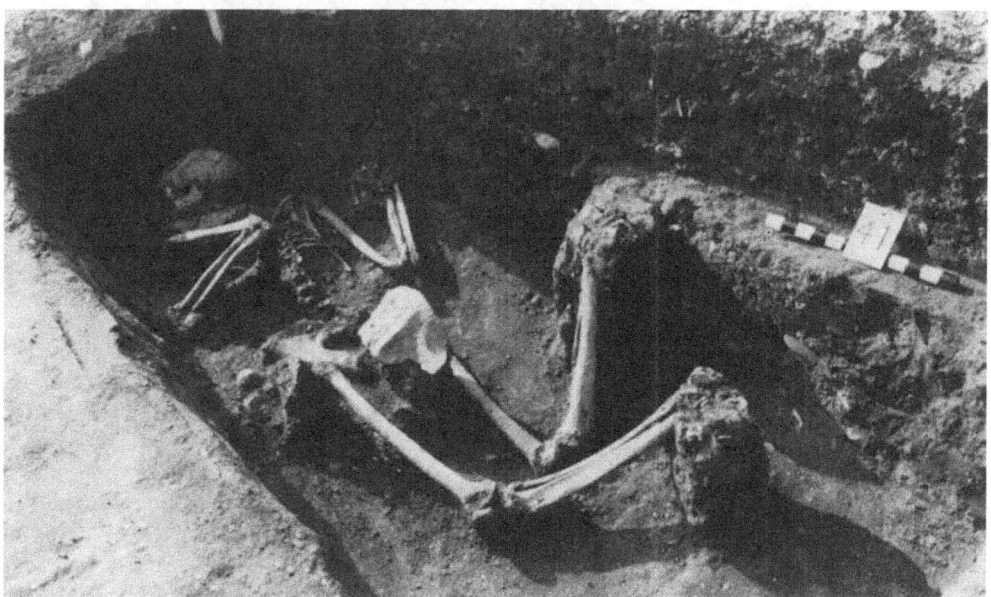

54 Contorted skeleton of a woman buried alive at Sewerby, Yorkshire. The stone was probably thrown down to stop her struggling up

Pagan Saxon England

55 Anglian 'wrist clasp' from North Luffenham, Rutland. Such objects are characteristic of the Anglian areas, and date from the mid-sixth century onwards

56 Stave-built wooden bucket from grave 600, Mucking, Essex. Such buckets are not uncommon finds in Anglo-Saxon graves. The facing masks on the vandykes should be compared with some of the other facing masks in Saxon art – e.g. those on the Kenninghall brooch (Plate 34). The grave also contained a sword and shield. Sixth century

East Yorkshire – the body had been contorted and weighed down with a piece of quernstone for grinding grain, no doubt to prevent her from climbing out of her grave. Beneath her lay the richly furnished burial of an old woman, possibly her mistress. The reason for the heavy flints being thrown on to the heads and bodies of children buried at Winnal, Hants, is less easy to find. Possibly the most extraordinary piece of detective work by modern scholars was carried out on a burial unearthed at Worthy Park, Hants.

Here a girl of about sixteen had been buried without grave goods. Careful examination of the bones showed that they had been damaged shortly before death in such a manner as to suggest that she had been raped – possibly as a result of a combined, violent attack by several men. In pagan Saxon England such a misfortune would have brought disgrace to the girl's family. A second burial in the same cemetery was of a woman in her late twenties who had been buried unceremoniously. The position of the skeleton suggested that she had been buried alive and had been attempting to get to her knees as the earth cascaded over her.

Horses and dogs, too, did not escape such atrocities, for they have sometimes been found sacrificed in graves. Joints of meat were occasionally provided, and duck eggs, hazel nuts and unopened oysters were among the foods left for

Pagan Saxon England

57 A glass 'claw' beaker with pedestal foot. Glass vessels are common finds in Anglo-Saxon graves. Most were imported from the Rhineland, but some may have been made in the neighbourhood of Faversham, Kent. This particular example is unusual in that it has a Roman-style pedestal foot. It may be an early import (of c. AD 400), but was not interred until the second quarter of the sixth century, in a woman's grave at Mucking, Essex

58 Bronze buckle, from Kent, decorated with 'Antique' cameo-style heads. This interesting object is an import into Anglo-Saxon England. It was probably made in the Byzantine world around the sixth century, and is paralleled by one from Akmim in Upper Egypt. The grave in which it was found was that of a normal Anglo-Saxon warrior, but he also was buried with a further three buckles manufactured somewhere in the Eastern Empire – their counterparts have been found in Bulgaria, the Crimea and Carthage

59 Bronze bowl, Sutton Hoo. Made in Coptic Egypt, it was an import probably from Alexandria. On the inside of the bowl are naturalistic engravings of a camel, a donkey, a lion and another feline animal. Several different Coptic vessels have been found in England, including one from the Taplow burial

the gastronomic delight of the dead. These last three unusual foodstuffs may have been symbols of rebirth, as indeed may the cowrie shells from the Indian Ocean which sometimes found their way into Anglo-Saxon graves.

The more regular inhumation grave goods fall into conformable categories. Men were usually buried with a knife, and the weapons of a warrior – usually spears, and a sword or perhaps a shield. Women were interred with jewellery, belt buckles, brooches and the like (though jewellery is also found in male graves). Females also took their chatelaine for suspending the household keys, and, especially in Anglian areas, were laid to rest with a 'girdle hanger' which symbolized their domestic authority.

The next most frequent grave goods are vessels – rough pots, drinking glasses or horns – which were no doubt originally filled with liquor. Pagan women's burials, just before the Conversion, contain circular bronze workboxes with hinged lids and sometimes a chain for suspension. There were frequently gilded: one from Kingston, Kent, contained two needles and another from Kempston, Beds, housed pieces of cloth when found. Graves occasionally contain iron 'strike-a-lights' to be used with tinder. In Anglian areas men's graves were frequently furnished with wrist clasps. Important women were buried with iron weaving swords used to beat the weft on a vertical loom. All these objects buried in Anglo-Saxon graves show that even in the pagan fifth and sixth centuries a reasonably comfortable standard of living must have been enjoyed. Many of the jewels are still attractive today and the objects of personal use have a particular poignancy.

Exotic objects show the extent of pagan Saxon trade. Some of the more richly furnished graves, such as those at Taplow and Sutton Hoo, contained bowls of bronze from Coptic Egypt, while Byzantine objects have been found in the Sutton Hoo ship. Three Byzantine buckles have been found in Kent and one in Sussex, while eastern, possibly Coptic, glass is not unknown in the England of the sixth to seventh century. Of course such exotic objects need not imply a direct trade with Byzantium or Coptic Egypt, for they could have reached England by way of France or the Rhineland, but some ships were coming to Britain from the Mediterranean in this period, as can be demonstrated by the finds of pottery from non-Saxon sites, so direct trade cannot be ruled out.

It is, however, to place-names that scholars must turn for the linguistic evidence of pagan Anglo-Saxon beliefs. The gods of the pagans are not well documented simply because, after the conversion to Christianity, church policy suppressed such information. An account of Paulinus' conversion of the people of Kent, for instance, describes how the newly converted priest rode a stallion instead of a mare when he deliberately desecrated a pagan shrine. From this it can be inferred that there were religious taboos amongst the pagans, at least as regards the priesthood, and that there were formal places of worship. Such information is of minor use, however, due to its sparsity. Archaeology

Pagan Saxon England has produced very flimsy evidence for pagan Saxon temples. A few structures within cemeteries have been interpreted as shrines – at Bishopstone a building was found in a grave-free area of the cemetery, a burial having been laid across its entrance. A possible sanctuary has been found at Blacklow Hill, Warwick, with arcs of posts in pits and possibly two associated burials. Pits filled with ox skulls, and an ox skull on a spearhead at Butley, may be similarly associated with pagan ritual. The modern inhabitants of *Harrow* on the Hill unconsciously recall the ancient *hearh* or hill shrine that was once venerated by their predecessors, every time they write their address. So too do the people of places like *Wey*hill, *Wee*don Beck, *Wee*ford or *Alk*ham commemorate the *weog* (an idol or hill shrine) and the *ealh* (a temple) that was originally an important part of life in the area.

It is noticeable from these examples that place-names have changed very considerably over the ages. In order for any meaningful conclusions to be made from elements in their make-up a study has to be made from the various forms they have taken over the centuries. The ultimate derivations of two similar place-names may be very different. The general conclusions are, however, that place-names which refer to pagan Anglo-Saxon religion tend to be more numerous in the south-east, decreasing towards the Midlands and beyond.

Some place-names refer to the gods of the Saxons by name. Woden, the supreme god and creator was worshipped, so it can be inferred, at Wednesbury, Wansdyke and Wednesfield. Tiw, the god of war, was obviously the object of veneration at Tuesley. Frig, the goddess of love and mother of both men and gods, is remembered in the much-changed place-names of Froyle, Frobury and Frydaythorpe. Thundersfield in Essex commemorates the worship of Thunor, god of thunder.

It will be noticed that several of these deities appear in the modern names for the weekdays – Tuesday (Tiw), Wednesday (Woden), Thursday (Thor), Friday (Frig), and a number of festivals celebrated in the twentieth century have ancient Saxon origins. Easter, for instance, as well as being a Christian feast takes its name from the Anglo-Saxon goddess Eostre, who might possibly be connected with Astarte the Babylonian and Phoenician goddess of the moon. The first of August, Lammastide, is a less familiar date nowadays, but may well be derived from the Saxon *hlafmasse* – the time when loaves (*hlaf* is a loaf) were made from the first corn, to give thanks.

Finally, in connection with pagan Saxon religion, mention must be made of the magical type of alphabet common among the early northern barbarians – runes. The runic alphabet seems to have been developed out of the Roman around the fourth century AD in Scandinavia. It was composed of twenty-four characters (the *futhorc*) probably devised in the first place for ease of carving on wood or stone. The form of the characters varied in place and time (the Vikings used different runes from the early Anglo-Saxons). Runes were not used for composing sentences until the seventh century, but were employed mainly for magical, talismanic or ownership inscriptions amongst the pagan Anglo-Saxons. Despite their pagan origin they were too used for magical purposes by the Christian Saxons and often appear on rings. In pagan Saxon England they sometimes appear on pots or swords. For instance, the god Tiw is invoked on pots from the cemetery at Loveden Hill, Lincs, and at Spong Hill, Norfolk.

Chapter three

Christian England
c. AD 600–800

In 669, a priest called Bassa was given the ruins of the Roman fort of Regulbium in which to build a minster. His benefactor was king Egbert of Kent. In 949 there is a record that the monks of Christ Church Canterbury were given the site by king Eadred, and by 1281 the ecclesiastical foundation had expanded so far that it was taxed on outlying chapels. The small church with its nave, apsidal chancel and porches was observed by antiquaries such as Leland, who noted in the sixteenth century that the sea was within a quarter of a mile of the ruins. A print of the early nineteenth century shows its extent at that time, with the two transitional Norman towers as prominent as they are today. The stone walls, partly robbed from the Roman ruins, survived through over a thousand years of history: but the threats to this masterpiece of Anglo-Saxon architecture were already gaining momentum. The sea moved inexorably closer – today it has eaten away a considerable portion of the fort. Were it not for a mother's influence over her son,

60 The Anglo-Saxon church at Reculver, Kent, as it appeared before demolition. The two prominent towers are Norman. The church was built in the seventh century but demolished in 1805, for no good reason, a remarkable act of nineteenth-century vandalism

however, it is probable that visitors to the site, Reculver in Kent, would be privileged to see more than the mere foundations and lower parts of the original walling that exist today. In the early nineteenth century the building was not only almost complete, but also had one of the rare triple arches that led from nave to chancel, which are known to have existed in other churches of the period, and are noted for their majestic simplicity.

It was in 1805 that the destruction of St Mary's church was destined to take place, and as the workmen deliberately pulled down the columns and bricks a piece of the English heritage died. The circumstances were described thus by the parish clerk of the time;

> October 13th 1802. The Chapel house fell down.
> Mr C C Nailor been Vicar of the parish, his mother fancied that the church was kept for a poppet show, and she persuaded her son to take it down, so he took it in consideration and named it to the farmers in the parish about taking it down: sum was for it and sum was against it, then Mr Nailor wrote to the bishop to know if he might have the church took down and is answer was it must be dun by a majority of the people in the parish, so hafter a long time he got a majority of one, so down come the church.

The clerk himself voted against.

In retrospect the vicar might have been better advised to reflect that mother does not always know best. Such was the state of Anglo-Saxon studies at the time that the vandals had little idea of the antiquity of the building they were pulling apart. Fortunately not all the churches of the Anglo-Saxon period were so destroyed. Indeed of the 400 or so which preserve some fabric of the period (from about 600 to the late eleventh century when the prevalent architectural style was Norman), many have survived simply because they were not recognized as ancient and were either ignored or inadvertently protected by later additions of plaster. The churches are simple, dignified and attractive to modern eyes used to uncluttered architectural lines. From the time the Anglo-Saxons were converted they began building their places of worship in stone as well as timber and as a result there are from this period onwards physical remains above ground to be seen of their achievements.

The sources

The Anglo-Saxons were converted to Christianity during the last years of the sixth century and throughout the seventh, a factor which had more than theological repercussions. Indeed it is only a slight exaggeration to say that the Conversion created English history, for with Christianity came writing, which led to the setting down of documentary records of contemporary events. With the Faith, too, came the disappearance of grave furniture from the burial grounds of England. Thus, even as the historical evidence increases, archaeological material diminishes and the inquisitive antiquarian must learn to evaluate the written page or the shape of a church window rather than the cinerary urns or the jewels of the pagans. Due to the absence of grave goods, only a minimum is known of the material side of life from about AD 600 to the Danish raids of about 800, the period known as the Middle Saxon.

The main historical sources are the records kept by monks for a variety of purposes. For the later sixth, seventh and early eighth centuries the narrative account compiled by the Venerable Bede, usually known as the *Ecclesiastical History of the English People,* is important. The earliest surviving manuscript of Bede's work was a copy made in Germany perhaps in 737, a mere two years after the author's death, and therefore it is fairly certain to be free of later additions. An annalistic history which takes up where Bede left off also survives, but is less useful simply because, by definition, it merely lists the main events of the day in chronological order. The *Continuatio Bedae,* as it is known, takes the story down to 766. Symeon of Durham wrote a book called the *Historia Regum* in which he provides entries until 802, but by far the most important source of information for the period is a work famous as the *Anglo-Saxon Chronicle.* This survives in no less than seven different versions and is an annalistic history of Britain spanning the Anglo-Saxon period. The first part starts with a traditional view of the Roman period and continues its year-by-year account to 891, drawing upon sources such as Gildas and Bede. All the versions to this date are roughly similar and are copies of a collection of annals compiled in the reign of king Alfred. Soon after 891 the texts diverge in detail, presumably because of differing information available or interesting to the people who were setting down the records in their various monasteries. The study of the various texts has proved complex, but from it the history of Anglo-Saxon England has been pieced together.

Apart from such 'direct' historical information, the documentary historian has other springs to tap. Certain biographies of saints are invaluable since they refer in passing to contemporaneous events in the areas in which their subjects operated. Bede, for instance, wrote a *Life of St Cuthbert* and *Lives of the Holy Abbots of Wearmouth and Jarrow,* which along with other texts such as Eddius Stephanus' *Life of Wilfred* shed much light on Northumbria of the Golden

Age (the seventh century). Equally important are charters and laws including wills, which explain a good deal about the organization of early England. Poetry too can be revealing.

The material evidence, sparse though it is, cannot be ignored. It consists mostly of works of art: sculpture, decorated manuscripts or metalwork which have never been buried, and the still-standing remains of stone-built churches. Below-ground archaeology is mostly confined to the material derived from one or two settlement excavations, including, rather unusually, a couple of royal palace complexes. Disappointingly these are for the most part unproductive of finds and not particularly informative about everyday life. Literature rather than archaeology provides the best picture of the Anglo-Saxon going about his business. If these, then, are the clues, what can be detected about early English history from AD 600–800?

The growth of the English kingdoms
The late sixth and early seventh century was dominated by the spread of Christianity from Kent throughout the rest of the Saxon world. The conversion from paganism was effected through the kings who were probably in some cases politically motivated to change their faith. It was the evolution of kingdoms out of the smaller warring factions of the previous two centuries which, too, coloured the history of the period. In the early seventh century the kingdom of Kent was in the ascendancy. It was but one of ten independent states which can be recognized at the time, south of the Humber (Map 2). On the east lay Lindsey, East Anglia, Essex (which also included much of modern Hertfordshire, Middlesex and Surrey) and Kent itself. In the south lay Sussex. In central England Mercia bordered on Celtic Wales and Middle Anglia embraced Leicestershire and extended as far as Northampton and the Cambridge Fens. In the southern Marches lay Magonsaetan and Hwicce, and Wessex grew up in the upper Thames and Salisbury Plain. How these kingdoms emerged from the pagan settlements is not traceable in any detail though the historical sources hint at the sort of political struggles that went on at the time. Many kingdoms were soon swallowed up in the growth of the 'Heptarchy' – Wessex, Mercia, East Anglia, Kent, Essex, Sussex and Northumbria. All were not equally important, and after their early boom, at the beginning of the seventh century, East Anglia, Essex, Kent and Sussex were relegated to the status of sub-kingdoms. The real story of Anglo-Saxon England in Christian times is of the power

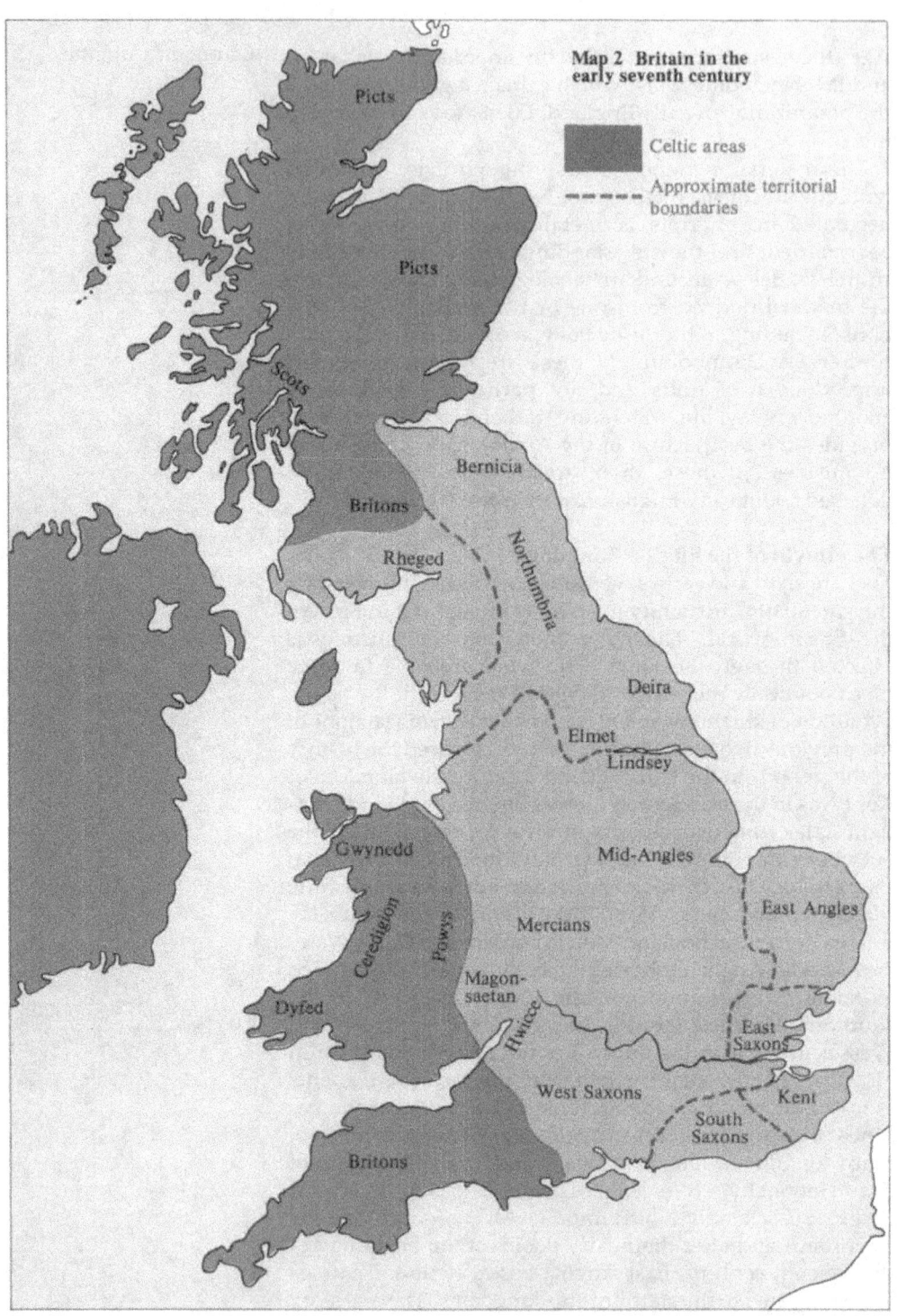

Map 2 Britain in the early seventh century

struggle between Northumbria, Mercia and Wessex, which flourished and waned in that order.

Northumbria grew out of the unification of the smaller Deira (focused on the Yorkshire Wolds) and Bernicia (focused on Northumberland). Anglo-Saxon sources distinguish very early on between the southern English and the northern (Northumbrians) even though both were ultimately of the same stock. The flourishing of Northumbria gave rise to a splendid artistic proliferation known as the Golden Age. Deira was traditionally founded in the later sixth century by a certain Aelle, and we are led to believe that an individual called Ida founded Bernicia slightly earlier.

Bernicia rose to prominence under Aethelfrith (593–616) who pushed his way into south-west Scotland and defeated the king of the Scots in 603. Soon afterwards Aethelfrith gained control of Deira and formed the united kingdom of Northumbria. His successor was the Deiran, Edwin (613–33) on whose death Bernician rule was restored under Oswald (633–41). During the first half of the seventh century Northumbria secured control in south-west Scotland and extended her northern frontier as far as the Firth of Forth. Soon after the middle of the century Northumbrians were pressing on the kingdom of the Picts, but retreated to the Forth following their defeat at Dunnichen Moss in 685. Meanwhile Edwin had been campaigning against the Welsh but had been killed by their ruler Cadwallon at Hatfield Chase on the Northumbrian border. As a result, early territorial gains in north-west England were lost and were not redeemed until the later seventh century. From this time onwards too Mercian pressure on Northumbria was seldom relaxed. The Northumbrians under Ecgfrith met the Mercians face-to-face near the Trent in 678 in an attempt to keep the upper hand but were defeated, and from 670 onwards Mercia was in ascendancy.

Mercia does not figure in the history books before the time of her king Penda (c. 632–55). This dynamic king waged war on his Northumbrian neighbours and proved a notable foe for the Welsh on his eastern borders. The Mercian royal dynasty claimed to be descended from the god Woden, through men who had ruled the entire Anglian race before their migration to Britain. The name Mercia is derived from a tribal name meaning 'boundary folk'. By 713 all the kingdoms in southern England were under Mercian domination. A vigorous phase of Mercian development was reached in the reign of king Aethelbald who succeeded to

Christian England

61 The Devil's Ditch, near Newmarket, Cambridge. One of a series of linear earthworks in East Anglia, it is believed to have been constructed to protect the area from attack from the south-west early in the Anglo-Saxon period. It runs for a distance of seven miles, and surpasses in size its later, longer counterparts of the Mercian Marches, Offa's and Wat's Dykes. The two figures silhouetted against the skyline to the left of the picture give some idea of the scale of the earthwork

the throne in 716. His successor Offa continued and maintained these achievements until his death in 796. Aethelbald was in many ways one of the last great barbarians; rebuked by contemporary clerics for his immorality and for the violence and extortion of his followers, he comes across the pages of history as an archetypal conqueror. Offa in contrast was positively a gentleman: he followed conquest by ordered rule and opened up Mercia to Continental stimulus. He was a contemporary of the great Frankish ruler Charlemagne who regarded him as a peer and who allowed the marriage of one of his sons to Offa's daughter. Offa welcomed papal legates in 786 (the first to set foot on English soil since St Augustine had arrived in 597) and an independent bishopric was founded at Lichfield. As will be seen (p. 128) Offa was active in the establishment of towns in his kingdom, and also introduced the first regular coinage of pennies.

The formation of Wessex, the last of the kingdoms to rise to ascendancy, can be traced back to the battle of Dyrham in 577 (p. 33) when Ceawlin took over the last of the British cities. Later tradition related that a certain Cerdic and Cynric landed near Southampton Water and founded a dynasty in the area in the fifth century (p. 32). By the end of Ceawlin's reign, Wessex embraced Berkshire, Hampshire, Wiltshire and much of Gloucestershire, and during the seventh century her influence extended increasingly

westwards. By 700 Exeter was in Wessex, but it was in the late Saxon period that the kingdom was of greatest significance. By the end of the eighth century the development of Anglo-Saxon civilization was destined to be shattered by the arrival of the Vikings.

Christianity

The Christian faith was probably introduced to Britain in the second century AD, gained impetus after 313 when it was adopted as the official religion, and thereafter flourished. The cumulative evidence suggests that the Romano-British church of the fourth century AD was organized and diocesan, probably urban-based and related to the civil administration. From the remains such as the justly famous frescoes in the chapel at Lullingstone villa, Kent, and artworks such as the mosaic from Hinton St Mary, Dorset, which depicts the head of Christ, it seems that the manifestations of Christian belief were widely accepted into everyday life, at least among the upper classes in Britannia. Christian and pagan symbols are often juxtaposed, resulting in the notorious difficulty of evaluating Romano-British Christianity – a symbol of apparently Christian significance could be favoured for many reasons, ranging from political expediency to aesthetics.

When an attempt is made to discover the fate of Christianity after 410 amongst the British population, the evidence becomes even more confusing and difficult to evaluate. The remains of a small timber building constructed within the Roman fort at Richborough, Kent, belong either to the late fourth century or more probably the fifth. A chancel in the ruined church of Stone-by-Faversham, Kent, is very similar to St Martin's, Canterbury, which Bede reported was built by the Romans. Stone-by-Faversham may therefore be contemporary – it could have been built on to an earlier and now perished timber nave. While no one building demonstrates a continuous use from the Roman period to the coming of St Augustine in 597, the evidence of church building complements that of history in continually shortening the gap between the two early periods of Christianity in England, which used to be thought of as several centuries long.

Cemeteries provide important evidence for the assimilation of Christianity in pagan England. Pagan burials have grave goods, while Christian interments are distinguishable by their general lack of grave furniture or their east–west orientation. A mixture of traditions is often found in burials of the Anglo-Saxon era, which make them very difficult to

Christian England

evaluate in terms of belief or the origins of the population. The evidence from Kentish cemeteries suggests that pagan Saxon burial practices continued almost unabated until the mid-seventh century, whereas objects of Christian significance were used as grave goods in the 'pagan' fifth century. A mount of late Roman Gaulish workmanship depicting Christ from a burial at Strood was probably deposited in the late fifth century, while a burial from Long Wittenham, Berkshire, contained a fifth-century bronze stoup with Christian scenes on it, presumably manufactured in northern Gaul. Such objects may have had little or no religious meaning for their owners, and they provide a useful caution against accepting as evidence for Christianity the objects bearing Christian symbols that appear in Kentish and other cemeteries after the Augustinian mission. There are, for example, an attractive pair of crosses from Kingston Down, a silver pendant from Chartham and a pin with the head in the form of a cross as a basic design from Breach Down. Examples of more ornate pieces such as the gold and garnet pendant cross from Wilton, Norfolk, set with a coin of the Byzantine emperors Heraclius and Tiberius (613–41), the similar pendant without a coin from Ixworth, Suffolk, and the superb pectoral cross from St Cuthbert's coffin (see p. 112) are notable in that they show the craftsmanship of the seventh-century pagan Anglo-Saxons being turned to the production of Christian pieces.

However ambiguous the archaeological evidence is, in 429 Christianity was certainly strong enough in Britain to concern Rome, when the heresy of Pelagianism was rife in the province. Pelagius (who is graphically but irrelevantly described by his biographer as being as broad as he was tall), was himself a Briton who had left for Rome around AD 380, in his youth. In the Eternal City he came into conflict with the doctrine of the reformed profligate St Augustine of Hippo, whose spiritual theology was in contrast to the simple morality of the Briton. Pelagius taught that man was master of his own salvation, thus denying the doctrine of original sin. Pelagianism, with its emphasis on individual initiative, may have had a political effect in encouraging the ejection of the officials of the British usurper Constantine III (see p. 29) and the attendant plea for reunion with the Empire. Whether or not this had been so, there can be little doubt that any Saxon arriving in Britain in the first half of the fifth century would have found Christianity, albeit heretical, well established among the Romano-British southern élite. It is significant that the problem was considered of sufficient magnitude to warrant St Germanus, bishop of Auxerre, crossing the Channel to deal with the heretics.

The mission provides an interesting insight into contemporary British Christianity. The deputation was received in St Albans by a richly clad delegation of city fathers who, according to Germanus' biographer Constantius, were converted from their heresy after a lengthy discussion. Having won this moral victory, Germanus converted the troops and taught them the war-cry of 'Alleluia' to which their subsequent victory over the combined forces of pagan Saxons and Picts, probably near Llangollen, was ascribed. Constantius relates the story in the following terms:

> the bishops cried out three times 'Alleluia!'; the whole army replied with a single voice, and the great cry rebounded, shut in by the surrounding hills. The enemy column was terrified; the very frame of heaven and the rocks around seemed to threaten them . . . they fled in all directions . . . the bishops won a bloodless victory, gained by faith, not by the might of men.

The conversion at St Albans and the Alleluia Victory were a short-lived triumph for orthodoxy. Pelagianism took hold again after Germanus' return to Gaul, and he found it necessary to return in 443 to drive out the Pelagian priests. Britain followed the practice of fixing Easter by rules laid down in 456, but when these were changed thirty years later the British Christians did not adopt the new method. In the following eleven decades the extent of Christianity cannot be adequately monitored through lack of evidence, but there can be little doubt that the majority of people in England lapsed into paganism, though as in the late Roman period it is almost impossible to evaluate the beliefs from material remains.

In the late sixth century, the Frankish-born queen of Kent, Bertha, was a Christian (see p. 100). Her chaplain, bishop Liudhard, is commemorated on one of the pieces from the small hoard of gold coin-ornaments found near St Martin's Church, Canterbury, but Christianity was of little significance until the Augustinian mission.

In AD 597 Pope Gregory, 'being moved by Divine inspiration . . . sent the servant of God, Augustine, and with him several other monks, who feared the Lord, to preach the word of God to the English nation' (Bede, *Ecclesiastical History*, Book 1, Ch. 23).

The apocryphal story of Pope Gregory seeing Angles in the slave market at Rome and being thus persuaded to send a mission to England ('Non Angli sed angeli' – 'They are not Angles but angels') is almost certainly a pretty cover-up for a more complex operation. Gregory probably saw the

Christian England

reunion of England with the Continent as politically expedient. The close ties between the Kentish and Frankish courts provided the vehicle by which this could be effected. Augustine presented himself to Aethelbert not as a simple priest but in the full panoply of the Roman Church – he was preceded by a silver processional cross, and the 'image of our Lord and Saviour painted on a board'. No doubt, too, Augustine and his followers (who came chanting a litany) were dressed in Roman vestments and carried books and other symbols of the Faith. Indeed, fragments of a Gospel book probably used by Augustine in England still survive. This, the Corpus Christi Ms 286, in Cambridge, contains a group of twelve gospel pictures on one page and a portrait of the evangelist Luke on another. The style is linear and Classical, and the closest parallels for the illustrations suggest a date in the late sixth century, which is compatible with the tradition that it was sent by Pope Gregory to Augustine. Certainly, similar books were reaching Kent in the years following the Augustinian mission, for by the mid-eighth century a school of manuscript illumination flourished in Canterbury and drew heavily on late Classical sources (see p. 108).

The process of conversion began at the top, with the baptism of Aethelbert, who in turn persuaded Raedwald of East Anglia to accept the Faith. A bishop from London and Essex was consecrated, but by Augustine's death around AD 640 Christianity was not well established. Raedwald's religion was a compromise, for he never abandoned his pagan beliefs completely, and Essex had lapsed back to paganism around 617, only thirteen years after its conversion.

In 625 one of Augustine's followers, Paulinus, left Canterbury to begin his mission in Northumbria. Here too king Edwin had a Christian wife (Ethelburh), through whom he was converted in 627. Thereafter Christianity was rapidly disseminated through Northumbria and the adjacent lands of Lindsey. Here too there were setbacks. At the end of his reign, Edwin was campaigning against the combined forces of the Christian Cadwallon of Gwynedd and Penda of Mercia. Penda won (see p. 93) and Edwin himself was slain in 633. Penda was a convinced pagan, though he advocated a policy of religious tolerance, and any progress that had been made during Edwin's rule was reversed during the confusion at his death.

It was at this point that Celtic Christianity took over the initiative from Rome in Northumbria. Celtic monks from Iona in western Scotland established a foundation at

Lindisfarne, and under the leadership of Aidan began the process of converting Northumbria to Celtic Christianity. In 664 a famous Synod was held at Whitby in Yorkshire, where the question debated was not whether Northumbria was to remain Christian, but whether it should adopt the Roman or Celtic forms of the religion. The Celtic cause was taken up by the gentle saint Cuthbert, the abbot of Lindisfarne, that of Rome by Wilfrid, bishop of Ripon. In the end Wilfrid won, and Northumbria adopted the Roman faith. The Synod of Whitby was ostensibly fought over such issues as the method of calculating the date of Easter and the form of the tonsure. The undercurrents were very probably politically motivated, the outcome of a fight for supremacy between king Oswy (who had been taught the Celtic faith) and his son Alfrid (who had been taught the Roman by Wilfrid).

Meanwhile, Christianity was making progress in the rest of England. The tolerant Penda allowed missionaries to operate in Mercia, and apparently raised no objection when his son Paeda was converted to the new faith. By the late seventh century the structure of the English Church had been created. Under Theodore of Tarsus (Archbishop of Canterbury 668–90) the country was organized into fifteen dioceses. Among the last areas to be converted was Sussex, which succumbed in 680 – to the same rhetoric of the humourless Wilfrid that had swayed the Whitby Synod. The structure of English Christianity received the official stamp of approval by the Council of Hertford in 672, while at Hatfield in 679 a profession of allegiance to Roman orthodoxy was made formally.

Paganism, of course, survived in various guises throughout the Anglo-Saxon period, even if there was no large-scale heathen revival. Even as late as the eleventh century legislation against the worship of woods, rivers and mountains, and against superstition, was deemed essential. In late Saxon writings spells and poems which invoke the gods of northern Europe occasionally appear, and staunch churchmen like Aelfric (see p. 152) found it necessary to bemoan the prevalence of black magic.

Church and monastery
The archaeological evidence for the spread of Christianity takes the form of the remains of churches and monasteries. The early Anglo-Saxon church was diocesan, but on to this framework was grafted another, monastic, organization which continued to flourish separately.

The term 'monastery' conjures up a picture of Gothic

ruins with ivy-clad walls, and of cool cloisters looking across a central garth. Such claustral planning however was not a feature of the early Dark Ages. It developed during the upsurge of monasticism in the eleventh and twelfth centuries, though some degree of planning in monastic lay-outs can be traced back to the eighth or ninth centuries. The monastic movement appears to have started in the east, where early hermits wished to sever themselves from everyday life and to devote themselves to God. Organized monasticism was already present in the eastern Roman Empire by the fourth century AD. Thence it spread to Gaul, where the monasteries founded by St Martin of Tours, John Cassian and Honoratus served as a model for British offshoots. While some Irish clerics seem to have taken vows of chastity and poverty in the fifth century, organized monsticism did not have any impact on Britain before the turn of that century. The first monasteries in Britain are found in the Celtic west, where they were the outcome of direct Continental contacts. Thence monasteries spread to Northumbria, where 'Celtic' Christianity had been maintained until the Synod of Whitby. The first Northumbrian monasticism did not have any impact on Britain before the reports that Augustine founded a monastery at Canterbury, but its early development cannot be traced from any material remains.

In essence, early monasteries comprised various communal buildings, individual cells and a church, grouped within an enclosure, and sometimes linked to a monastic farm. Of the communal buildings, a refectory, dormitory and guest house recurred. Some early monasteries were 'double houses' for both monks and nuns, ruled over by an abbess – Whitby, Yorkshire, was one such. In contrast to many later ecclesiastical establishments, there seems to have been no objection to women guests in male communities.

A few churches are contemporary with the Augustinian mission and its aftermath. The church of St Martin in Canterbury was built (according to Bede) in Roman times, used by Queen Bertha and her chaplain and subsequently taken over by Augustine. Material evidence points to the church being pre-Augustinian, though a Roman date cannot at the present state of knowledge be proved or disproved. The western and earliest part of the church was built of flat Roman tiles laid in courses. To the south, an annexe was floored with *opus signinum*, a composition popular in Roman times and occasionally found in Saxon England, compounded of cement with chips of tile and stone. None of the early work is now visible, but at the most recent exposure, in 1954, it was noted that while some tiles appeared sharp, others looked re-used. The use of Roman materials and a Roman type of flooring argues for St Martin's early date in the development of Anglo-Saxon churches, especially since the workmanship is not in keeping with that of known Augustinian buildings.

The earliest post-Augustine churches are mostly confined to Kent, and share certain features in common. The most important group are to be found in Canterbury itself, and consist of the complex ruins on the site of St Augustine's Abbey. This site was extensively excavated in the early part of this century. The most important building uncovered was St Augustine's own church, dedicated to SS Peter and Paul. In keeping with the other early Kentish churches, it consisted of a rectangular nave with a porch or narthex and a chancel with a stilted apse. The main body of the church was flanked by side chapels known as *porticus*, in which burials were laid, as at this period burials were not permitted inside the nave or chancel. Bede informs us that the north-east *porticus* contained the bodies of Augustine and his successors, while the south-east one contained those of Ethelbert, Bertha and bishop Liudhard. Aligned on St Augustine's church were the churches of St Mary and St Pancras.

All the Augustinian churches share certain features in common. They are all small – missionary churches, in fact, designed for a few followers. They share the same basic plan and are simply built, sometimes re-using Roman materials. All, however, are modelled on the Roman basilica, and all are stone in contrast to the tradition of timber building which was seen to symbolize the heathen world.

The churches of Reculver and Bradwell-on-Sea had differing *porticus* from other churches of the group. They partly flank the chancel, and this feature is not to be found elsewhere in western Europe at this date. Significantly, both churches are about fifty years later than the main Kentish group, and in those fifty years Syrian civilization had collapsed with the arrival of the Persians in 610. The outcome was the dispersal of Syrian monks and craftsmen throughout Christendom, and it is to them that the unusual arrangement of the *porticus* at Bradwell and Reculver can be ascribed. They are in fact not for burials but are the *diaconicon* and *prothesis* of the Syrian church – chapels used as a vestry and for the receipt of offerings from the faithful and their preparation for the altar.

Christian England

The church at Bradwell-on-Sea, dedicated to St Peter-on-the-Wall, has survived the encroachments of the sea with walls 7.3 m high, buttressed from the start. It rises out of the faint remains of the west gateway of the Roman fort of Othona, its height exaggerated by its width of a mere 6.6 m. Much Roman material was incorporated in its construction. Until 1920 the church was used as a barn, a relic of which days is the huge patched area in the south wall through which farm waggons were manoeuvred. The *porticus*, and

62 Early foundations of the Mercian church at Repton, Derbyshire. Current opinion believes that these belong to a mausoleum of the eighth century, later incorporated as a crypt below the chancel of the new church built by Wiglaf of Mercia (827–40)

the apsidal chancel excavated in 1877, have disappeared, but the nave is reconsecrated and restored and the plain whitewashed walls invoke the spartan atmosphere in which the seventh-century Christians worshipped. The 15.1 m long south and north walls are pierced still by three of the original four windows. The entrance to the chancel, now the east wall, is blocked by the tall tile and stone jambs which turn near the top at an angle which suggests a triple chancel arch, as originally at St Pancras, Canterbury and Reculver.

The remains of the apsidal chapel are almost certainly those built by St Cedd, bishop of the East Saxons, in 653, even though this cleric would presumably have favoured a rectangular east end in keeping with his Celtic northern traditions. The apse probably reflects the taste of his Kentish masons.

Christian England

63 Brixworth, Northamptonshire. The polygonal apse of the church, with its semi-subterranean ambulatory (behind the low wall), was added to the late seventh-century church in the late Saxon period.

The finest of all the early churches is that at Brixworth in Northamptonshire, still monumental despite the demolition of its outer *porticus*. Sir Alfred Clapham described it as 'perhaps the most imposing architectural memorial of the seventh century surviving north of the Alps'. It is usually assigned to the period around 670–700, though the dating evidence is far from certain. In its present form, its polygonal apse and ambulatory (the latter now open to the air) are the work of the late Saxon period (i.e. after 950), when its porch was rebuilt to form a belfry tower to which was added a circular staircase. The church is 48.8 m long, and the blocked arches which originally led to the side chapels (*porticus*) are monumental and impressive, despite the somewhat ghostly appearance of the blocking. Roman bricks and tiles were used among the softer colours of the Northamptonshire sandstone.

Christian England

In Northumbria, church archaeology is dominated by the excavations in two great monasteries: Monkwearmouth and Jarrow. These have been made for ever famous by their association with Bede, who was born in the former place around 673 and who became a priest in the latter around 703, where he wrote his ecclesiastical history and died.

At Monkwearmouth the monastic church of St Peter still stands, though the partly excavated monastic buildings are no longer above ground. Much is known about its original character from Bede, who told how Benedict Biscop, a Northumbrian noble, incorporated into it all the best elements of the monasteries he had seen on his travels abroad. It was begun in 674, and the work carried out by masons and glass makers brought specially from Gaul. Its sister monastery at Jarrow was begun in 681. By the early eighth century both between them housed over 600 monks. From the excavations at Monkwearmouth and Jarrow it is known that stone and timber buildings existed at Jarrow. Finds of painted plaster, coloured window glass and decorative stone carving hint at their original richness, and Jarrow produced evidence for ornamental glass working, including millefiori.

The church of St John in Escomb, Co. Durham, is still intact from the early Saxon period, though it was not mentioned by Bede which has caused some to assume that it post-dated his death. The chancel and nave still stand despite the fact that it was unroofed during the nineteenth century. The chancel arch is almost certainly re-used Roman, and the window construction has given rise to the term 'Escomb fashion' jambs, since it is typical of the Anglo-Saxon mason.

Middle Saxon art

Christianity had little effect on ornamental metalworking, except in so far as the Cross became an increasingly popular motif. It did, however, introduce painting and sculpture to the Saxon's repertoire. All the extant examples of painting from England before 800 are found in manuscripts executed by monks under Church patronage. Sculpture too was usually produced for Church requirements, but probably commissioned from lay artists, and at least one example of secular carving survives.

The earliest examples of Anglo-Saxon painting are found in Gospel books executed in the great monasteries of Northumbria. In the Golden Age Continental manuscripts were imported to enrich monastic libraries. These works were illustrated in the late Antique (i.e. Classical) style fashionable in Italy. Benedict Biscop was a particularly active collector, and according to Bede, brought 'furniture, vestments, relics and a library of valuable books' from the Continent.

Manuscript illumination
The earliest surviving Northumbrian manuscript dates from the early seventh century but is radically different from any Classical volume. Known as the Durham Cathedral AII 10, only twelve pages now survive, but one of these is very richly decorated, with abstract interlace ornament in yellow and red dots, and with yellow, red, blue and green knots. This can be seen on the opening page of the text of St Mark, which also carries trumpet-pattern ornament and an intertwining snake with two heads. Despite its early date, the AII 10 displays the Northumbrian

64 Folio 3 verso of the Durham Cathedral MS AII 10. This is the oldest surviving decorated Northumbrian manuscript, and only twelve pages remain. It dates from slightly before AD 650, and shows a variety of plain interlace as well as the Romano-British-derived pelta pattern ornament. The interlace may be of Syro-Coptic inspiration

Christian England

65 The Book of Durrow, folio 3 verso. This Northumbrian manuscript owes much in its ornament to a Romano-Celtic past. The triskele roundels on this page recall the hanging-bowl escutcheons produced in Romano-Celtic workshops of the sixth century, while the trumpet spirals and other ornamental elements similarly echo Romano-Celtic art. It was probably executed around AD 650, though a later seventh-century date has been claimed for it. Page width *c.* 15.5 cm

taste for pelta ('shield-like') pattern (inherited from the Celtic origins of her monasteries), for lacertines (inherited from the Anglo-Saxon past, see p. 71), and a taste for the abstract interlace which in this case was borrowed from some eastern Mediterranean book.

The first major masterpiece of Northumbrian painting was a volume illuminated around 650, known as the Book of Durrow because it was kept for a long time in the Irish monastery of that name. This work of awe-inspiring intricacy is a copy of the Gospels, preceded and followed by canons of concordance and summaries of the text. Each gospel starts with a picture of the evangelist's symbol, followed by what is known as a 'carpet page' – an all-over abstract design perhaps inspired by ideas from Coptic Egypt. Facing this, the first page of the text has an ornamented initial capital. The canon tables are framed in borders of interlace. The colours are limited to rich orange-red, green, yellow and brown. Taken as a whole, the Book of Durrow is an encyclopedia of the influences current in seventh-century English art. Some elements are borrowed from Romano-British and Dark Age Celtic metalwork, some from Anglo-Saxon jewellery. The interlace recalls that on the Sutton Hoo buckle, and the eagle evangelist symbol looks like a Gothic cloisonné brooch. In the animal figures can be seen the hip and shoulder spirals favoured by Pictish sculptors whose repertoire was descended from the art of the Steppe nomads centuries before. There is influence from Coptic Egypt and from late Antique manuscripts. The carpet pages have strong similarities to Roman mosaics. The robe of the Man symbol recalls millefiori glass or mosaic.

Some of the elements of the Book of Durrow are also found in a book known as the Echternach Gospels. It takes its name from the late seventh-century monastery of Echternach near Luxembourg, where it was taken and served as a model for some Continental versions of the Northumbrian style.

The Lindisfarne Gospels made around 700 is the finest of all Northumbrian artistic achievements, and in it were developed all the elements already discussed. A marginal inscription explains that it was the work of a Saxon abbot called Eadfrith. It was made at Lindisfarne, in the same scriptorium as the Echternach Gospels. Basically it follows the layout of the Book of Durrow but has portraits of the evangelists as well as their symbols, and in this respect more closely follows Antique models. The initials are so elaborate that they occupy much of the first page of each Gospel, and the colours are rich and varied. The 'trade mark' of the Lindisfarne artist is a long-beaked, long-legged bird. Although the figures are stiff, with tubular draperies reminiscent of Romano-British sculptures, they represent a marked step forward in realism from the little figure in the Durrow manuscript, with its legs pointing sideways, its geometric body and regular, expressionless face.

The Durrow–Lindisfarne style owed a lot to native artistic tradition, but other books produced in Northumbria copied their classical models more slavishly. None did so more than the Codex Amiatinus, which was one of three copies of the Gospels made at the command of Ceolfrith, the first abbot of Jarrow. One copy was to stay in Jarrow, one was to go to Monkwearmouth and the third, the Codex Amiatinus, was to be presented to the Pope. Ceolfrith set out for Rome with the intention of delivering the book himself, but he died in France in 716 and the book ended up in an Italian monastery, having failed to reach its destination.

Christian England

66 The Lindisfarne Gospels, the most famous of all the Northumbrian manuscripts of the Golden Age. This page (folio 25 verso) shows St Matthew at work on his Gospel. Under the inspiration of imported books the Lindisfarne Gospels show a marked advance in naturalism from the stiff figure of St Matthew to be found in the Book of Durrow. The draperies, however, are stiff and tubular, and recall late Romano-British sculptures. The knotted curtain is a Mediterranean device which occurs, for example, in mosaics. Date *c.* AD 700. Size: 34.3 cm by 24.8 cm

After 700, Northumbrian manuscript art declined. However the Lichfield Gospels (also known as the Book of Chad) which was made soon after this date has some fine ornament, including a cruciform carpet page which is a swarming mass of Lindisfarne-style birds.

The manuscripts brought to Canterbury by St Augustine gave rise in the eighth century to a Kentish school of book illumination. The Canterbury manuscripts are much closer to their classical models than the Northumbrian. Influences from Celtic art are minimal, though the earliest surviving product, the Canterbury Psalter, which dates from around 750, has some very fine Celtic patterns on the arch framing the very classical-looking composition of David as Musician.

Superb and richly coloured is the Stockholm Codex Aureus, now in Scandinavia but produced in Canterbury around 760. Although some interlace ornaments the frame of the chair in which St Matthew sits to preface his Gospel,

concession to native taste stops there. Here the vellum of the pages has been sumptuously coloured purple. Purple vellum was used also in the Gospel book known as the Royal IE VI, where it sets off silver lettering.

Throughout the eighth century Canterbury remained the leading centre of manuscript production, though some books such as the very Northumbrian-looking Rome Gospels, decorated around 800, may have been produced in Mercia. The old vigour was spent, and in the words of one authority, Dr Margaret Rickert, 'the birds look like hung game, and the confronted animals, instead of glaring at one another, gnaw contentedly on their own legs or graze peacefully nose to nose'.

The tomb of St Cuthbert

Even as Northumbrian monks were ruining their eyesight tracing intricate patterns, artists in other media were caught

67 The Canterbury Psalter, produced around the mid-eighth century, probably in St Augustine's abbey. This page (folio 30 verso) depicts David as Harpist. Good Mediterranean models were available for the Canterbury artists to copy, so there is greater naturalism than in the early Northumbrian manuscripts. Celtic influence was also less apparent in Kent, though some Celtic influence is detectable in the peltas and other motifs ornamenting the arch. Compare David's harp with Plate 27. Size: 23.5 cm by 17.8 cm

up in the fever of creation that attended the flowering of the Northumbrian Golden Age. Just how successful they were can be seen from a remarkable discovery in Durham.

On 17 May 1827 a solemn party stood by the platform projecting behind the High Altar of Durham Cathedral, while a stone slab was slowly raised. The slab lifted, the anxious spectators saw an inscribed oak coffin, and below this, amid other relics, a 'dark substance of the length of a human body, which, after a moment's investigation, proved to be a skeleton, lying with its feet to the east, swathed apparently in one or more shrouds of linen or silk'. The body was that of St Cuthbert, the gentle Celtic monk who had upheld his faith in the Synod of Whitby.

There was no doubt that the burial was genuinely that of the saint. First, during re-excavation in 1899 the remains of the body were found to display evidence of a tubercular leg, which would explain Bede's description of Cuthbert walking with a limp. Second, the coffin's decoration is exactly right for the traditional date of its manufacture, AD 698. Cuthbert's body had a chequered history. On his death in 687 it was attired in vestments and laid by the altar in the monastery church at Lindisfarne. In 698 it was disinterred, and found to be miraculously incorrupt (presumably because it had been pickled in brine). It was reburied in a new coffin and in new robes in an above-ground shrine, where the faithful could come near to it. Between 875 and 995 it travelled far afield, resting for a while at Chester-le-Street. Eventually, on the building of the new cathedral in the eleventh century, it was laid to rest in Durham.

In 1538, at the Dissolution of the Monasteries, Cuthbert's peace was disturbed again. The *Rites of Durham* describes his fate:

> After the spoil of his ornaments and jewels, coming nearer to his body, thinking to have found nothing but dust and bones and finding the chest that he did lie in very strongly bound with iron, then the goldsmith did take a great fore hammer of a smith and did break the said chest open; and when they had opened the chest they found him lying whole, uncorrupt, with his face bare, and his beard as it had a fortnight's growth . . . then when the goldsmith did perceive that he had broken one of his legs when he did break up the chest, he was very sorry for it.

Once more reburied, it was undisturbed until the re-opening of 1827. Other bones were found at this time, including a head which was probably that of St Oswald.

The coffin and other relics buried with Cuthbert shed brilliant light on the art and culture of seventh-century Northumbria. A few of the relics belong to the late Saxon period, but the coffin, portable altar, comb, pectoral cross and the Stonyhurst Gospels all belonged to the saint. The Gospel book is a seventh-century Italian or Italianate book, bound in ornamental leather in Northumbria. It had been removed from Cuthbert's coffin in 1104, and is now at Stonyhurst College. The binding is ornamented with interlace, and a plant-motif of Mediterranean inspiration. It is the finest example of English leatherwork to survive from the period.

St Cuthbert's coffin is quite unlike any other example of

68 The end panels from the coffin of St Cuthbert. They depict the Virgin and Child and the Archangels Michael and Gabriel. The coffin dates from c. 687, and compares with Merovingian Frankish work to be seen at Poitiers

Northumbrian art. Its sides and lid are incised with representations of Christ and the symbols of the evangelists, with their names in Roman and runic characters, along with a seated Virgin and Child and half-length figures of archangels and apostles. It deliberately strives after a Roman ideal, and compares closely with an ornamented stone coffin dated to around 600 found at Poitiers. It is ironic that Cuthbert, who strove so fervently to maintain the Celtic ideal in life, should be laid in a Roman-inspired coffin in death.

Cuthbert's comb is an austere object, totally without decoration: combs had a ritual function in the early Church. Simple too is the plain wooden portable altar. Such objects, ready-consecrated, were taken by peripatetic saints to set up on a pile of stones or mound of earth to form an 'instant altar', for in the wilds it was obviously impracticable to consecrate an altar for every service. After Cuthbert's death

Christian England

the altar was encased in silver, but the original wooden tablet is engraved with five consecration crosses and an inscription IN HONOREM S PETRI (in honour of St Peter); on one side the silver casing shows St Peter holding a scroll (which perhaps dates from 698). A roundel was added to the back in the ninth century, perhaps to protect a circle left open to display the wood to the faithful and which had been under attack from relic-hunters seeking splinters.

Cuthbert's pectoral cross belongs to the secular tradition

69 The pectoral cross of St Cuthbert, executed in gold and garnet and repaired in antiquity. From St Cuthbert's coffin, it represents the last fling of polychrome jewellery adapted to Christian use. Breadth: 6 cm

of metalworking. The gold symbol has been repaired, and is set with cloisonné garnet inlays. It was probably made in seventh-century Northumbria.

Sculpture

Dating from early in the Golden Age are a series of sculptures, of which the earliest and finest are two crosses at Ruthwell in Dumfriesshire and Bewcastle in Cumbria. The Anglo-Saxons probably borrowed the idea of erecting free-standing crosses from the British, who may have been in the habit of putting up wooden ones. Stone versions were peculiar to the Anglo-Saxons at this period.

The sculptor's art came to the Anglo-Saxons from the Mediterranean, and the models behind the ornament on the early crosses are equally exotic. The Ruthwell Cross was made in about AD 700. It is decorated with Christian themes, amongst them St John with his symbol, John the

Baptist, Christ in Glory, the hermit saints Paul and Anthony, the Flight into Egypt, the Visitation, Christ with Mary Magdalene washing His feet, and the Crucifixion. There are frequent allusions to the desert fathers and to desert themes, suggestive of contacts with the Eastern hermits. Vine scroll ornament inhabited by birds and beasts occupies the sides, and Anglian runes border it, with the text of the Old English poem *The Dream of the Rood*. The figural work is classical, but a little stiff.

The Bewcastle Cross was made slightly later, and is still buffeted by the weather in a bleak setting in a Cumbrian graveyard, looking out over the grassed banks of a Roman fort. Its head is missing, but it has a long, slender shaft, 4.4 m high, with decorated panels depicting Christ, John the Baptist and John the Evangelist. The back shows Northumbrian inhabited vine scroll, and the sides are ornamented with interlace, chequer patterns and animals. It too bears

70 The Bewcastle Cross, Cumbria: (a) shows a side panel with interlace and characteristic Northumbrian vine-scroll ornament; (b) shows Christ, with a runic inscription beneath. It was probably erected by St Wilfrid in the 680s, and the runic inscriptions include a poem in Northumbrian dialect which may refer to Alcfrith, the Deiran king who died c. 709. It is very 'classical' in its treatment, and the mastery of the sculptor is astonishing in view of the fact that he had few models to depend on

Christian England

extensive runic inscriptions, including a poem in Northumbrian dialect and a possible reference to Alcfrith, the Deiran king who died c. 709. It may have been erected by St Wilfrid in the 680s, and like him its design is uncompromising.

The inhabited vine scroll which appears on these crosses for the first time was to stalk through later Anglo-Saxon sculpture. Any similarity it originally possessed to the Mediterranean plant was soon forgotten, and it took on fantastic shapes. The birds and animals feeding off the fruit

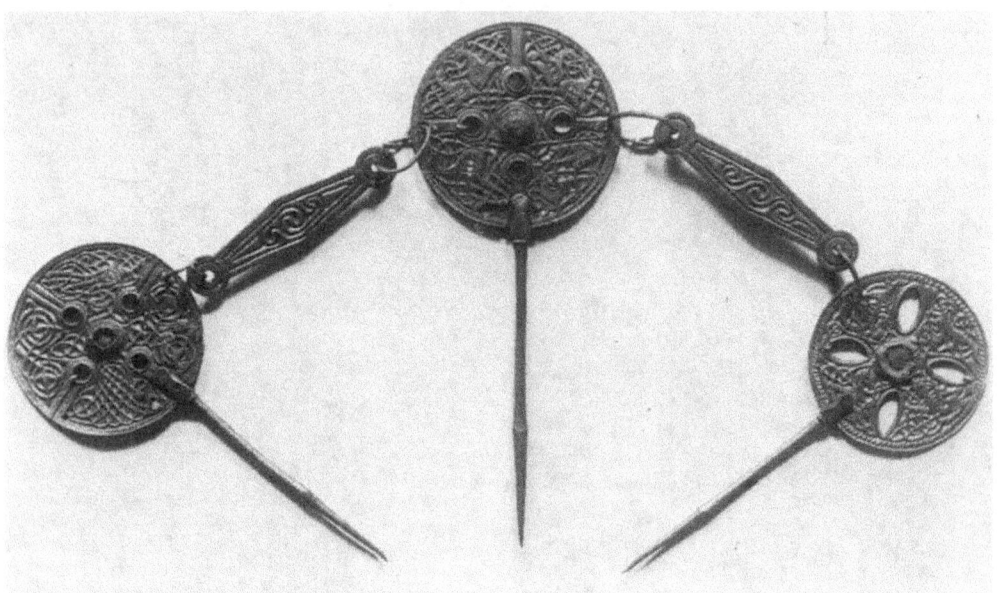

71 A set of three joined pins from the River Witham, Lincolnshire. The heads of the pins are ornamented with interlace and with confronted pairs of animals with eyes originally inlaid with glass studs – the last survival of the cloisonné technique. They are of gilt bronze, and typical of eighth-century 'chip-carved' work. Length of central pin: 12 cm

which represent Christ in the Eucharist nourishing Creation soon intertwined themselves into the overall patterns, and the leaves, flowers and fruits became lesser elements.

During the early eighth century, although most sculpture was not up to the standard of the Ruthwell and Bewcastle crosses, it was in general good, and is well exemplified by works such as Acca's Cross at Hexham or the Abercorn and Aberlady shafts from the Anglian-occupied areas of Scotland. By 800 however the tradition was in decline, eclipsed by the rising sun of Mercia (see p. 93).

Metalwork

Ornamental metalworking continued to develop along familiar lines in the later seventh and eighth centuries. Cuthbert's pectoral cross shows the survival of the cloisonné technique into the later seventh century, and though gold was by this time becoming scarce, the smiths of the period liked to gild many of the products which were now made of silver or bronze. Animals, by this time fairly naturalistic, adorn such pieces as the linked pins from the river Witham. These pins date from the eighth century and show a last fling of the cloisonné technique with their use of blue glass insets for the animals' eyes. There are, however, three fine pieces of metalwork which stand out in this period. The first is the gilt-bronze Tassilo Chalice, made by Carolingian smiths under Anglo-Saxon influence. Ornamented with chip carving, it depicts Christ. A disc brooch from Ixworth, Suffolk, shows the continuation of old Kentish tradition, and even has bosses and a cruciform design, within which chip-carved animals cavort. Perhaps the finest product of the age is the silver sword hilt from Fetter Lane, London, richly ornamented with parcel gilding and niello, a black silver-oxide paste. Purchased for half-a crown from a workman who found it in the nineteenth century, its ornament includes four snakes in a whorl on the front of the grip.

Christian England

The Franks Casket
One great gem of Northumbrian art of the Golden Age is the Franks Casket, a whalebone box, named after its donor to the British Museum, Sir Wolaston Franks, who was Keeper there in the late nineteenth century. It is decorated all over with narrative scenes that were perhaps copied from a manuscript such as a World Chronicle.

Pagan and Christian tales jostle together cheek-by-jowl, and include the Saxon story of Egil, the Adoration of the Magi, the Siegfried Saga, Romulus and Remus and the

(a)   (b)

72 Silver sword pommel from Fetter Lane, London, parcel gilt with niello (a black silver oxide paste) inlay. Late Saxon smiths excelled in their use of silver and niello to produce black and white effects. On one face (a) can be seen an animal spreadeagled, and on the other (b) four snakes in a whorl. Leaf and tendril ornament, a feature of late Saxon work, appears here. Ninth century. Length: 8.7 cm

73 The Franks Casket. Named after Sir Wolaston Franks, it is a whalebone box which in the eighteenth century was used as a workbox by a family at Auzon in France – how it got there is not known. Of Northumbrian work of around AD 700, the back panel here illustrated shows the siege of Jerusalem by Titus in AD 70. The inscription is partly in Roman letters and partly in runes – the runes at the bottom left-hand corner and bottom right-hand corner have been taken by some to be the signature of the carver, and read DOMGISL. The rest of the inscription relates to the scene. The building in the centre may be the Temple with the Ark of the Covenant. The animals with their segmented snouts are Pictish in character, as are some of the figures, and the box may have been carved by someone trained in a Pictish workshop. Length: 22.3 cm

Wolf, and the Capture of Jerusalem by Titus. Anglian runes provide some captions. The style of some of the figures is curiously Pictish, with their dumpy bodies and large heads.

The Anglo-Saxon as king's subject

> Our spirits shall be sterner, hearts the keener, courage the greater, as our strength fades. Here on the ground lies our lord, a good man cut down. The man who thinks of leaving the battle now shall regret it for ever, I am old. I will not run away, but intend to lie dead alongside my lord, so dear a man.

Here the tenth-century poem *The Battle of Maldon* epitomizes the theme of loyalty which was such a cohesive force through the entire span of early English society. Life was united by two great bonds – of a man for his family and for his lord, the latter being of paramount importance. It was a process of mutual protection, and wrongs were avenged by blood-feud. As constant blood-feud was wasteful both of life and time, vengeance could, as time wore on, be assuaged by the payment of a 'man-price' or *wergild*, which was paid to the kin of a dead man by the killer or his family. Every man had a wergild calculated on his importance in society – in Wessex there were three classes, 'twelve hundred men', 'six hundred men' and 'two hundred men', the figures referring to the number of shillings that were payable as *wergild* if they were killed. Injury was similarly compensatable, and the laws of king Alfred stipulate a series of appropriate payments to discourage would-be attackers. If the nail of the little finger was lost, one shilling was payable, but if a back tooth were knocked out four shillings were due.

The class structure of England depended on a variety of factors, which took into account birth, rights, wealth, duties and occupation. At the top of the pyramid was the king: in early times some kings had more importance than others, and such over-kings were known as *bretwaldas*. In pagan times kings liked to claim descent from gods. The king's men transferred not only their possessions but their honour to their king – thus when the hero Beowulf triumphed over the monster Grendel in the poem, the victory became that of his king Hygelac. The monarch, however, gave his men war gear (which was sometimes returnable at death as a sort of death duty, and known as *heriot*), gifts of land, gold and protection.

Next in the hierarchy was the nobleman, called variously *thane, ealdorman* or *gesith. Thanes* were distinguished from the rest of the populace by their ownership of land and their birth.

Below this level were the free peasants or *churls*, whose *wergild* was fixed at 200 shillings. They too owned land which they passed down to their heirs, and they were free to go where they pleased. They had various obligations to fulfil, paying dues to crown and church and being required to give military service and to take part in the *folc-gemot* ('folkmoot' – popular meeting).

At the bottom of the pyramid were slaves who could be bought, sold or bequeathed. They could be born into serfdom or become enslaved as a punishment (such was the price if a fine could not be paid). By the time of Alfred, however, they were allowed to own some property. His laws also made provision for them to sell things they had been given, or had produced in their spare time – 'on the four Wednesdays in the ember weeks' they were allowed holidays. They could buy their freedom, but were more often released by manumission often at the death of their owner. They had no *wergild* but were valued at eight oxen.

The administration of the country lay in the first instance in the hands of the king and his council, known as the *Witan* (which means 'wise men'). This met wherever the king might be, often at festival times. On a local basis justice was overseen by an *ealdorman* (later known as an *eorl*), appointed for life and responsible for one or more shires. Local feuds were arbitrated, thieves judged and other such matters attended to under his direction at a district assembly. Beneath the *ealdorman* were the king's reeves (from whose title the later shire reeves or sheriffs are derived) who ran the king's estate, presided over the local *folc-gemot*, regulated local trade taxes and dues, and undertook other minor legal activities. Town reeves in later times were confined in their responsibilities to particular towns.

The king and his subjects at home

Few settlements of the period 600–800 have been excavated, but those few buildings which have been uncovered, for example at Maxey, Northamptonshire, and North Elmham, Norfolk, are little different from the earlier examples at Chalton and Catholme. However, for reasons which are not yet properly understood, many of the villages occupied in pagan times seem to have been abandoned sometime in the seventh century. New villages were founded, which grew into the settlements of medieval and later times. How real this 'Middle Saxon Shuffle' of settlements is remains difficult to determine. The Anglo-Saxon villages which can be sampled by excavation are atypical in that they are 'failed' settlements which were not overlain by medieval and later villages. Some settlements were deserted in the Middle Ages and would seem to be useful places to study, but such sites have seldom brought to light evidence for pagan Saxon predecessors. A few deserted medieval villages, such as that at Wharram Percy, Yorkshire, have produced evidence for existence in the middle Saxon period. If indeed there was a general shift from old villages to new sites around the seventh and eighth centuries, various economic and social factors might be evoked to explain it. For example, the choice of pagan Saxon settlements may have been dictated by existing Roman estates, but with progressive opening up of forest, new land may have become available.

Although little is known about the lifestyle of the middle Saxon commoner, something about the living standards of his royal liege has been discovered from the remarkable palace complex excavated at Yeavering in Northumberland.

Yeavering was the residence of king Edwin (616–32). Various buildings were grouped around a timber grandstand shaped like the segment of a circle: it may have been from this that Paulinus preached to the Northumbrians in 627. Not far off was one of the timber forts that are rare from this period, and between it and the grandstand stood a large aisled hall, supported by external buttresses and with a section partitioned off. Doors pierced all four sides. The structure measured about 27 m long internally, the measurements being based on a modified Roman foot (the so-called 'Yeavering foot'), which was used to space out other halls at distances of eighty 'Yeavering feet'. One building of Edwin's time had a sunken floor, another seems to have been a temple which was converted into a church. The whole complex was burnt down, perhaps when Northumbria was ravaged in 632 during the campaigns of Cadwallon (see p. 93). The destroyed buildings were replaced by further halls, and incinerated again, probably during the raids of Penda of Mercia.

Yeavering is not unique. Similar complexes of halls are known from Hatton Rock in Mercia, which may date from the eighth century, and at Millfield in Northumbria, not far from Yeavering itself, both of which have been detected by aerial photography. At Old Windsor, Berkshire, a middle Saxon watermill and some stone buildings with glazed windows may belong to another palace complex.

The Anglo-Saxon as craftsman

Anglo-Saxon England was predominantly a farming society, but in the country and, when they had developed, in the towns, various traditional crafts occupied the people. Because of the difficulties of dating and sparse finds, the

Christian England

74 The Northumbrian palace of Yeavering, from the air, showing up as crop marks. The curved crop marks on the extreme left belong to the native-style enclosure. Immediately to its right is a hall, of which the buttress posts are clearly visible, as are the internal divisions. This was rebuilt several times. Other rectangular buildings are also clearly visible. The palace complex, known to Bede as *Ad Gefrin*, was occupied by king Edwin, and was excavated between 1953 and 1957

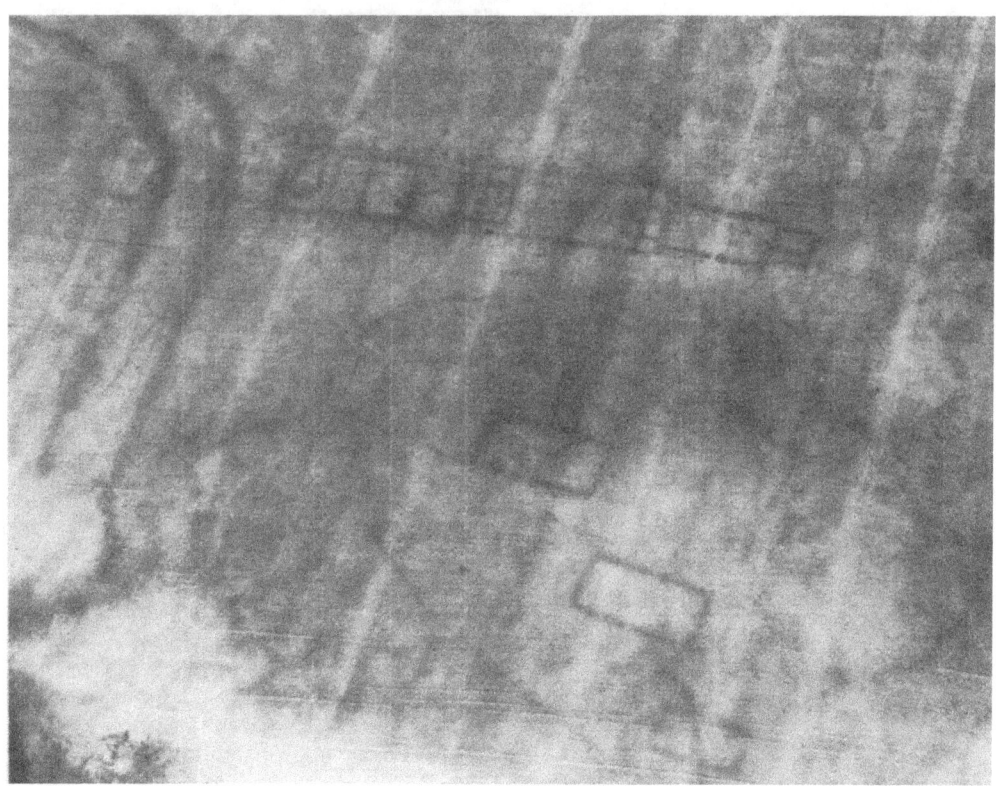

Christian England

picture of craftsmanship that can be pieced together has to span pagan to late Saxon times, and not be confined to one period.

Some crafts were minority activities, such as soap-making (which is recorded in the place-name of Sapperton in Yorkshire), charcoal-burning, salt-making (which is preserved in the *wich* place-names of Cheshire) and bell-founding (in late Saxon Winchester). The main crafts, however, were woodworking, weaving and metalworking.

Of all the crafts of the Anglo-Saxons, carpentry was perhaps the most important. Wood was used for a variety of things, from buildings to tableware and tools. Many of the surviving woodworkers' tools have a curiously modern look about them: hammers, drills, axes, adzes, augers, sawblades, a chisel and even a plane found in a pagan grave at Sarre in Kent would be regarded as quite serviceable by a craftsman today. Toolkits have been found at Hurbuck in Durham, Westley Waterless in Cambridge and Crayke in Yorkshire (these all date from the ninth or tenth centuries but can be assumed to have existed in middle Saxon times). Wedges were used to split wood, and axe-hammers are

75 The Anglo-Saxon watermill at Tamworth, excavated by Prof. P. A. Rahtz. The box in the top left-hand corner formed the mill pond, the box at the bottom right was the outfall channel. Between the two were two troughs, the one on the left feeding the water mill. The projecting beam (*bottom left*) was probably a foundation. Remains of an earlier mill can be seen beneath. The wheel was horizontally mounted, as in recent 'Click Mills' in the Northern Isles. Millstones (some of Rhineland lava) and parts of the mill mechanism were also found. Eighth century

known from Horton Kirby in Kent and Alfriston in Sussex.

Few wooden products survive, but pagan graves have yielded stave-built buckets, and in York the cooper's skill is represented by a barrel top. Wooden combs and spoons have been found in York, where bowls and platters serve to remind us that in Saxon times most tableware was of wood. Very advanced carpentry is displayed in the construction of a well-lining at Portchester and in the timbers of a water mill at Tamworth in Staffordshire. Oak was split to make roof shingles at Winchester.

Textiles were home-produced and linen and woollen cloth have occasionally been found by archaeologists. A tablet for weaving braids was found at Kingston Down in Kent. Some rich ladies had braids interwoven with fine gold threads. Such braids show great variety in their patterns, and were used for borders of clothes or for hair bands.

Iron-working was of great importance, for metal was needed for most tools. Shaft furnaces have been found and excavated at Mucking, Stamford, West Runton (Norfolk) and Wakerley (Northants). This is a Roman type of furnace, in contrast to the bowl furnace popular among the contemporary Celts and at least some of the pagan Saxons. Few smiths' tools have survived, though hammers, chisels, tongs, pritchels and a file have been recorded. The blacksmith was a stalwart of any Anglo-Saxon community for he made and repaired tools, nails and horseshoes. Weland Smith is a prominent mythological figure in Anglo-Saxon lore. Specialists must have made swords and armour, and may have been responsible for the ornamentation of iron by tinning (through fusion plating) or inlaying with silver, bronze or copper. Pewter and lead were more popular in the later Saxon period than in pagan times.

No jeweller's workshop has been found (though a pagan period mould for a brooch has come from Mucking; see p. 65). A ninth-century jeweller's hoard has been found at Sevington, Wilts, with objects ranging from an ingot to a finished strap-end. A jeweller's grave at Barton-on-Humber (Lincs) contained a lead die for stamping a thin piece of metal, and a set of weights with a balance.

Glass was made in pagan Kent, in the region round Faversham, and some window glass seems to have been made in the Northumbrian monastery of Monkwearmouth. Glass-making was also carried out at Glastonbury, Somerset, where three smelting ovens have been found.

Bone was far more commonly used in Anglo-Saxon times than in later ages, for many different objects. Composite bone combs are particularly characteristic products.

Christian England

Coinage and towns

Although town life continued within the walls of Roman towns during the fifth and sixth centuries and settlements of Anglo-Saxons took place within their walls, the Anglo-Saxons did not develop beyond a village economy until the seventh century. A flourishing urban economy cannot exist on barter – a universally recognized coinage, backed by some central authority is needed. During the first period of the Anglo-Saxon settlements, no such authority was established and there was no precedent for coinage in the Continental homelands. For most of the fifth and into the sixth century the only coins coming into England were the occasional Byzantine or other exotic gold pieces which were valued for their gold content and ornamental quality rather than as currency.

With the rise of Kent, however, south-east England's overseas trade blossomed, and Englishmen became acquainted with the Merovingian Frankish gold tremisses: tiny coins modelled on Roman predecessors which were little larger than aspirins and which were struck at a great diversity of mints. The earliest group of tremisses were

76 Merovingian tremisses, found in the purse at Sutton Hoo. Typical of the small gold coins current in the Frankish world, they were struck by a variety of mints and are difficult to attribute and date due to the similarity of Frankish names, but metrology (the study of their weights) helps. Their dating has been crucial to the dating of the Sutton Hoo burial. At the time of their deposition coins were not in regular use in England – they were a ritual deposit, perhaps to pay the 'oarsmen' of the dead king's ship. First quarter of seventh century

those found with three blanks and two ingots in the purse at Sutton Hoo. All different, they were struck between 625 and 630 and were ritual objects, not currency, perhaps intended to 'pay' the ghostly crew of the dead king's ship. The coins were all tiny because at this time gold was becoming scarce, and the tremisses were progressively debased during the seventh century until they were frankly silver pieces. Certainly during the period from 550–75 onwards large numbers of Merovingian gold coins were being absorbed into eastern England, and it is reasonable to suppose that at least by the seventh century the first gold

Christian England

coins were being issued in England. There seems to have been a variety of mints, mostly in the south-east, of which London was the most important, though York also seems to have been striking some coins. These early gold pieces,

usually called *thrymsas*, were modelled on Roman prototypes and are represented in a hoard of 100 found at Crondall in 1828.

Increasing scarcity of gold led to the rapid debasement of the early *thrymsa* coinage, and by the 690s it had been replaced by silver coins with the same fabric known as *sceattas* which were probably called 'pennies' by their users. *Sceattas* were struck in London, Canterbury, Rochester, York and Southampton, as well as at a mint or mints in East Anglia, and continued in use until 750 or even later. Alongside the English-struck *sceattas* were others, issued in Frisia, which circulated widely. The *sceattas*, and the larger silver pennies

77 Gold *thrymsa*, from the Crondall Hoard, Oxfordshire. The Crondall Hoard, found in 1828, comprised 100 small gold coins and 2 cloisonné pins (see Plate 4). The coins are the earliest struck in Anglo-Saxon England, and the reverse of this one carries the abbreviated name of the city of London where it was struck. The hoard dates from around AD 650–75.

78 Towards the end of the seventh century, the early gold *thrymsas* were progressively debased and became small silver pieces which are usually termed *sceattas*, though they were probably called 'pennies' by their users. Many have types modelled on earlier Roman coins, and many too show considerable artistic merit. The first coin is one of the 'Standard' series, which is modelled on a coin of Constantine with a vexillum (a type of standard) and two captives on the reverse. That on the right has a fantastic animal on the reverse which fortuitously recalls some of the backward-looking beasts on early metalwork and a facing bearded head which can be compared with those on the Mucking bucket (Plate 56). The *sceatta* coinage continued until the mid-eighth century. (Enlarged)

Christian England

which succeeded them, circulated east of an arc from the Wash to the Southampton Water. Beyond this line coins do not seem to have been used much if at all as a regular means of trade until the ninth century.

The ultimate models behind the *sceatta* coinages were Roman, but the interpretation of the designs was purely English. Many of them are superb examples of the minor arts. The patterns include strange stalking birds, backward-looking beasts, grotesque monsters, abstract whirling patterns, centaurs and men. Some seem to illustrate scenes from Anglo-Saxon mythology, others were merely ornamental. Few are inscribed: some of those struck in East Anglia carry runes which translate as the personal names of moneyers, while a few others bear the name of the London mint.

It is to Offa that the establishment of the true penny can be attributed. Just as the *sceattas* and the *thrymsas* before them had been struck for trade with the Continent and mirrored Continental trends, so too were the first pennies English versions of Frankish *deniers*, which had first been struck in 755 under Pepin III. In fact, Offa did not devise the

79 Penny of Offa (AD 757–96), king of Mercia. Offa took over the custom of striking pennies from the Kentish kings Heaberht and Ecgberht whom he conquered. Offa's coins were the first widespread issues of pennies in England, and were of very high quality, also enjoying some use on the Continent. This example bears his portrait, name and title on the obverse and an ornamental pattern on the reverse, with the name of the moneyer, Dud. The obverse portrait shows certain features in common with those of Roman emperors. (Enlarged)

penny, but took it over, ready patented as it were, as a subsidiary benefit of his conquest of Kent, for here the co-monarchs Heaberht and Ecgberht were already following Frankish precedent and striking pennies from around 770. Offa began his own coinage of pennies around 780, and from then on silver pennies remained the main coin of the realm until the time of the Tudors, though some halfpence were struck by Anglo-Saxon kings along with the occasional gold piece, and a regular coinage of gold and of other silver denominations came in during the reign of Edward III.

Offa's coins were intended for overseas trade, and were clearly modelled on Roman antecedents – he even struck coins in the name of his wife Cynethryth as did Roman emperors. Offa's pennies were larger and thinner than the old *sceattas*, and very accomplished artistically. They were mostly issued at Canterbury. The new coins did not reach

Christian England

80 *Sceattas* became progressively degenerate, as this 'Porcupine' *sceatta* shows. The 'standard' still appears on the reverse, but the obverse whorl of lines is all that is left of a 'wolf and twins' reverse of Constantinian coins commemorating Rome. Eighth century. The coin on the right is a Northumbrian *sceatta* of Eanred (810–41), struck in bronze. In Northumbria *sceattas* were debased until they became small bronze pieces and continued to be struck until the Danish raids, even though pennies were popular elsewhere. The reverse bears the moneyer's name, EADUIHI (Eadwine). (Enlarged)

Northumbria, where *sceattas* continued to be issued, progressively debased until they were tiny copper pieces with inscriptions but no design beyond a tiny central cross. These *stycas*, as they are usually (but inaccurately) termed, circulated in Northumbria until the Vikings' arrival put an end to their issue shortly before the mid-ninth century. They may have been issued to make tax collection easier.

Among Offa's coins the most remarkable is a gold piece, imitating a *dinar* of Caliph Al Mansur, struck in AD 774. It was found in Italy, and even has Arabic legends. The oil likely to have figured in eighth-century trade was from olives, and this English *dinar* may have been struck because Arab coins were the main gold currency of the western Mediterranean, following the Arab conquest of Spain. A now lost silver penny of Offa bore the legend S PETRVS, and was perhaps intended as a tribute to the Pope. Offa's coins enjoyed a wide circulation in Europe – two have been discovered in Russia, and others have been found in Norway and Italy, where one of his issues was imitated at Lucca.

Towns

The growth of a money-based economy went hand-in-hand with town development, and the earliest Anglo-Saxon towns can be ascribed to the late seventh century.

Among the earliest are a group of trading posts which

seem to have been linked to inland royal and religious centres, which themselves grew into towns. Hamwih, for instance, the Saxon predecessor of modern Southampton, seems to have begun life in the late seventh century and was connected with the ecclesiastical centre at Winchester. Fordwich, Dover, and slightly later Sarre seem to have been the trading posts for Kent, and were linked to Canterbury. Ipswich served East Anglia. These were new foundations. London and York were in a class by themselves, growing up on existing Roman sites and combining both mercantile and ecclesiastical functions. London was a bishop's see as early as 604, and the Kentish kings had a palace there by 675; its mercantile importance is attested by the gold *thrymsas* struck there with the London mint-name around the middle of the seventh century. By the same token York had a bishop by 625, and may have had a royal residence by then. Although few finds prior to the ninth century have so far been made there, it is known that the Roman town defences were refurbished in the seventh or eighth century (perhaps as early as 650) when a stone tower (the 'Anglian tower') was built on the line of the Roman legionary fortress wall.

London and York probably had similar status to Continental towns such as Cologne. Undefended trading centres, such as Hamwih, can be matched by the Frisian trading centres of Dorestad and Quentovic.

A clear picture of life in an eighth-century English trading centre can be pieced together from the excavations at Hamwih, which was deserted in the medieval period in favour of the site of modern Southampton, not to be built over again until the industrial boom of the nineteenth century. More information than usual was available to archaeology for this reason. Its site on the bank of the river Itchen meant that it was ideally situated for Continental trade. At its peak Hamwih covered some 72 acres (30 ha) and was regularly laid out with parallel gravelled roads that ran at right angles to the shore of the Itchen. Along these highways (which underwent frequent repair) the plots of land contained houses with the wells, rubbish pits, and industrial workings to their rear. Among the excavated buildings were some which were bow-sided, and which may owe their shape to Continental influence, for similar bow-sided buildings have been excavated at Dorestad and elsewhere, though there is some evidence for them in the earlier Anglo-Saxon period.

The inhabitants of Hamwih engaged in a variety of industries. Some *sceattas* were coined there, though the site of the mint has not yet been found. Bronze was cast in a variety of objects, and a forge and furnace have been excavated which had been used for the production of domestic ironwork. The evidence for carpentry included an oak cask made out of staves with hazel binding, and a bucket of similar manufacture. Textile manufacture was demonstrated not only by the spindle whorls, pin beaters for packing down the thread on the loom, and loom-weights, but by a piece of worsted wool. The main industry in the town appears to have been bone-working. Single- and double-sided combs, weaving tools, gaming pieces, comb cases and pins were all made from this material. Not all the bone-work from Hamwih was made locally, however – a flute, handled combs and a decorated handle are best matched in Frisia, though the handle was of a type used to top the apple-wood canes used as walking sticks by elderly Franks.

Although industry was carried out in all areas of Hamwih, trade was its *raison d'être*. Considerable quantities of glass were imported from the Rhineland and probably the east too. Pottery from the Meuse, the Pas-de-Calais and the Ardennes are common finds on the site. The ceramic finds include Tating Ware from Germany, decorated with diamonds of tinfoil stuck on the sides of the pot, and some vessels from the region round Rouen and other pottery from the Trier district. From the great lava quarries at Niedermendig came querns for grinding grain. More exotic was the bone of a green turtle (which is now found no nearer Southampton than the Canary Islands) and the handle of a classical cup, perhaps brought back from the Mediterranean by a trader as an antique souvenir. A rune-inscribed bone probably came from Frisia.

Trade was not directed exclusively towards the Continent. Among the stone objects recovered were some whetstones of Palaeozoic limestone, of which the nearest outcrops were in south Wales, the Mendips and Derbyshire. A piece of millstone grit came from Yorkshire, Derbyshire or south Wales. This builds up to a possible picture of trade through Oxford to the central Midlands (a route in operation in the Middle Ages), perhaps prompted by the Midland salt supplies.

Among the host of everyday articles found are keys (implying door locks), window glass (though this was very rare, and most houses would have had shutters), pottery and stone lamps, knives, a strike-a-light, the iron tip for a spade, and a chisel. An unusual gadget was a fork-spoon, which can be compared with the famous fork-spatula and spoon-spatula from a hoard at Sevington.

81 The defences of the Saxon town of Hereford. In the foreground are two corn-drying kilns, probably of Dark Age date. The line of the rampart's original surface can be seen running diagonally up the section beside the ranging pole. It was built on top of the kilns, and shows several phases of construction. The most significant was that of Period 5, which had a timber wall at front and back and was composed of alluvial clayey soil with layers of peat and possibly turf. Finds of late Saxon pottery from above it suggest that it might be the defence put up by Aethelflaed in 913–15, when she is known to have fortified the *burh*.

The mercantile centre of Hamwih was not defended. It was in Mercia that the beginnings of deliberate urban planning set within a defensive earthwork can be found. At Tamworth there are hints of an early earthwork enclosure. Some time in the eighth or ninth centuries Hereford was furnished with a small delimiting earthwork. This was followed by a substantial gravel and clay rampart, enclosing a rectangular area of some 33 acres (13.6 ha). The shape of the Hereford defences and the regular layout of the street within it indicate a deliberate, planned foundation. It is not impossible that Offa was the genius behind such planned towns – he had plenty of experience of rampart construction in connection with the building of his famous Dyke, and was also much aware of Continental life. Not until Alfred was the Mercian idea developed further, as we shall see in the next chapter.

The greatest single achievement of middle Saxon England was the construction of the great linear earthworks of Wat's and Offa's Dykes. These Mercian frontier works along the border with Wales were not the only dykes found in post-Roman Britain, but they were certainly the most ambitious. Similar territorial boundaries had been built in East Anglia (including the Devil's Ditch on Newmarket Heath) and in the south-west (Wansdyke) in the early centuries following the arrival of the Anglo-Saxons in England, but they were slight compared with the Mercian

Christian England

82 Offa's Dyke, on Llanvair Hill, Shropshire, looking south-east. The great earthwork, 192 km in length, was built by Offa of Mercia to demarcate the boundary with the Welsh kingdom of Powys. It runs from near Treuddyn in Clwyd to a point near Chepstow, and consists of a bank and ditch without any forts, turrets or other defensive structures

frontier works. Unlike the Roman frontier works of Hadrian's and the Antonine Wall, the Mercian dykes were not furnished with forts, turrets or other military installations. They were simply composed of an earth bank and a quarry ditch, though some sections at least of Offa's Dyke may have been crowned with a wall. Offa's Dyke is a staggering 192 km in length (Hadrian's Wall is a mere 116 km long), and runs through some of the finest scenery in England, from near Treuddyn in Clwyd to a point near Chepstow on the Severn, with a number of gaps where dense forest probably made the dyke superfluous. Wat's Dyke, somewhat shorter, extends from near Holywell to the middle Severn, and was probably built by Offa's predecessor, Aethelbald (AD 716–57). Together they are surviving testimony to the power of eighth-century Mercia, the power that was eclipsed in the ninth by Alfred's kingdom of Wessex.

Chapter four

The Late Saxons
c. AD 800–1066

From the greatest treasures of the Ashmolean Museum in Oxford one Anglo-Saxon jewel can be singled out. Found in 1693 near Athelney in Somerset, it is edged by an openwork inscription: AELFRED MEC HEHT GEWYRCAN – 'Alfred had me made'. The style of the object suggests a date in the late ninth century, and the fact that in 878 king Alfred the Great was in residence in Athelney, and set out from there to win his great victory over the Danes at Ethandun, suggests strongly that the king himself ordered the jewel to be made. Since he later established a monastery at Athelney it is not impossible that the jewel was there.

The Alfred Jewel displays a figure in cloisonné enamel behind a protective plate of rock crystal. The inscription is

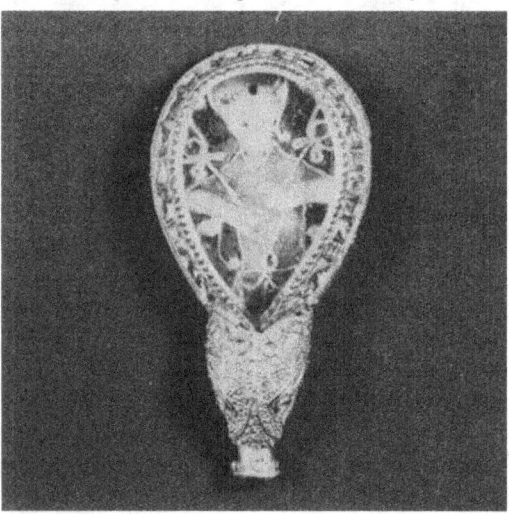

83 The Alfred Jewel (*right*) was found in 1693 near Athelney in Somerset, and carries an Anglo-Saxon inscription to the effect that 'Alfred had me made'. Although it is not certain, it is generally accepted that this indicates it was made on the order of king Alfred (AD 871–99). Current opinion holds that it is the top of an *aestal* or reading pointer, of which the Minster Lovell Jewel was the foot. The figure on the front of the jewel is a personification of Sight (compare it with the same personification on the Fuller Brooch, Plate 111), which appears to have been cut down to fit the jewel from an earlier object. It is covered by a piece of rock crystal. On the back is a foliage pattern of Carolingian derivation

set off with gold filigree and granular work, and on the back is a gold plate with engraved foliage and scale decoration. The pear-shaped head terminates in a gold socket, fashioned in the form of a boar's head ornamented in granular work, through which a gold pin still remains from the original fastening to a shaft of wood or ivory. It cannot be a pendant from a necklace, for this would have been contrived so that the enamelled figure would be visible the right way up (not upside down) when suspended from a chain or string. In any case, it would have had a loop rather than a socket. There can be little doubt that the Alfred Jewel adorned the top of a staff – it could have surmounted a manuscript roller, a sceptre, a stylus for writing on wax tablets, or a pointer. Fortunately the object provides a clue: it displays a representation of a man, his eyes looking to the left, a branch with a floral head in each hand. Some have interpreted it as a depiction of king Alfred, the Pope, or even Christ, but the craftsman would have made these look straight ahead. A similar personification adorns a late Saxon silver brooch depicting the Five Senses, known as the Fuller Brooch (see p. 182) and the Alfred Jewel must be depicting a personification of Sight. Alfred proposed to give a copy of his translation of Pope Gregory's *Cura Pastoralis* along with an ornamental pointer called an *aestal* to each of the English bishoprics. This is just such a pointer.

The Alfred Jewel is symbolic of the culture of late Saxon England. The gold boar's-head socket is an echo from the pagan past, a barbaric thing, like a refugee from the Benty Grange helmet crest or from Sutton Hoo. The technique of its manufacture, in filigree and granular work, survives from the fashion of seventh-century Kent and East Anglia, and the use of brightly coloured enamels laid beneath a piece of rock crystal recalls the polychrome jewellery of days gone by. That is all that belongs to the barbaric past. The use of a personification of one of the Five Senses belongs to a Classical past. The inscription, though in Anglo-Saxon not Latin, reveals a tradition of learning – Alfred after all was traditionally instrumental in the fostering of Anglo-Saxon as a written language instead of the hitherto universal Latin. Before this time, non-Latin inscriptions had tended to be talismanic and magical, but from now on Englishmen were to use their own tongue proudly, to record their history and their culture. The back plate tells another story. The foliage pattern stems ultimately from Classical acanthus ornament, but it is in no way a slavish copy of an Antique form. Its style shows that it was done by a Carolingian craftsman, either in England, or, more probably, France. One other feature of the Alfred Jewel is anomalous – it does not appear as it was originally conceived. The enamel plate was cut down to fit the piece of rock crystal, which may have come from another jewel. It was in fact old wine in a new bottle, like the dynamic new society that produced it.

In late Saxon England the uneasy relationship between civilization and barbarism was resolved, if briefly. Though barbaric in their origins, much of their thinking, their secular literature and their social structure, the late Saxons con-

The Late Saxons

sciously endeavoured to emulate their civilized neighbours on the Continent and further east. Contact with civilization was first made with the Christian mission from Rome; it was later extended through the proximity of Anglo-Saxon England to the Merovingian and Carolingian empires. The Saxons had adopted the Roman faith, Roman art, Roman thinking: Charlemagne regarded Offa of Mercia as his equal. Yet inside every civilized Saxon was a restless barbarian. The social system of late Saxon England itself, for all the civilized trappings of its complex, efficient administration, was rooted in the past. A Saxon king was little more than a tribal war-leader, dressed up in civilized clothing.

Sources

The documentary sources for late Saxon England (c. 800–1066) are in the main similar to those for the middle Saxon period, except that they are more copious. Once again the *Anglo-Saxon Chronicle* provides the main historical framework, which can be filled out with laws, charters, poems and some independent chronicles, incorporated into the writings of a later medieval monk, Symeon of Durham. Asser's *Life of King Alfred* is a unique record of his time, and there are other informative *Lives* of notable late Saxon personalities, such as the clerics Aethelwold, Dunstan and Wolfstan of Worcester. The letters of the monk Alcuin are also very informative on some aspects of English history.

The material evidence is very much more copious than for the middle Saxon period. More late Saxon churches survive than those of earlier periods, and there are more known late Saxon settlement sites which include town sites which have produced a variety of evidence for late Saxon urban life. Although the plans of secular buildings are known from urban excavations and from the excavation of some aristocratic sites and a royal palace, the evidence for late Saxon villages is surprisingly meagre still, and though some late Saxon rural settlements, such as Little Paxton and St Neots, have been excavated at least in part, there has still not been any extensive excavation of a village site occupied predominantly in the late Saxon period.

Due to large numbers of specimens turning up in Viking-period and later hoards in Scandinavia, late Saxon coinage is very well understood. So too is late Saxon pottery, and there is a fine collection of ornamental metalwork of the period. Late Saxon and Anglo-Scandinavian sculpture, particularly in the north of England, is almost embarrassingly plentiful, and many outstanding decorated manuscripts have survived. Other art treasures such as ivories survive from the late Saxon period though absent before, and from such evidence a clear picture emerges of the mastery of late Saxon artists.

History – the wrath of the Vikings

Late Saxon England was driven to assume the mantle of civilization by the threat of Viking invasions. The cleric Alcuin writes of the 'savage' Vikings, complaining that

> We and our forefathers have lived here for about 350 years, and never have such terrors as these appeared in Britain, which we must now suffer from the pagans: it was not thought possible that such havoc could be made.

How like the words of Gildas, three centuries before (see p. 22) describing the coming of Alcuin's own people; he had no real right to cast the first stone. Curiously enough, Alcuin, like Gildas before him, attributed the arrival of the savages to God's retribution on an iniquitous race: the wheel had come full circle.

> 793. In this year terrible portents appeared in Northumbria, and miserably afflicted the inhabitants: these were exceptional flashes of lightning, and fiery dragons were seen flying in the air, and soon followed a great famine, and after that in the same year the harrying of the heathen miserably destroyed God's church in Lindisfarne by rapine and slaughter. (trans. G. N. Garmonsway)

This entry in the *Anglo-Saxon Chronicle* heralds the last of the great barbarian incursions to Britain – the coming of the Vikings (Map 3). Even today, the word 'Viking' has an immediate impact on the listener – it conjures up images of violence and bloodshed, of burning churches, of ferocious bearded warriors slaughtering innocent peasants and raping their wives and daughters, of long dragon-prowed ships with brightly coloured sails, of gold and savage art. But the English word for law is derived from the Vikings, and all over England some of the most English-sounding names such as Grimsby, Scunthorpe, Staxton or Derby are evidence for peaceful Scandinavian farmers tilling the soil and living in villages little different from those of their Anglo-Saxon neighbours. Like the Saxons themselves, the Vikings have a myth of their own and, as with the Saxons, the reality was not always like the fantasy.

The Vikings were the last of the barbarian invaders of Britain and are thus the best documented. Their raids began in the late eighth century: a time when monks were in the habit of noting events if only to help them remember dates that would be useful when it came to calculating Easter. Had the Vikings not been interested in looting churches and monasteries, the chances are they would not have attracted

The Late Saxons

such attention from chroniclers. The recorders were all clerics, and it was precisely these members of the community who had most to fear from Viking plundering. It was the Church, too, that could least sympathize with Viking paganism; had the raiders been Christian the chances are they would have been less feared.

It was not only the Church that was responsible for our picture of the Viking sea raider. In Iceland, the Christian descendants of the early Scandinavian adventurers looked back from the comparative tranquillity and respectability of the twelfth and thirteenth centuries to what they imagined were more romantic and exciting days, when men were men and the treasures of Europe were theirs for the asking. Accordingly, they tried to relive the great days of the Vikings through their sagas – tales like that of Burnt Njal, or the Vinland Saga, or even the great epic of the Norse in Scotland, the *Orkneyinga Saga*. These were usually based on truth, but were ornamented in the interests of the telling of a good yarn; just as the apparently historical records of the contemporaries of the Norsemen were elaborated to make the threat sound more fearsome.

Like some of the Anglo-Saxons before them, the Vikings came from the north, many coming from the same areas as some of the fifth-century settlers. Like the Anglo-Saxons too, their seafaring was brought about partly by overpopulation in their homeland linked with internal political squabbles, and partly by the desire to prey on richer cultures. Like the Anglo-Saxons, they were primarily farmers with a social structure which depended on family ties and loyalty to the lord. Like the Anglo-Saxons they had sophisticated law codes and a vigorous art based on animal forms.

However, one feature of the Viking movements does distinguish them sharply from their Anglo-Saxon predecessors. While the Anglo-Saxons had been content with England, for the Vikings the known world was not big enough. The Norse colonized not only the remote islands of Scotland, but sailed on to Iceland, Greenland and eventually to America. The Swedes were great traders, and apart from establishing bases in northern Europe they forged a route which led through Russia (the territory of the Rus) to Byzantium and beyond. Scandinavians served in the Imperial royal bodyguard of Byzantium, the Varangian guard, while along the Russian trade route Arab silver coin flooded into Scandinavia and overflowed into Europe. The Norse ravaged the kingdom of the Franks, sacking Rouen, Nantes and the trading port of Quentovic in the Low

The Late Saxons

Countries; in 911 they wrested Normandy from the Franks and made it one of their territories. They raided Spain in the mid-ninth century, even as Swedish traders were engaging in more peaceful business in the eastern Mediterranean – a marble lion, taken from the Piraeus near Athens to Venice in the Middle Ages, bears on its shoulder a Swedish runic inscription. Europe was to witness other barbarian folk migrations before the end of the Middle Ages – the Magyars for example – but never again was she to see so extensive a movement.

The 'Vikings' comprised the Norse or Norwegians from Norway, the Danes and the Swedes. The term 'Northmen' or 'Norsemen' is sometimes used to embrace all raiders of Scandinavian origin, and contemporary chroniclers seem to have been fairly indiscriminate in their choice of a label for the incomers. Raiders from all three areas are represented in Britain, but the Swedes were in a minority and were just one element in raids and settlements which were predominantly either Norse or Danish. The Norse settled in Scotland, the Isle of Man and Ireland, and established a kingdom at York, as well as conducting sporadic raids on the Atlantic coast of northern England and Wales. The Danes were primarily active in England, first establishing themselves in the east, where they occupied what became known as the Danelaw (Map 3, p. 134). They also played some part in the colonization of Ireland.

The Danish colonization of England is documented most clearly in the *Anglo-Saxon Chronicle*. It was concentrated between 865 and 954, when raids gradually gave way to peaceful settlement, and again shortly before AD 1000 until Cnut (Canute) the Dane became king of all England for the period 1016–35. The earliest (but suspect) record of the Danish raids is of an attack on the south coast which led to the murder of the king's official representative in 789. This was followed by the raid on Lindisfarne in 793 which we have already seen recorded in the *Anglo-Saxon Chronicle*. It led the saintly Alcuin to write in horror:

> Behold the church of St Cuthbert spattered with the blood of the priests of God, despoiled of all its ornaments; a place more venerable than all in Britain is given as prey to the pagan peoples.

From 835 onwards raid after raid is documented in the *Anglo-Saxon Chronicle*. In 851 a Danish army spent the winter in England – raids of the tip-and-run variety had given way to something more serious – concerted attack. Between 865 and 880 the Danes gained control of most of Northumbria, eastern Mercia and East Anglia. They tem-

The Late Saxons

porarily seized London, and penetrated the heart of Anglo-Saxon England, Wessex. Here they were met by the formidable Alfred, who drove them back and established a political frontier along the line of the old Roman road, Watling Street. This line (from Chester through Shrewsbury, Lichfield, Bedford and Hertford to London) was reclaimed and held by the Mercian *ealdorman* who had married Alfred's daughter. To the east of this line the Danes were allowed to settle by the treaty made at Wedmore between Alfred and the Danish leader Guthrum. This region was known as the Danelaw, and within it the Five Boroughs of Nottingham, Lincoln, Stamford, Derby and Leicester were established. Some Angles still held on to Bernicia, and the Danes did not cross the Pennines. However, north-west England did not long remain free of Scandinavian domination: people from the Irish-Norse kingdom centred on Dublin settled extensively from the Wirral to Carlisle, from where offshoots were established to the east of the Pennines. York was taken from the Danes by the Norse in 919, the army having arrived from Dublin through southern Scotland. Although by 927 the kingdom of York had reverted to the Anglo-Saxons there was still the threat of a Norse kingdom extending from Dublin to York until the death of the great Norse scourge, Eric Bloodaxe, in 954.

By the middle of the tenth century the first phase of Scandinavian England had waned under the ascendancy of Anglo-Saxon Wessex. Alfred died in 899, and his son Edward the Elder began the process of reclaiming land from the Danes with the help of his sister Aethelflaed. The Danes had grown soft through almost a generation of peace, and Aethelflaed and her brother proved worthy children of an illustrious father. Aethelflaed had Mercian interests on account of her husband, and adopted a policy of restoring lost lands to Mercia by a process of attrition, while her brother carried the same tactics to Essex and Hertfordshire and later further afield. By 920 Edward controlled all England south of the Humber, for in that year conquest was completed. At Bakewell in Derbyshire Raegnald, ruler of the Viking-held York, Ealdred, the Northumbrian ruler of Bamburgh, and the rest of the Northumbrians, the Strathclyde Britons and Constantine, king of the Scots, all submitted to Edward, making him the most powerful ruler in Britain.

His successor, Aethelstan, who came to the Wessex throne in 925, became one of the legendary figures of saga lore, and governed Dane and Saxon alike. Aethelstan's

The Late Saxons

reign was troubled by disturbances in the north of his kingdom. He was forced to invade Northumbria and devastated York, accepting the submission of the kings of Scotland, Strathclyde and the ruler of English Northumbria in 927.

It was thus that Aethelstan extended his kingdom to include Lancashire and Westmorland. Not content with this, he decided to press on northwards into Scotland, and in 934 his army reached as far as Kincardine. The threat of Aethelstan's forces united all the northern elements hitherto squabbling among themselves for supremacy, and in 937 the combined forces of the king of the Scots, the king of Strathclyde and the Norse king of Dublin invaded England and met Aethelstan and his brother Edmund at Brunanburh, the modern location of which is not known. The Anglo-Saxons won an overwhelming victory, and the battle was commemorated in one of the finest poems in Anglo-Saxon, which even found its way into the usually cryptic entries of the *Anglo-Saxon Chronicle*.

Aethelstan, who is usually regarded as the first King of all England, died only two years later. His successor, Edmund, was beset until his death in 946 by further troubles in the north, which only came to an end in 954 with the expulsion of Eric Bloodaxe from York by his successor Eadred. Henceforth Northumbria was ruled by earls acting as deputies of the English king.

The second Viking age

In 978, Aethelred succeeded to the throne following the murder of his half-brother, Edward the Martyr. He was burdened with guilt for the murder and his subjects regarded the crime as the most serious since the coming of the English. Aethelred handled all affairs of state with uncertainty and treachery, a fact which earned him the epithet 'Unready' (i.e., unwilling to accept advice). His

84 Silver pennies of (a) Aethelred II, the Unready (978–1016) and (b) Cnut (1016–35). Both were struck at the London mint. Aethelred's reign was characterized by constant Danish raids, despite his efforts to buy peace with enormous payments known as *Danegeld*. Cnut became the first Danish king of England, having defeated Edmund Ironside, Aethelred's son, at Ashingdon in Essex

reign is characterized by a new phase of Danish menace, during which England was subjected to a constant series of attacks culminating in the campaigns of Swein Forkbeard, the son of Harald of Denmark. Swein drove his father out of Denmark some time before 988, and conducted two raids on England before his first organized campaign in 1013. His army made a base at Gainsborough, Yorks, and he was immediately accepted as their king by the Northumbrians and by the Danes in eastern England. He pressed into Mercia, and thence into Wessex, receiving the surrender of Oxford and Winchester. In 1013 London surrendered to him, and Aethelred fled to Normandy, Swein being recognized as king of England. Swein did not live long enough to enjoy his triumph, and was succeeded in 1014 by his younger son, Cnut. Aethelred returned, and Cnut withdrew to Denmark, where he mustered more forces. In 1015 he returned at the head of a considerable army, to carry out a campaign first against Aethelred and then, on the latter's death in 1016, against his son Edmund Ironside. In spite of early successes, Edmund was beaten by the Danes at Ashingdon in Essex, and in November 1016 Cnut became master of England.

Throughout his reign Aethelred had paid vast amounts of money to the Danes to keep the peace. In 991 he paid 22,000 pounds weight of gold and silver, and in 1012, 48,000 pounds weight. Much of this took the form of silver coin, with the result that more Anglo-Saxon coins have been found in Denmark than in England. The levy was known as the *Danegeld*, and Cnut saw no reason to stop bleeding the conquered England of her silver. In 1017 he dismissed his fleet with a 10,500 pounds weight hand-out exacted from the unfortunate inhabitants of London, and demanded a *Danegeld* of 72,000 pounds weight from the rest of England, which he divided up into four parts for ease of administration. In 1017 he married Aethelred's widow, the sister of

(b)

The Late Saxons

the Duke of Normandy, to secure his position against possible claimants, and set about ruling England efficiently. In 1019 he became king of Denmark, and in 1028 assumed the throne of Norway. Until his death in 1035 England enjoyed peace and stability, maintained by his standing army and fleet which was paid for by taxes. For the government of England, he devised a law code based on the laws of the earlier Anglo-Saxon kings.

Cnut intended that England and Denmark should be ruled by his son, Harthacnut, but troubles in Scandinavia kept the latter from coming to England on his father's death, and a dispute broke out as to who should govern the country. Harold I, the illegitimate son of Cnut, was made king of England, but he died in 1040 just as Harthacnut was preparing to cross to England. This he finally did, but although his succession was uncontested the reign was brief as he died 'as he stood at drink' at the wedding feast of Tovi the Proud. He was probably about 25 years old.

Edward, known to history as the Confessor, was elected by popular acclaim in London as his successor, and was crowned at Winchester in 1043. He was the son of Aethelred the Unready, and with his accession England was to enjoy, if briefly, a return to Anglo-Saxon rule. Rather in contradiction to his reputation for saintliness, Edward possessed himself of his mother's lands and money, and settled down to rule England. In 1051 it looked as though civil war might break out when earl Godwine, one of the most powerful men in England, refused to obey Edward. The king, however, drew on the support of his two powerful allies, Leofric of Mercia and Siward of Northumbria, and the outcome was the exile of the Godwines for a year on the Continent. In their absence Edward set about strengthening his ties with Normandy for, until his accession, he had lived there for twenty-five years and was accordingly pro-Norman. He appointed Norman clerics, including one Robert of Jumièges, whom he made first bishop of London and then archbishop of Canterbury. In his latter years the Confessor paid less and less attention to affairs of state and more and more to his own concern with the Faith (he was subsequently canonized), and England moved slowly towards the Norman Conquest. Indeed, long before William the Conqueror arrived with his army, the Normanization of England was well in hand.

Saxons, Danes and Norwegians

The decline of the Danelaw came about through the recognition by the Danes that they needed an ally against

The Late Saxons

the Norse menace, and through their conversion to Christianity. Just as the Scandinavian threat made the Anglo-Saxons more consciously civilized, so did the greater barbarism of the Norse make the Danes feel more akin to the English. The Danes gradually became absorbed into England; even in the twelfth century the laws which gave the Danelaw its name were still recognized. The assimilation was probably possible since there was land enough for both Anglo-Saxon and Dane in the Danelaw – there is no evidence for a massacre of the English population, nor of its displacement.

The way of life of both peoples was similar, and they probably did not find it too difficult to understand each other's language. Danish influence penetrated even Wessex, where in the eleventh century there were complaints that the Danish hairstyle had become popular.

History and place-names tell much more about Scandinavian England than archaeology. It is remarkable that there are very few Viking finds from large areas of England. There are a couple of poor Danish cemeteries, one of them at Ingleby in Derbyshire, a few graves of warriors buried with their weapons, such as that at Repton in Derbyshire, and a concentration of finds from the Thames at London. Nearly all the other remains have come to light in York (see p. 148), though the enormous number of Anglo-Scandinavian sculptures in northern England speaks plainly of the cultural fusion of Angle and Dane in the north at least (see p. 176).

The general dearth of Danish finds in England may be explained in a number of ways. The general scarcity of pagan graves, for instance, may be due to the early conversion of the newcomers to Christianity. The lack of settlement evidence has to be accounted for in other ways.

First, we have relatively few excavated settlements of the late Saxon period in England as a whole, and only a handful of these are rural settlements, as opposed to urban or noble residences. The recent discoveries of Viking-period farmsteads in east Yorkshire, coupled with the excavation of one at Ribblehead, shows that they did exist and that in some areas at least they were similar in character to the Scandinavian settlements in Atlantic Britain. Second, it is likely that many of the Scandinavian incomers rapidly adopted the material possessions of the native Anglo-Saxons and materially at least assumed an Anglo-Saxon lifestyle. The late Saxon wheel-made pottery of the Danelaw known to archaeologists as Thetford, St Neots and Stamford Ware, is as likely to be Danish as Anglo-Saxon, and related vessels such as York Ware have been found in Anglo-Danish contexts in the city. The Vikings, like many peoples before and since, knew how to profit from the culture of the lands they settled, and without doubt Danish stimulus prompted urban development in Anglo-Saxon England as part of a two-way traffic of mercantile ideas.

The density of Scandinavian settlement in England is most clearly reflected in place-names. The greatest concentration of Danish place-names is to be found in a broad belt immediately behind the line held by the Danish army along what had been Watling Street in Roman times. This belt of dense settlement extended from Grimsby to Leicester. Next most densely settled was north Yorkshire, with the East and West Ridings intensively settled, but not quite as thickly as the North. In Northumberland the names are thinly scattered, while in East Anglia, Norfolk was the most densely settled area, the form of the place-names (ending in -*by* and -*thorpe*) indicating an early colonization. In Suffolk Danish names are fewer, and in Essex, in the extreme south-east of the Danelaw, fewer still. Hertfordshire boasts hardly a single Danish name.

Place-names were only part of the Danish linguistic contribution to late Saxon life: the English language itself, the form of personal names, field names and even stream names were changed through Danish influence.

Words as English as 'take', 'call', 'husband', 'sky', 'window', 'anger', 'low', 'scant', 'loose', 'ugly', 'wrong', 'happy', 'hence', 'though', 'thrive', 'ill', 'die', 'bread' and 'eggs' are all Scandinavian. This surprising survival is due to the fact that modern English is descended from a Midlands dialect, in which Anglo-Saxon and Danish speech was mingled. In parts of Yorkshire even today the local dialect is Scandinavian in origin.

Also many English institutions were transformed. The Danes introduced new methods of accounting, land measurement and social organization. They even brought about changes in the law, and in late Saxon England the laws differed in the Danelaw from the rest of England, even when both were once more united, being stricter if simpler than the traditional law of the Anglo-Saxons.

The Danes were the most significant of the Scandinavian incomers. But they were not the only ones. The Norwegians were also present in England, and played their own important role in the shaping of English history. Unlike the Danes, their settlements were not the outcome of an intensive series of military campaigns, but of gradual infiltration. One of the areas most densely settled by the

Norse was north Yorkshire, where place-names attest their presence. Some enclaves of Norse were to be found in the Danelaw, and a scatter of place-names suggests settlement in the East Riding of Yorkshire also. But the main area of Norse settlement was in the north-west, which was colonized by extension from the Isle of Man. Norse names abound in the Wirral, in Lancashire, and in Cumbria, extending across the Pennines into the western parts of Yorkshire. These Norsemen were later settlers than the Danes, first making their landfall in the tenth century. Here the land was generally thinly populated, much of it densely forested or, in the case of southern Lancashire, flat and waterlogged, while the Lake District was too rugged for intensive early settlement. The native population was not ousted – Anglo-Saxon remained the language of place-names in most of Lancashire and Cheshire – though in the forested Wirral Norse names predominate, names like Greasby, Irby, Heswall, West Kirby and Thingwall. Archaeological evidence for Scandinavian presence is afforded by a scatter of finds, notably from the puzzling settlement at Meols, drowned by the Irish Sea but from which has been recovered evidence of successive Roman, Celtic, Anglo-Saxon and Scandinavian occupation.

Late Saxon towns

The Danish attacks accelerated the growth of Anglo-Saxon civilization by giving impetus to town growth. Alfred had profited by studying Danish methods of warfare, and had noticed that they avoided pitched battles and made use of earthworks behind which to hole up. Like all good tacticians, he employed their own methods against his foes, and set about building defensive works which could serve as campaign forts.

Of the Danish earthworks almost nothing is known from archaeology. Various sites have been claimed as Danish fortifications, but none has produced conclusive evidence of Danish occupation, which is not really surprising since they were of the nature of temporary camps, not permanent settlements.

In contrast, much is known about the earthwork defences of the English. We are very fortunate in possessing a document known as the 'Burghal Hidage'. This was drawn up in the time of Alfred's successor, Edward the Elder, but described a situation already established, which presumably goes back to Alfred's time. The earthworks that Alfred set about establishing were for the most part not forts but fortified towns – *burhs*. It was his intention that no part of

85 The Saxon *burh* of Cricklade, Wilts, looking south-west. The grid-iron street plan is clearly visible, as is the rampart of the late Saxon defences on the left of the picture

Wessex should be more than 32 km from one of these *burhs*, and evidence suggests that most of them were established between 879 and 892.

The *burhs* were unique in Europe at the time, and show outstanding foresight on the part of Alfred. They were not simply defences put around existing towns to meet the demands of the moment. They were new planned towns, sometimes on existing sites, sometimes on new, which were conceived of as growing economic units and which were to set the pattern for town plantations in Europe for centuries to come. That they were founded to last shows the confidence of Wessex in their future success, and that many such as Oxford and Winchester have survived as major towns to this day shows that the confidence was justified.

In some cases, where there was an existing site, the new *burhs* were simply built on top of what was already there. Where such sites were not available, promontories which had natural defences were often chosen. Where these were lacking, Alfred's builders laid out their defences on a rectangular plan, rather like a Roman fort, as for example at Oxford, Cricklade, Wareham or Wallingford.

The defences of *burhs* consisted of a rampart of earth or turf, reinforced where necessary with timber, sharply scarped at the front, more gently sloping at the rear. Outside the rampart lay one or more ditches. Inside, the burghal towns were carefully planned with a regular gridiron street plan which divided the interior into blocks and which provided ready access to the defences from any part of the town. Round the inside of the rampart was a wall-street, which facilitated the mobilization of forces and which emphasizes the military origin of the town. In the case of the *burhs* built within pre-existing Roman towns it is notable that apart from the main thoroughfare (which was probably dictated by existing gateways placed centrally in the Roman defences) the old Roman street plan was not followed. This proves beyond reasonable doubt that the regular planning was a new, deliberate feature.

Of the interior features of the burghal towns little is known. There are hints that in some cases a church may have stood near the gateway, and that there was internal specialization. Street names at Winchester show that by AD 1000 specialization of crafts had already given rise to particular groupings according to trade – Tanner Street, Shieldwright Street and Fleshmonger Street are all recorded by this time. People were probably attracted to the new towns by financial considerations – tax concessions, low initial rents, and freedom of tenure may have been some of these. The whole process has a modern ring about it. Once founded, Alfred's *burhs* boomed.

Aethelflaed and her brother introduced *burhs* into Mercia. A document, the 'Mercian Register', provides a record of what was done, and a reference to Towcester under the year 917 makes mention of the building of a stone wall there. At Hereford, recent excavations have shown that the initial defence consisted of an earth bank with some turf, consolidated with horizontal branches, which still survived to a height of 2.5 m high and which originally would have been about 3 m high (see p. 128). This was fronted with a timber revetment and breastwork, and another, smaller, stone wall was constructed at the rear of the rampart. This pattern of defence was similar to that at Tamworth, Staffordshire. Here the turf rampart of Aethelflaed had been held together with timber strapping. Near the gateway it doubled in thickness, and may have been stepped up, with a bridge over the gate providing a continuous wall-walk.

An innovation of Edward the Elder was the establishment of double *burhs* which faced one another across a river with the intention of controlling it and were joined, as at Nottingham, by a bridge.

From such para-military beginnings late Saxon towns mushroomed. If it were necessary to isolate any single achievement of late Saxon England it would have to be the acceleration of urban growth. By the Norman Conquest, very few people in England had to travel further than 24 km to reach a town. Over 100 urban communities can be recognized, which from recent estimates can be calculated to have housed around 10 per cent of the population. These towns set the stage for later urban development in England. They not only equalled most Romano-British towns in size, but in many cases exceeded their medieval successors. Population estimates are notoriously unreliable, but in the time of the Domesday Survey of England in 1086 (which is more a reflection of the population of late Saxon than of Norman England), it is likely that towns such as Norwich sheltered upwards of 6,000 people, Oxford and Colchester 2,000–3,000, York at least 8,000 and London only perhaps 12,000. If these seem small to modern ears, it is worth remembering that until the Industrial Revolution most English towns were hardly larger than modern villages. In the late Middle Ages the great majority of English towns had populations of between 3,000 and 4,000 each, many of the smaller market towns having as few inhabitants as 1,500. In 1545 only one provincial town in England contained in excess of 10,000 people, and only fourteen others more than 5,000. These figures can be compared with those calculated for Roman Britain, where, with the exception of the great towns like Cirencester or St Albans, which may have numbered over 20,000 inhabitants, towns probably had around 5,000 occupants if they were major centres, and around 2,000–3,000 if they were of lesser importance.

That urban growth was accelerated in late Saxon England is clearly reflected in mint operation. Boroughs were accorded the right to issue coins, and the possession of a mint is one of the surest indicators of borough status. Before 973, when Edgar reformed the coinage, there were 27 mints in England striking coins. By 975, at the end of his reign, there were 40, of which 12 were in what seem to be new boroughs. By the end of the century a further 30 mints were in operation, and by AD 1000 a grand total of 70 towns were issuing coins. Eighteen others were in production at the time of the Norman Conquest.

In spite of the urban excavation during the past two decades, very little information has come to light about the buildings, industries or way of life in late Saxon towns. This is partly because many of the towns of late Saxon England are important today, and have an uninterrupted history. Eighteenth-century and more particularly Victorian building programmes demanded the sinking of very substantial foundations and cellars, which have often removed all but the earliest remains on urban sites. Therefore, although the traces of Roman predecessors have often escaped all but the deepest foundations, not so the Saxon remains. Except for churches, virtually all the buildings in late Saxon England were of wood, and traces of these can easily be missed by all but the most experienced excavators, whilst the stone walls of medieval and later merchants' houses can hardly escape detection when sewers are being laid or gas pipes repaired.

The clearest picture of life in a late Saxon town is being provided by the current series of excavations in Anglo-Scandinavian York. The town is exceptional for a number of reasons – it was occupied by the Danes as well as the Romans, and as such is likely to reveal more about Scandinavian-style urban life than purely Anglo-Saxon. Nevertheless it must have shared much in common with its purely Anglo-Saxon contemporaries.

The Danes were instrumental in the development of the urban community at York, though Norse too played their part. While occupation continued on the site after the abandonment of the Roman fort and blossomed in the middle Saxon period into something akin to an urban community (see p. 38), very little has survived of this phase. One excavator as recently as the 1970s has pointed out that all the pre-Danish pottery from Anglian York can be contained in one fairly small bag.

After 800 York was a boom town, and particularly between 876 and 1068 Jorvik, as it was known, was one of the key trading centres in Europe. Around 900 the Scandinavians, who had hitherto relied on the still extant Roman defences for their protection, put up an embankment crowned with a palisade along the line of the Roman northwest and north-east walls. The other walls of the Roman fort were not deemed to be in need of refortification. The

86 Timber buildings at Coppergate, York, during excavation. These are the best-preserved Viking period structures so far excavated in Britain, and date from the later tenth century. The horizontal planks are supported by uprights of timber. A sill beam provides the foundation. York was an important trading city, Jorvik, in Viking times, and the current excavations are revealing much important information about its character in the period

87 Anglo-Scandinavian disc brooch from Coppergate, York, from the recent excavations. Disc brooches were very popular throughout Saxon times, and examples like this were the descendants of the cloisonné brooches of pagan times. Tenth century

Danish bank extended from the River Foss to the River Ouse, taking in both the fort and the area between it and the rivers. To the south-west of the Ouse was the Roman civil settlement, reached originally by a river bridge.

Inside the Roman fort area the ecclesiastical centre of the city grew up, eclipsing commercial expansion, but a vigorous commercial quarter rapidly developed along the present Micklegate–Ousegate–Pavement axis of the city. It is from this area that most of the spectacular remains of Anglo-Scandinavian York have come to light, almost unbelievably well preserved due to waterlogging.

All the evidence points to York being a somewhat unpleasant environment in which to have lived during the Scandinavian period. It was an industrial and trading centre

89 Wooden bowls and (*centre*) the cores left after turning them on a lathe, from the recent excavations at Coppergate, York. Tenth century

Few other cities have produced much material evidence for their late Saxon occupation. In Thetford, however, it has proved possible to uncover larger areas than in other towns. One section investigated in the 1950s had narrow cobbled roads with a large house and smaller buildings in a peripheral area of the town near the defences. Here and elsewhere in the town smiths and other industrial workers were active, some manufacturing the fine, wheel-turned pottery known as Thetford Ware that was popular in eastern England. In the western part of the town the rectangular timber properties were demarcated by boundary ditches. One building was 36 m long and other smaller houses had cellars. One had a mortared floor. Traces of an external staircase, and similar evidence from elsewhere, suggest that some late Saxons enjoyed two-storeyed buildings. Window glass was found in Thetford, and though rare it is not unknown in other late Saxon secular contexts.

Whatever their status, a general feature of late Saxon towns is their wealth of churches. Norwich, for example, had twenty-four, and even small boroughs had two or three.

Trade and industry

In September 1970, while a large drainage channel was being dug on the Graveney Marshes in Kent, the remains of an oak boat emerged. Early boats are always exciting, for they are rare finds, and rarer still are those of Dark Age date. Only three had previously been unearthed of the Anglo-Saxon period in England, two from Sutton Hoo and one from Snape, all of them dating to the seventh century and all three surviving only as impressions in the soil. The Graveney boat's timbers had been preserved through being waterlogged, and as such their discovery opened up a new chapter in the study of British seafaring.

Radiocarbon dating showed the boat to have been made around the late ninth century. Unlike contemporaneous Viking ships, the Graveney boat was not a warship but an ordinary cargo vessel. Only 10 m of it survived intact, but it is reasonably certain that it was once more than 14 m long, with a beam of less than 3 m, its keel made from a flat, fish-shaped plank. It was luted with cattle hair, and expertise had gone into its construction. Originally a sailing vessel, suitable for cross-Channel trade, it may have been converted late in its life into an estuarine barge. A clue to the trade in which its owners may have engaged came to light on the very bottom of the boat, where the excavators found scattered sherds of pottery of French or Belgian origin that were made in the tenth century.

The discovery of the Graveney boat highlights the importance of overseas trade in the economy of late Saxon England. In Aelfric's *Colloquy* a merchant is described as saying

> 'I go on my ship with my cargo and traverse the realms of the sea, and sell my merchandise and buy valuable things which are not produced in this land, and I bring it hither to you with great risk across the sea, and sometimes I suffer shipwreck with the loss of all my goods, hardly escaping alive.'

The goods he brought back were 'purple and silk, precious gems and gold, rare garments and spices, wine and oil, ivory and brass, copper and tin, sulphur and glass and suchlike things'. In return, English exports included hunting dogs and slaves (which were, incidentally, some of the chief exports of Roman Britain), furs, silver, linen, horses and weapons.

Not all furs were sold out of the country. At Chester the king's reeve had the right of pre-emption on marten pelts brought into the town. A law code of about AD 1000 concerning London trade permitted foreign merchants to buy wool, fat and three live pigs for their ships. The wool had to be bought after unloading, instead of direct from the ships coming in to port from other parts of the country.

The Late Saxons

Around the same time timber, fish, wine and blubberfish are recorded as coming in to the port of London, though the first two items may have come from Britain rather than the Continent. At the end of the tenth century merchants from Rouen were supplying wine for English meals, and slaves were being exported from Bristol even in the late eleventh century. At this period an Anglo-Scandinavian lady is recorded as selling English girls to Denmark.

Naturally enough, most of this overseas trade has left no tangible evidence. Near Eastern glass has been found in London, Chichester and Yorkshire, attesting far-flung contacts. Arabic coins are common in Viking hoards in Britain, and one was found in a late Saxon context in Winchester in 1964, though such coins were the result not of direct contact with the east but of Scandinavian trade to Byzantium and beyond. The silver Arab dirhems were popular with the Vikings for their metal content, as coins were not used as currency until quite late in Scandinavian history.

Pottery tells a story of merchant vessels battling their way through North Sea storms. From the Rhineland huge amphorae (storage jars) decorated with rouletted straps, known as Badorf Ware, had been trundled off ships as early as the eighth century, while Tating Ware, decorated with stuck-on lozenges of tinfoil, was being shipped into southern English markets, albeit in small quantities, from the Low Countries. In the tenth century the overseas potters grew rich as trade figures increased – the English were eager to buy red-painted vessels (Pingsdorf Ware) from northern France and the Rhineland, up to and after the Norman Conquest.

Schist whetstones were imported from the Eiffel, and lava querns from the same region were a sought-after commodity among Saxon housewives. Such querns are not only found in major ports, but have turned up at sites like St Neots in Huntingdonshire, where they must have been obtained from the nearest town, Cambridge or Thetford.

Much of the overseas trade was in foreign hands. There are many references to Frisian merchants, and men from Rouen, Flanders, Ponthieu, Normandy, France, Huy, Liège, Nivelles and the Holy Roman Empire are recorded in London around AD 1000. Laws carefully regulated trade with foreign merchants, and agreements were reached between kings for their protection whilst abroad. When on a pilgrimage to Rome, Cnut negotiated greater protection and a reduction in tolls for his subjects from various Continental rulers. Aelfric mentions English merchants in Rome, a fact

The Late Saxons

90 Pot of red-painted ware, characteristic of the Pingsdorf kilns in the Rhineland. This type of pottery was imported to Anglo-Saxon England from the Continent from the beginning of the tenth century, though red-painted wares of similar types were produced in France and Germany from the end of the ninth until the twelfth century

supported by the discovery of Anglo-Saxon coins there. The export of some commodities was sometimes banned, as for example horses in the time of Aethelstan. It was sometimes necessary for a foreign ship to obtain a licence to enter port, as at Chester, where the penalty for breaking the rule was a fine of forty shillings to the king and earl from each man on board. If entry had been prohibited by royal decree, ship, crew and cargo were all confiscated.

Internal trade was equally subject to legal restriction. Tolls were levied, and laws tried to ensure that trade was conducted before proper witnesses in order to prevent accusations of theft. Edward the Elder tried to ensure that all trading took place in a town, and though this proved impossible to maintain, Edgar decreed that all purchases were to be made before official witnesses.

Raw materials often travelled over wide areas. Salt was always at a premium, for it was needed for preserving meat and fish as well as for flavouring: it was obtained from Cheshire. The main centre of production was Droitwich, where the majority of salt pans belonged to the king or earl, but where commercial interests were held by people from many parts of England, and even by the church of St Denis in Paris. Iron was mined in Kent, Sussex, Northamptonshire, Lincolnshire, Yorkshire and the Forest of Dean, and was traded far afield in the form of blooms from which tools could be forged. Lead was mined in Derbyshire, and in 835

Wirksworth was annually paying lead to the value of 300 shillings to the archbishop of Canterbury.

In spite of its weight, stone seems to have been traded quite far afield from the quarries. A millstone quarry is recorded in Sussex, and a study of the building stone used in late Saxon churches has produced surprising results. Saxon builders thought nothing of transporting good building stone up to 112 km – this is particularly true of the Jurassic oolitic freestones, which were taken west into Devon and the Welsh borders and east into Hampshire and the lower Thames valley, while Barnack stone from Northamptonshire was transported over East Anglia probably by Fenland waterways. The half-ton imposts of the church at Breamore in Hampshire were brought 112 km from their source near Bath.

It is in the English pottery industry that substantial evidence can be found for the intensification of trade and industry in late Saxon England. Shortly before the arrival of the Scandinavians, a new type of pottery had been put on the market in East Anglian towns. This was wheel-thrown, and fired in a fully-developed kiln. Despite local variations in fabric, it was made in a surprisingly uniform variety of shapes. In the course of the ninth century it caught on in the whole of England with the exception of London and Kent, parts of Wessex and the extreme south and north-west. Its spread in popularity must without doubt be ascribed to the influence of the Danes. Known from its date span not its characteristics as Saxo-Norman pottery, its buyers remained loyal until the twelfth century, despite the availability of other ceramics. Its decline may have come about through the increase of country-based kilns and the decline of town pottery industries. Seventeen local 'industries' have been recognized in England, all sharing features in common. While it would be misleading to regard these as the products of a mass industry of the type that flourished in the

The Late Saxons

91 Shallow bowl with spout from Thetford, Norfolk, in Thetford Ware. This type of gritty, hard-fired ware, usually grey in fabric, belongs to the family of Saxon-Norman wares which first began to be produced in the Danelaw in the last years of the eighth or the early years of the ninth century. They were in use in most parts of England (with regional variations) down to the twelfth century

92 Glazed bottle, imitating leather, in Winchester Ware, from Winchester, Hants. Winchester Ware was produced mainly in the eleventh century, and is one of a series of late Saxon glazed wares, of which Stamford Ware is the best known. Glazed pottery spread to England from the Continent around the time of the Danish Raids

Roman period, nevertheless they are the nearest thing to it in Anglo-Saxon England. The pots were no doubt manufactured in groups of kilns localized in towns which maintained some kind of monopoly over the pottery trade in the local market.

The three largest groups of Saxo-Norman pottery are known, after the towns in which they were first recognized, as Stamford, Thetford and St Neots Ware. The Stamford products are as good as much of the best pottery produced in north-west Europe in the period. They display an important technological innovation – the use of glaze. At best, Stamford Ware is a whitish, hard pottery, not unlike some modern 'folksy' wares; the glaze is a pleasant pale green, pale yellow or orange.

The Late Saxons

Coinage

The expansion of internal and overseas trade necessitated good coinage, and the monetary system of late Saxon England was second to none. After the major coinage reform under Offa (see p. 124) ninth-century English money was generally monotonous and instable: pennies continued to be struck in Mercia and elsewhere in the south and scruffy but copious bronze *sceattas* were turned out by a succession of Northumbrian rulers and the occasional archbishop of York. Alfred was responsible for establishing in Wessex a good coinage of pennies. The earliest issues of these bore his portrait and the title ALFRED REX, as well as the monogram of the city of London which commemorated his establishment of a West Saxon garrison there. In the meantime, the Danes were also busy establishing their own coinage in the areas within their control. The Danes of East Anglia struck a copious series of commemorative pennies for Edmund, whom they elevated to a saint. In the seven Danish boroughs English pennies were copied, and other issues were struck by the Vikings of York and by Guthrum (see p. 137) who briefly managed to gain control of the London mint.

Although the Vikings of York periodically issued coins, most of the Anglo-Scandinavian coins disappeared in the early tenth century. It fell to king Aethelstan to regularize the coinage, which he did by setting up a single coinage for the whole of England, and by attempting to control the issue of coins south of the Thames by his Grateley Decrees, which proclaimed that all places of importance were entitled to a mint. Aethelstan also banned the circulation of foreign coins.

The real institution of an advanced monetary system,

93 Penny of Alfred the Great (871–99). The reverse bears the monogram of the city of London and the moneyer's name. (Enlarged)

The Late Saxons

however, was the work of king Edgar. In or around 973 he proclaimed that all coins in circulation were to be demonetized and called in, to be remelted and restruck as pennies of uniform type which would remain in circulation for a fixed number of years. To control this, more mints were opened up and all dies were produced in one centre, the names of the mints to which they were issued being incorporated into the legend along with the moneyer's name. This set the pattern for English coinage until the twelfth century. The recoinages were first fixed at six- but subsequently at three-year intervals.

By the time of Cnut the need for more coins to meet the demands of the *Danegeld* and the *heregeld* (tax levied to support the Danish army) had led to a proliferation of die-cutting centres. During his reign these were once more reduced, and the weight of the penny stabilized. Although it was to suffer some vicissitudes, the Anglo-Saxon monetary system remained the best in Europe, and William I took it over without modification at the Conquest. Penalties against forgers were outstandingly severe and forgeries are extremely rare. The coins had a purchasing power above

94 Late Saxons pennies of (a) Burgred of Mercia (AD 852–74) and (b) Edward the Confessor (Hammer Cross type) (1042–66). (Enlarged)

their face value of the silver, and this fact alone prevented coins being exported as silver bullion or melted down.

The Late Saxons

Palaces and manors

Although few remains have survived of village houses of the late Saxon period, their absence has generally been compensated for by the discovery and excavation of royal and noble residences. The most exciting was the palace occupied during the ninth and tenth centuries at Cheddar, Somerset. Although the positive evidence associating the site with king Alfred is ambiguous, it was certainly occupied by kings Edmund, Edwy and Edgar. The earliest palace complex comprised a long hall with slightly bowed sides and entrances opposite one another in the long sides, with associated outbuildings set within palisades and furnished with a large drainage ditch to carry off storm water. In the tenth century a new hall was built, somewhat smaller but more regularly constructed, with entrances in the short sides. There was also a stone chapel and some further outbuildings. The whole of this complex was approached through a stockade and ditch, furnished with an elaborate

95 The twelfth-century hall of the great palace complex at Cheddar, Somerset, after excavation by Prof. P. A. Rahtz. On the right-hand side of the picture can be seen the recuttings of the post-holes when the hall was rebuilt. Its predecessor (in background), was rebuilt. Its predecessor was occupied by kings Edmund, Edwy and Edgar in the tenth century

entrance flanked by a 'flagstaff' or pole on a plinth of Roman brick. The overall appearance must have been something akin to a Wild West cavalry fort, and the halls were small even by the standard of Edwin's at Yeavering (see p. 118) and minute compared with the recorded dimensions of Edward the Confessor's hall at Westminster, a grand 76 m or so by 22 m at its widest point (it also had slightly bowed sides). Another building within the Cheddar complex has been interpreted either as a fowl house, as seems more likely, or as a mill with a grain store at one end and a bakery at the other. In the centre was the circular mill platform, with the track for the weary pony to trudge round (if indeed it was not man-powered).

At Sulgrave, Northamptonshire, a noble residence of the same period which in many ways was more impressive than the hall at Cheddar was excavated. Here for the first time in Saxon archaeology there was evidence for some stonework in a secular building. The complex comprised a stone and

96 The Fowl House at Cheddar. In the foreground is a store, in the centre is the hen run and in the background is the fowl keeper's house

timber hall, a kitchen and an outlying rectangular stone building later incorporated into the entrance of a Norman ringwork. At Portchester, Hants, an aisled hall was among the late Saxon buildings. At both Cheddar and Sulgrave there were hints of upper storeys.

The Church in late Saxon England

The Danish raids were a dark and terrible phase in the history of the Anglo-Saxon Church. In the early ninth century, church after church and monastery after monastery was sacked and left deserted, and the subsequent extensive settlement of heathen Danes in eastern England disrupted Church organization. Fortunately, however, the heathen incomers were rapidly converted. There were Christian Danes in the Danelaw by the end of the ninth century, and by soon after the middle of the tenth paganism was relatively rare, though there were sporadic outbreaks until the Norman Conquest.

The Church had other problems as well as heathenism. The raids and subsequent heavy taxation led to general impoverishment, and also corruption had set in in many monasteries. By the ninth century these were frequently in the hands of secular clerks, many of whom were married and far removed from the ideal of Christian piety. But new winds were blowing on the Continent that were soon to be felt in England. The teaching of the sixth-century monk St

Benedict was being adopted and was resulting in monastic reform. Nowhere was this reforming zeal felt more strongly than in Winchester, where the cathedral became its focus.

The nucleus of the Old Minster at Winchester had been a cruciform church built by king Cenwalh in 648, with the main altar at the crossing, between two side chapels. In plan it was fairly typical of its period, constructed of re-used Roman material. It was greatly admired, presumably because unlike other Saxon churches it was adorned with worked stone. In front of the entrance was the shrine of St Swithun, bishop of Winchester between 852 and 862, who had requested to be buried in a humble place. Beyond was a structure known as the tower of St Martin which had been erected by 971. In the 960s and 970s monastic reform and revival at Winchester led to the rebuilding of the old church as the Old Minster. The finished cathedral was dedicated in 994, and linked the tower of St Martin to the original nave, the tower being enlarged to form the nucleus of a West Front, which probably had two taller flanking towers. The focus of the new nave was the shrine of St Swithun, with a crypt beneath. Pilgrims could probably visit his bones kept in a reliquary on a raised altar above the crypt. On either side of the new nave were chapels, and the plan was further complicated by other projections.

The key figures in the Winchester Revival were St Dunstan and St Aethelwold. Dunstan was born in 909 and brought up at court, where he became acquainted with Continental ideas. After some doubts, he became a monk and rose, after a brief period of exile on the Continent, to become archbishop of Canterbury. He was an Anglo-Saxon in the mould of Leonardo da Vinci – he was a skilled metalworker, manuscript illuminator, theologian and politician, as well as a singer and harpist. He introduced Benedictine reform to England. Aethelwold was a more fiery reformer than Dunstan. He became bishop of Winchester in 963 (the most important office in the Anglo-Saxon church after the archbishopric of Canterbury) and also controlled the monasteries of Peterborough, Ely and Thorney. He maintained close contact with the Benedictine abbey of Fleury on the Continent; he died in 984.

Further north the Benedictine reforms were carried out by the archbishop of York, Oswald (d. 992). He was a close friend of the abbot of Fleury and spent some time abroad.

Through the efforts of these men England was influenced by fresh artistic and intellectual stimulus from the Continent, which was to become focussed on Winchester. To some extent the atmosphere conducive to artistic innova-

The Late Saxons

tion had been fostered by royal patronage. Alfred had himself been a notable patron of the arts, and is reputed to have given a sixth of his revenue to the support of various artificers. He presented numerous gold shrines to churches and monasteries and patronized the erection of new ecclesiastical buildings – many of the architects and designers were foreign, but they trained Anglo-Saxons rather than executing the designs themselves. Aethelstan was also a great patron of the arts. He gave gifts to libraries, and his court was a cultural centre. Continental links were strengthened when an Anglo-Saxon princess, Edith, married Otto I (936–73), the founder of the Ottonian Empire of Germany that had succeeded the Carolingian Empire.

Late Saxon churches

The majority of churches which survive in England from the Saxon period can be dated to the period between the ninth and the eleventh centuries. Many of these, as would be expected, date to the latest decades of this era. Many too have been destroyed with the exception of a few features, the rest being replaced over the centuries by later work. Dating churches of this period is extremely difficult unless some document exists to prove their origins. The Norman Conquest too did not suddenly bring about architectural changes, so many 'Saxon' features were in fact probably built after 1066. There seems to have been a lull in church building during the ninth and early tenth centuries, presumably as a result of the Danish raids, but thereafter came a renewed interest in erecting stone places of worship.

In general the more elaborate an Anglo-Saxon church, the more likely it is to date to the late Saxon period, though very simple buildings were still being built throughout the period. Anglo-Saxon churches can usually not be dated more closely than to the nearest half century and many of the finest are subject to perennial learned disputes. There is a wide variety of regional features; so wide that very few conclusions have been made about the architectural traditions.

Perhaps the most celebrated church which dates to the late Saxon period is that first noticed by Rickman in 1819 at Barton-on-Humber (see p. 4). This dates to the eleventh century in its earliest features, and to soon after the Conquest in others. It displays a number of very typical Anglo-Saxon architectural features. The building is simply a tower with a western annexe which originally had other annexes, and it is now in process of restoration by the Department of the Environment. The lowest two stages of the tower and the western annexe both date to around AD 1000 and are typical of Anglo-Saxon architecture in having very thin walls (a mere 76 cm). Both too, display that feature so familiar to students of the architecture, long-and-short work on the quoins. This is a technique of finishing the corners of stone buildings by using long stones alternately with short ones. Anglo-Saxon work of this method is distinguishable from that of other periods chiefly by the

The Late Saxons

97 The tower of the Anglo-Saxon church at Earl's Barton, Northamptonshire, showing characteristic triangular-headed windows, baluster shafts and pilaster strip work. This late church is a classic example of Anglo-Saxon architecture

massive size of the masonry involved. Other techniques of quoining which immediately denote Anglo-Saxon architects, but which are not visible in this church, are side-alternate work and random megalithic quoining. The first is distinguished by rectangular stones of roughly the same proportions being placed alternately running along the faces of the two walls which meet at the corner of the building. The second style of quoining simply uses huge stones, up to 2 m tall, placed at random.

A very typical feature of Anglo-Saxon architecture to be seen at Barton-on-Humber is pilaster work. This too is well displayed on such famous towers as that at Sompting or

The Late Saxons

Earl's Barton. This feature immediately shows a church to be of pre-Norman workmanship and is thought to be derived from the half timbering of timber churches. Also at Barton-on-Humber there are a number of characteristic windows of the period – the simple round openings on the annexe, the triangular-headed belfry windows in the second stage of the tower, the similar but round-headed openings below them and the simple round-headed door,

98 Detail of the tower at Earl's Barton, Northants, showing the quoining, doorway and blocked windows

now blocked, in the east wall. The tower stages are divided by ornamental stonework known as a stringcourse.

A feature of Anglo-Saxon churches is that doors or windows may often lead from impossible heights into a void. This stems either from a change in liturgical needs, or from demolitions of the features that made them necessary in the first place. It can, however, be confusing for the observer to disentangle.

The Late Saxons

99 Haddiscoe Thorpe, Norfolk, a classic example of an East Anglian round tower church of the late Saxon period. The building material (flint) made angles difficult

The Late Saxons

Of the more simple remains, the Norfolk round towers are notable. Many date from the Saxon period, as is demonstrated by their Saxon windows and doors, and many lie in villages that seem to epitomize rural English life in the mould of the Anglo-Saxon myth.

An unusually finely decorated church in Norfolk, with a square tower, can be seen at Dunham Magna. Here the church of St Andrew originally boasted a Saxon chancel, but this has been rebuilt, and it is therefore the tower and nave built in the very latest phase in the eleventh century to which attention should be given. The tower is axial and without decoration, under a medieval topping, and is lit by late Saxon double-belfry windows, with round windows on the east and west above the main windows which are round-headed. Long-and-short quoining can be seen on the tower. Amongst the other late Saxon features, the arcading inside the nave is of great interest, having been produced for decorative effect.

A church with remains from all phases of Saxon ecclesiastical building is that at Wing in Buckinghamshire. Although this church has considerable additions of post-Conquest date, the aisled nave, apsidal chancel and underlying crypt were first built in the seventh or eighth centuries and additions were made in the late tenth or eleventh centuries.

A very complicated church architecturally is that at Deerhurst, Gloucestershire. Here the nave, west porch and side chapels were built early in the Christian period. The west porch was raised to three storeys and the side chapels extended some time after. In the tenth century or thereabouts the porch was further raised to form a tower and the chancel was replaced by an apsidal version which is at present in ruins. This very substantial church has many Saxon features still extant and is in contrast to the simple Odda's Chapel of the Holy Trinity nearby. Here the late Saxon nave and chancel were incorporated into a house and not discovered to be of ecclesiastical antiquity until 1885. It is assumed to be the edifice referred to on a stone found in the nearby orchard in 1675. The inscription states that a hall was built and dedicated to the honour of the Holy Trinity by Earl Odda, the date being given as the second of the Ides of April in the fourteenth year of the reign of King Edward of the English. This, being interpreted, is 12 April 1056 and is thus a very unusual example of a close dating for an Anglo-Saxon building. The farmhouse is still attached to the church and the centuries of domestic usage have left their mark within the building.

Also associated with an historically known personage is the church at Bradford-on-Avon, which, though started in the eighth century, probably by St Aldhelm, was extensively altered in the late Saxon era. It displays very fine blind arcading outside and pilaster work as well as a very fine and typically simple chancel arch inside. It is famous for its carvings of two angels.

Late Saxon art

English artists have always excelled at drawing and delicate tinting: they have seldom been noted for their skills in handling areas of strong colour, probably on account of the subtle northern light. It was English drawing that led the fashion in twelfth- and thirteenth-century Europe, reaching its finest expression in the work of Matthew Paris. It was penmanship that distinguished Hogarth and it was engraving and line drawing coupled with pale washes that assured the everlasting fame of William Blake. Although skilled with oils, Turner's finest achievements were in watercolours, which was also the favourite medium of Victorian and Edwardian artists both professional and amateur.

Confidence with line was also the hallmark of the late Saxon art, and it was this period that was one of the most important in the history of English art, an epoch in which English artists led the rest of Europe. Such was the fame of English artistry that the Normans carried off many treasures to the Continent, but even so a wealth of superb manuscripts and sculptures has survived to attest to its greatness. The centre of late Saxon art was Wessex, centred on Winchester, with other flowerings in Mercia and Northumbria.

The art styles manifested themselves in two separate traditions which kept up a vigorous dialogue until after the Norman Conquest. The first was classically inspired and became known as the Winchester School. It was characterized by its naturalism, inherited from ancient Rome by way of Carolingian Europe. The other was as barbaric as the Winchester School was civilized: it was the animal art of the Vikings, an artistic tradition which grew up from the same root as that of the Anglo-Saxons and which therefore appealed to something deep-rooted in the early English mind. As a reaction against this, the Winchester School grew increasingly classical, a clarion call for civilization.

In Northumbria, however, people were even further removed from the influences of the Carolingian world, and the Scandinavian style took hold and manifested itself in a

The Late Saxons

sculptural tradition which revitalized the moribund art of the Northumbrian crosses and gave rise to a new art style that was neither Danish nor Anglo-Saxon, but truly Anglo-Danish. Despite the efforts of the Winchester School artists of Wessex, an uneasy and not very successful assimilation of Danish traditions also came about elsewhere. The infiltration of Scandinavian taste can be seen in the era of Danish rule under Cnut – Urnes-style tendrils curl across the pages of English manuscripts as late as the twelfth century.

But it was without doubt the ninth-century Carolingian Renaissance that was the greatest influence in stimulating late Saxon art in Wessex. Charlemagne modelled his Empire on that of Rome and consciously copied late Antique works in all aspects of the civilization that he fostered. The Carolingian abbey church of St Denis echoed Roman basilicas, while the church built at Fulda was modelled on St Peter's basilica in Rome. Charlemagne was himself an educated man – he could pray in Latin and knew some Greek – and he knew that real learning was not to be found in France. It was, however, to be found in Britain, and the emperor gathered around himself Saxon, Irish and other scholars, including Alcuin of York, who, being a keen student of Virgil and to a lesser extent of that most secular of writers, Ovid, laid equal stress on the value of pagan Classical and later Christian writings. Out of this convergence of learned men in Charlemagne's court came the blossoming of Carolingian art, several schools of which in turn contributed to the late Saxon traditions. Two schools were pre-eminent. First there was the Ada School which was itself partly influenced by Northumbrian art and which contributed a monumentality and feel for colour to the figures drawn at Winchester. Second there was the Rheims School, which contributed a technique of flickering line drawing, which 'began at once to inject . . . a kind of palsy by which everything to do with the subject, space, landscape, evangelist, desk and pen quivers and vibrates' (J. Beckwith, *Early Medieval Art*, London, 1964).

The earliest manifestation of Carolingian classicism in Anglo-Saxon art can be seen in a remarkable group of masterly embroideries sewn at the orders of king Aethelstan for presentation to the shrine of St Cuthbert in Chester-le-Street, some time between 909 and 916. The embroideries consist of a stole and two maniples, executed on narrow bands (about 6 cm wide). England was famous for needlework throughout the Middle Ages, though little has survived: Popes had their vestments made in *opus*

Anglicanum ('English work') by Englishwomen. The colours have now faded to uniform tans, but were originally rich. Gold thread was combined with coloured silks, and the embroideries depict full-length figures of prophets and saints standing on conventionally sketched rocks. They are completely naturalistic, and owe something not only to Carolingian art but also to Byzantine models.

St Dunstan himself was no mean artist, and we are fortu-

The Late Saxons

100 Tenth-century embroidered stole, presented to the Shrine of St Cuthbert, Chester-le-Street. It depicts the prophet Jonah, and was executed between 909 and 916. In style it reflects Carolingian and Byzantine models, and is a good example of *opus Anglicanum*, English embroidery, of the period

The Late Saxons

nate in having a drawing done by him, executed perhaps at Glastonbury before 957. It shows Dunstan kneeling at the feet of Christ, his huge hands clasped and his face earnest. The figures have a monumental solidity, and in this sketch and in a similar-styled Crucifixion in a book known as the 'Sherborne Pontifical' we have the first real demonstration of the Anglo-Saxon artist's ability to convey solid form with line.

101 The Harleian Psalter, folio 3 verso. This superb example of Winchester School art shows line drawing at its most accomplished and sensitive. Produced at Winchester at the end of the tenth century in tinted outline, it measures 23.5 cm by 17.9 cm

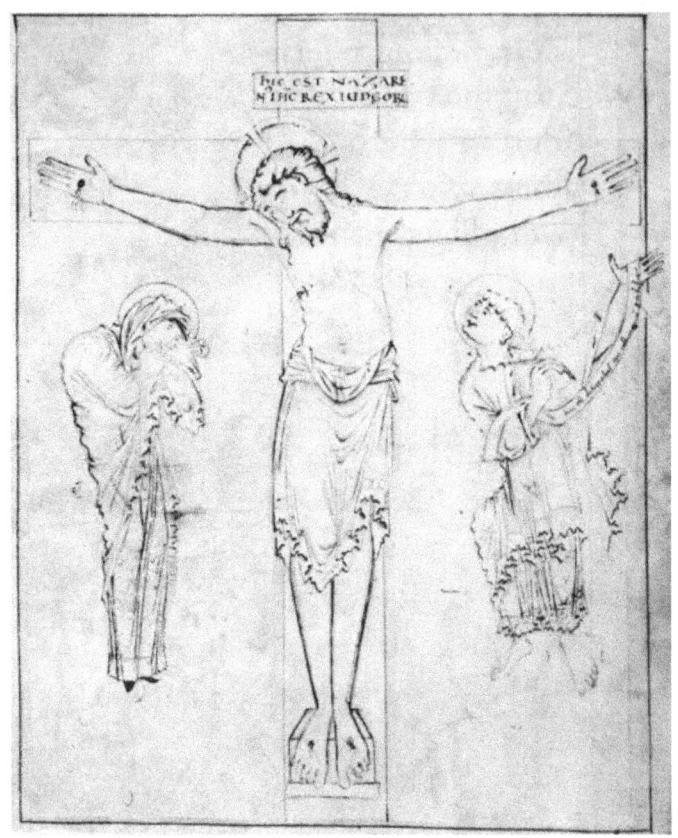

The Dunstan drawing has no colour – it is done in brown outline, combined with some rubric red. Around the time that it was being made, however, other manuscripts, such as the Bosworth Psalter (made at Canterbury for Dunstan) were using dull colours to infill the drawing. From the end of the tenth century two innovations in technique appear. The first was the use of different coloured inks to write the text and pen the drawings (coloured outline); the other was the use of coloured infilling for outline drawings done in brown ink (tinted outline). These two techniques were often combined.

The first manifestation of tinted outline can be seen in the brilliant Harleian Psalter (one of the British Museum manuscripts), which has a superb Crucifixion done in reddish-brown, with subtle tinting. It has been described as a sketch with colour notes for painting, and the figures have both solidity and something of an ethereal quality. It was a Winchester product.

The scene was set for the emergence of the Winchester

The Late Saxons

102 The Benedictional of St Aethelwold, folio 102 verso. Made at Winchester around 975–80, it is a classic example of Winchester School art. The scene here represented depicts the Death of the Virgin. Size: 29.2 cm by 21.6 cm

School proper, under the patronage of bishop Aethelwold. The first Winchester School product that has survived is a miniature in a charter granted to the New Minster of Winchester by king Edgar in 966 (a second cathedral was built alongside the Old Minster at Winchester in the tenth century, both Old and New Minsters being supplanted by the present Norman cathedral in the eleventh century). This, the New Minster Charter, is done on purple vellum and depicts king Edgar between the Virgin and St Peter, offering his Charter to Christ on a mandorla supported by angels, the whole in an acanthus-decorated frame. The

The Late Saxons

right ingredients are there, even though it has its crudities. The angels flutter free of the frame (which is a *trompe l'oeil* modelled on a solid frame, possibly Carolingian ivory), and Edgar is lively, even though the artist did not know how to paint him turning round and has produced an impossible corkscrew effect which defeats anatomy.

The teething troubles shown by the artist of the New Minster Charter have been ironed out in a manuscript which epitomizes the full flowering of the School, the Benedictional of St Aethelwold, made around 975–80. The illuminations in this book explode on the page in a cascade of deep colours. Gold abounds, juxtaposed with strong rich tones. There are two types of miniature in its pages, one contained in a rectangular frame in which the painting imitates a solid ivory frame right down to the chamfered corners ornamented with fleshy acanthus. The figures within this frame are solid, in the Ada School tradition, and have a certain Byzantine quality with restrained colours. The miniatures in the other type of frame (formed by an arch supported on columns on which acanthus burgeons) are

103 MS Harley 603, folio 4. This Winchester School manuscript was executed at Canterbury around AD 1000, and is a copy of a Rheims School Carolingian manuscript which still survives. Both are inspired by some kind of roll manuscript of earlier date, and use a 'strip cartoon' device to illustrate the psalms. The English figures are much more lively than their Continental prototypes

more flamboyant, with harsher colours and more crowded compositions.

In marked contrast is the Harley 603 manuscript, a copy of a Carolingian manuscript done in Canterbury around AD 1000. It is populated with strip-cartoon figures which prance around amid flickering draperies to illustrate the Psalms. Done in red-brown ink they are ultimately inspired by some Roman roll manuscript, but have all the vigour that the original almost certainly lacked.

While monks were experimenting with the new ideas in their scriptoria, Continental influence was beginning to be felt in the sculpture of southern England. It is detectable in the cross-shaft from Codford St Peter, near Salisbury, which depicts a man holding a branch in one hand and an uncertain object, possible a musical instrument, in the other. It dates probably from the ninth century, and shows Mercian influence. By the later ninth century Carolingian art was affecting some Wessex sculpture, but this 'civilized' tendency had to compete with a more barbaric rival, well exemplified by the superb carving from Colerne, Wiltshire, carved at the very end of the ninth century. Decorated with a pair of interlocked lions with spiral shoulders, segmented-off heads, snub snouts and hatched bodies, it recalls nothing so much as the Pictish beasts that confront one another on some objects in the St Ninian's Isle treasure.

The Colerne sculpture and some contemporary pieces show that within Wessex the barbarian spirit was alive and flourishing at the time of the Danish raids. In the ensuing period it was ousted by the neo-Classical Winchester style, though 'barbaric' sculpture continued to be produced in the early tenth century in Wessex.

The Late Saxons

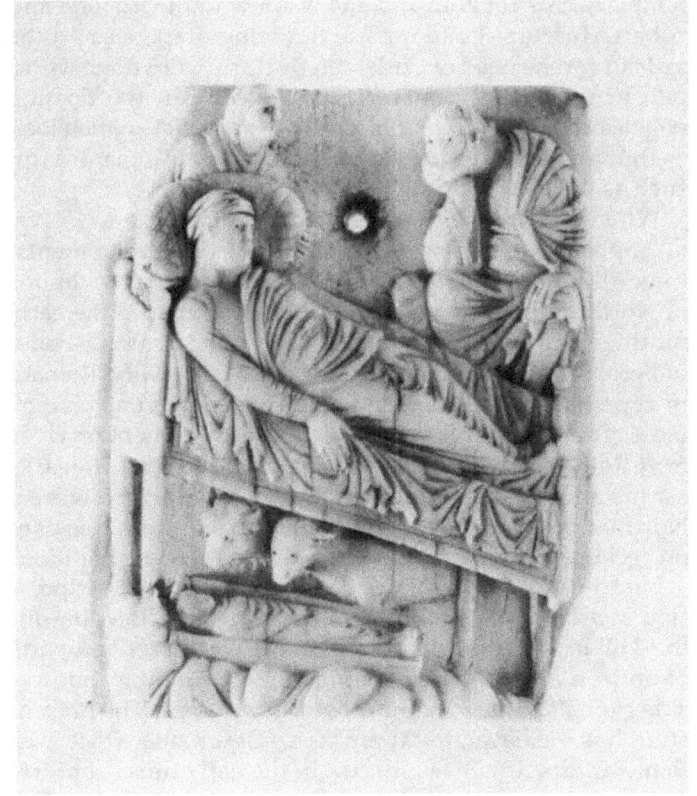

104 Winchester School ivory of the Nativity, which can be compared with the Death of the Virgin in the Benedictional of St Aethelwold (Plate 102). Winchester artists were as skilled at carving as at painting. Mid-tenth century

The Late Saxons

The earliest example of the Winchester style in stone can be seen in a pair of angels displayed high up in the east wall of the nave of the church at Bradford-on-Avon. They at once recall the angels which flutter on either side of Christ in the New Minster Charter, and, if this comparison is valid, they must date from around the second half of the tenth century.

The best Winchester style carvings are not executed in stone but in ivory. The very finest are a pair of ivories depicting the Virgin and St John, which date from the beginning of the eleventh century and are now in St Omer. The delight the artist has taken in carving the folds of the draperies and vitalizing them with movement is clearly apparent, and contrasts with the serenity of the figures themselves. Similar expertise is displayed in an ivory of the Baptism and in a plaque of the Virgin and Child, both dating from around AD 1000. A superb Nativity with charming cows adorns an ivory now kept in Liverpool.

Great mastery in depicting emotion can be seen in an ivory carving of the Crucifixion mounted on to a German reliquary cross of gold and enamel now in the Victoria and Albert Museum, London. The flickering draperies and the sad but serene head of Christ can rival any work done with a pen in a late Saxon manuscript. So too can the floating angels on a triangular mount from Winchester, which look as though they have just flown off the page of a manuscript such as the New Minster Charter.

While Wessex was developing her distinctive art, the rest of England was experiencing other artistic developments. In Northumbria crosses that belonged to the old traditions of Northumbrian art were still being produced in the early ninth century. Some of these are quite accomplished – in Bernicia the figural work on some crosses is very 'Roman' in appearance, with deeply moulded draperies and chubby faces. The style is well exemplified by the fragmentary cross from Rothbury, which has a Crucifixion on the head, the earliest instance of this arrangement in English art. However, Northumbrian art rapidly went into decline from this date on, eclipsed by the rapidly developing Mercian tradition.

Ninth-century Mercian art can be seen at its most expressive in architectural sculpture. The church at Breedon-on-the-Hill in Leicester stands within the weathered ramparts of an Iron Age fort, dominating the surrounding countryside from its vantage point above a quarry face. The present church is medieval, but it replaces a Saxon one which was richly adorned with sculptures in the early ninth century. These sculptures are now incorporated into the later fabric.

The Breedon carvings offer a diversity of styles. The most notable series of carvings appear on friezes – narrow bands a mere 18–23 cm wide, which now run round the inside of the church. Birds and animals follow one another in a cartoon strip, while men and animals are locked in combat. One scene shows mounted spearmen and their captives. Alongside the friezes are more monumental carvings, done in panels, and very richly modelled figures.

Eighth- to ninth-century Mercian art was not confined to stone sculpture. It can be seen on two superb products of Saxon artistry, the Ormside Bowl and the Brunswick Casket. The Ormside Bowl was found in a Viking treasure hoard in Cumberland, and consists of an outer bowl of bossed silver and a lining of gilt copper, with jewelled discs of gilt copper inside and outside the base of the cup, decorated with filigree and repoussé interlace. The rim carries glass inlays in rectangular settings, an embossed metal ribbon and applied twisted wires. The ornament on the bowl itself comprises a menagerie of fantastic animals, full of exuberant energy, in a foliage forest. Some of the mounts

The Late Saxons

105 The Book of Cerne, folio 21 verso. This Mercian manuscript dates from around 818–30, and is imitating a Canterbury School product. Note the 'trial' sketch at the bottom of the page, and the elongated body of the bull – the artist had a model for the forepart, but not the hindquarters

The Late Saxons

are additions of around 900, but the whole is a descendant of the hanging bowls of earlier times.

The Brunswick Casket is in a more sober tradition. Made in Ely before 866, it is a whalebone casket a mere 12.7 cm in height, edged with metal strips, those on the base carrying an inscription in runes. The bone panels carry vine scrolls inhabited by long-necked birds and lizards with interlaced tails, descendants, like those on the Witham Pins (see p. 114) of creatures from a pagan past.

The ornamental style of the Breedon carvings and the Ormside Bowl can be seen too in Mercian manuscripts of the early ninth century. Of these, one stands out – the Book of Cerne. Decorated around 825, the Book of Cerne is in the old Northumbrian tradition of manuscript illumination, though the number of illustrations in it are sadly sparse. The best is a full-page decoration to preface the Gospel of St Luke. An evangelist figure crowns an arch above his symbol, the winged bull. But what a bull! The bottom half is out of all proportion, is stiff and at quite the wrong angle. The explanation is that the artist had only the top of a bull to copy (a version of this survives) and had to improvise the bottom – his preliminary sketch to try it out can still be seen unerased at the bottom of the page.

The arrival of the Danes revitalized northern Anglian art. Hitherto, sculpture had been commissioned by monasteries for the most part, but now a new, secular patronage led to the proliferation of sculpture. The lay patrons required funerary memorials, and often favoured secular ornament or motifs derived from pagan mythology, even though these were now adorning Christian monuments. Huntsmen and warriors abound, and representations of Thor, the Valkyries or Weland Smith all make their appearance. This Anglo-Scandinavian sculpture blends together elements of both the earlier Anglian and the new Scandinavian styles. Ornamental elements were inter-borrowed by sculptors, and to the existing repertoire of sculptural forms the Anglo-Danish artists added the wheel-headed cross and the hogsback recumbent gravestone, shaped like a chapel or house gripped by three-dimensional animals (usually bears). Modelling tended to be executed in shallow relief, but it must never be forgotten that these, like other Dark Age sculptures, were originally painted in bright colours – red, black and white.

The Scandinavians found in English art some elements that were to their taste. Ribbon-like animals with double contour lines, spiral joints, hatched bodies and interlace proliferated in England (see p. 71). The pre-Danish starting point can be seen in the cross from St Alkmund, Derby, a Mercian sculpture with a barbaric lion. From such creatures the Danes developed their own 'great beast' that is to be found tangled in interlace in later Anglo-Danish sculptures.

The 'great beast' appears fully fledged in the so-called Jellinge Style of Viking art, a style developed in England under Saxon and Irish stimulus but which is named from a site in Denmark which has produced a silver cup ornamented in characteristic fashion. The Jellinge style employed animals with sinuous double outlines and with pigtails and lip-lappets. It began in the late ninth century, and continued until c. AD 1000. In the early eleventh century it gave way to Ringerike, which was typified by animals from which come tendrils of acanthus leaf foliage. In England a distinctive type evolved which blended with the Winchester style in the early eleventh century under the rule of the Danish Cnut. Finally, Ringerike gave way to Urnes style, named after a decorated wooden church in Norway. Urnes ornament developed around 1050, and is typified by tendrils which are even more elongated and in which the foliage is less apparent.

The Jellinge style is clearly exemplified on a bone belt fitting found in the Thames in London, which depicts a little man (unfortunately headless) clad in a suit of armour. His legs have been turned outwards and then upwards to make

The Late Saxons

106 Sculpture from the recent excavations in Coppergate, York, done in an English version of the Jellinge style. This particular type of 'bound dragon' makes its appearance at York in the tenth century, and was developed in Ryedale where similar creatures can be seen. Such sculptures were manifestations of a hybrid Anglo-Danish tradition in the North of England

The Late Saxons

him fit into the circle – his arms hang down. Arms and legs are both loosely bound to his body by twin interlacing serpents. The Jellinge 'great beast', as it was perfected in England, can be seen combined with Anglo-Saxon elements on a cross from Sockburn in County Durham, and in purer form on a fragmentary cross-shaft from Otley in Yorkshire, where a tighly-knitted Jellinge beast adorns one face while Anglian interlace appears on one side.

107 Ivory carving of a man on a bone belt fitting from London. This is in the Jellinge style. The man's head is missing. Diameter: 8.3 cm. Tenth century

The finest example of Ringerike comes not from the north but from London. Here, in St Paul's Churchyard, was found a grave-slab 61 cm wide, datable to around the time of the death of king Cnut (1035). Originally richly painted, its field is occupied with a dynamic combat scene in which two lions try to pull down a beast. Tendrils are everywhere, and the whole composition is bursting with energy. Of the same period, and purely Scandinavian in design, is a bronze weather vane found in Winchester, with foliage derived from English acanthus and hints of something more exotic. This Ringerike was to find its way into contemporary manuscripts. It can be seen particularly clearly in a manuscript of Caedmon's poems in the Ashmolean Museum known as the Junius II, which was made between 1030 and 1050. At the end of the book a blank space has been filled with a sketched design for the book binding, and in this sketch Winchester acanthus and Viking Ringerike are

The Late Saxons

108 The Gosforth Cross in Cumbria is the most outstanding example of Anglo-Scandinavian sculpture. It dates from the tenth century, and stands nearly 4.6 m tall. The ornament includes Manx-style ring-chain patterns, and a combination of Christian and pagan scenes

happily combined, each as accomplished as the other. Elsewhere in the same book Ringerike influence can be seen in the ornament of capitals to columns.

Urnes style ornament was more popular in Celtic Ireland than among the English. True Urnes designs are only apparent in some metalwork, notably a series of small openwork bronzes, book mounts and the like, several of which have been found in the Danelaw and which are probably made in Britain, copying Danish originals. Urnes influence, however, is to be seen in a few sculptures, such as in the beasts at Christ's feet in the fine sculpture from Jevington in Sussex, and in the tracery of the capitals of the church at Kirkburn in eastern Yorkshire, both of which can be dated to the eleventh century.

The finest achievement of Anglo-Scandinavian art is the Gosforth Cross from Cumbria, which dates from the tenth century. It is extremely tall (nearly 4.6 m) and graceful, with

The Late Saxons

a rounded lower section, a sliced-off, square-sectioned shaft, and wheel-headed cross head with prominent central boss. It can be compared with some Manx sculptures, and displays the ring-chain pattern developed there by the sculptor Gaut. The scenes depicted are pagan, with the exception of a Crucifixion, and though Jellinge influence is apparent, the diversity of creatures that adorn it are naturalistic and well observed. It is at once a blend of all the

109 There is nothing Scandinavian about this late cross head in Durham Cathedral. Executed between 995 and 1083, it represents the continuity of the earlier traditions of Northumbrian crosses. The panel in the centre depicts the Lamb of God

traditions of Britain that were current around AD 1000, a blend which is distinctive of its age and totally individualistic.

Metalwork

While sculptors and manuscript illuminators were experimenting with new ideas from overseas, and blending them with native styles and skills into new and exciting expressions, the ornamental metalworkers were not idle.

Anglo-Saxon metalworkers were famous in Europe for

110 This silver and niello mount for a drinking horn comes from the Trewhiddle Hoard, Cornwall. Deposited c. 875, the hoard includes a number of pieces decorated in what as a result has been termed the 'Trewhiddle style'. The animals are ultimately descended from those of pagan Saxon times, but are now much more naturalistic

their skills, and some of the examples of their work that have come down to us can rate as among the finest of their age in Europe. Their best medium was silver, which had ousted gold in the middle Saxon period, and this was to be combined with a black paste inlay (niello) to produce outstanding effects.

The finest style of late Saxon ornamental metalwork is named after a hoard found at Trewhiddle in Cornwall,

The Late Saxons

111 The Fuller Brooch. The most outstanding example of late Saxon metalwork, this depicts personifications of the Five Senses, with Sight in the centre. It dates from the ninth century, and is of silver inlaid with niello. Diameter: 11.2 cm

dated by coin finds to c. 875. The hoard includes an undecorated silver liturgical chalice, a liturgical scourge, strap ends, strap slides, a pin and curved drinking horn mounts, which are ornamented with small yapping animals twisted into triangular and other frames, their fur indicated with dots. They are descendants of the animals of Anglo-Saxon art of earlier ages, but they are, despite their contortions, relatively naturalistic. Foliage motifs were also used by the Trewhiddle artists, and these can be seen along with animals on the ring from Poslingford, Suffolk, here executed in gold. Nielloed silver inlays in Trewhiddle style were set into two of the finest Anglo-Saxon swords to have survived, that from Abingdon and that from the river Witham, in Lincolnshire. The style also appears on the sword found near Richmond in Yorkshire in 1976.

Nielloed silver was used to different effect on two ninth-century disc brooches. Disc brooches, made from a plate

The Late Saxons

with bosses, were the descendants of the gold and garnet brooches of pagan times, but the bosses (usually five) were now of minor importance. The Strickland Brooch, named after Sir William Strickland, a nineteenth-century collector, has inset gold plates, and is ornamented with backward-looking animals in a style reminiscent of Trewhiddle. The Fuller Brooch, on the other hand, has somewhat different animals interspersed with rosettes and human faces round its border. The rest of the ornament is human, and comprises personifications of the Five Senses.

The story of the Fuller Brooch is fascinating, and a fitting end to this survey of the Anglo-Saxons. With its classical personifications it epitomizes the final triumph of Anglo-Saxon civilization over centuries of barbarism. Alas, the triumph was short-lived, for in 1066 the Normans came. However, the Fuller Brooch survived this occurrence if much of English culture did not. Its history is unknown until 1910 when it was said to have been bought by a London junk dealer who claimed to know nothing of its antecedents. It was placed on display in the Ashmolean Museum in Oxford, but pronounced to be a fake by some of the leading experts of the day. After this it was sold for the price of the metal to Captain Fuller. In 1949 the Strickland Brooch came to light and was recognized as being similar to the nearly forgotten Fuller Brooch. Captain Fuller allowed the British Museum to carry out tests on it which proved its authenticity. He then nobly allowed the museum to buy it for a nominal sum with the stipulation that it would be known henceforth as the Fuller Brooch since he was the only person (apart from the archaeologist E. T. Leeds) who had believed in it.

Epilogue Chapter five
The Normans and after

In many respects the Norman Conquest was a non-event. If it is deemed essential to break up the pattern of history into convenient units, it is arguable that the date to be sought is AD 800 or AD 1200, not 1066. The modern view of history is in large measure dictated by that of contemporary chroniclers. It was not in the interests of the contemporaries of the Normans to paint them as they were, uncultured Norsemen descended from the Vikings. The extant chronicles are mostly the work of churchmen, for they above all others carried the Classical flag of literacy through the Middle Ages. However, an educated cleric's view of his society would have been very different from that held by landowners or peasants, who were the upholders of a tradition which stretched back through the post-Roman centuries into the prehistory of northern Europe, little affected by changes at the top of the social pyramid.

This is not of course to assert that the Norman Conquest had no effect on England: the Normans certainly introduced new elements into English life which were gradually absorbed, and brought about the gradual disappearance of others. They introduced a new ruling dynasty to England: almost all the top people were replaced by Normans. By the time the Domesday Book was drawn up in 1086 only two out of 1,400–1,500 tenants-in-chief who held land from the king were English, and only 8 per cent of the land was in English hands.

Most English institutions were entirely taken over by the Normans, including the basic structure of courts of shire and hundred, though William strengthened the position of sheriff to bring it more in line with that of the Norman *vicompte*. The Anglo-Saxon fiscal system was also continued, and though the legal system was extended the basis remained that of Anglo-Saxon England. There were few immediate changes in Church organization, though William regarded the Church as part of the State, and considered bishops as instruments of government.

Culturally, England remained firmly Anglo-Saxon. In the field of the arts it was only vernacular literature that was to suffer badly from the Norman Conquest. Painting and

Epilogue
The Normans and after

sculpture continued as before, and until the end of the eleventh century churches were being put up that were Anglo-Saxon in all but date.

Just how strong the Saxon tradition was in Norman England is underlined by the fierce debates that have surrounded the dating of several major sculptures and churches. Are they pre- or post-Conquest? The problem is well exemplified by the Chichester Reliefs, now usually regarded as being of the twelfth century, but which have also been claimed as pre-Conquest. One depicts the Raising of Lazarus, the other Mary and Martha greeting Christ at the gate of Jerusalem. The art-historical arguments have tended to cancel one another out, and in the final analysis the late dating is preferred on account of the fact that they are carved from imported Caen stone. Similar arguments have surrounded the dating of the larger of the two Roods at Romsey Abbey, Hants, and other, less famous, controversies could be cited. When we turn to churches, it is apparent that many of the features that are regarded as 'Norman' in English architecture were already present before the Conquest. Edward the Confessor's church at Westminster, built between 1045 and 1050, was in Norman style, with a full triforium and clerestory.

In manuscript illumination the same blurring of the divide between Saxon and Norman is apparent. The later eleventh century was a period of relative stagnation no doubt partly due to the ecclesiastical reforms. Changes in styles of handwriting have been used to distinguish the pre-Norman from the early post-Conquest manuscripts illuminated at Canterbury. A copy of one of the earlier drawings in the Harley 603 manuscript (originally illustrated c. AD 1000, see p. 172) was added after the Conquest on a blank space at the end of the text, and its style, though differing from the original, is nevertheless purely Anglo-Saxon.

If changes might be expected in institutions and art, the general pattern of life in England need not be expected to have changed much, and this seems to have been the case. The Domesday Book provides a picture of life in rural England as true to the late Saxon age as the Norman, and there is no reason to suppose that village life was disrupted. Many everyday articles in use in medieval England go back to Saxon or Viking origins: axes identical to those that appear wielded by carpenters in late Saxon manuscripts, were still in use as late as the fourteenth century. If this seems natural enough in the case of basic tools, it is less natural in weaponry. In Norman England two types of sword were fashionable, the one which was derived from Viking prototypes in Normandy, the other which had similar Viking origins but was developed in late Saxon England. Saxon style disc-brooches were still being worn for some time after the Normans landed, and on a humble level archaeologists have found little change in fashion. In material terms, the Saxo-Norman overlap can most clearly be seen in the pottery. Anglo-Saxon types (such as Thetford Ware and Stamford Ware, see p. 156) continued to be made and used alongside other 'medieval' forms which themselves can be traced back before the Norman Conquest. Saxo-Norman pottery was certainly still fashionable in the twelfth century in many areas, and derivative versions were being produced probably until the end of the century.

Recent studies have shown that the Normans were not responsible for the growth of towns in early England, as was often formerly supposed. It has been demonstrated how towns blossomed in late Saxon England: the Normans merely took them over, following the late Saxon layout and overall plan.

It is true, however, that the Normans also continued what the Anglo-Saxons had begun. They founded new boroughs, and established colonies of French traders in some of the old ones. French words appear more frequently in the language of trade (as they did in government and legal spheres), but this may be as much due to the continuing pattern of trade with France that had started in Saxon times as to the Conquest itself, and the town development might easily have continued without Norman encouragement. The growth of international trade was certainly not the product purely of the Norman Conquest. Recent archaeological studies of imports show very clearly that instead of a Saxon trade with the Rhineland switching to a Norman trade with France as previously thought, England traded with both areas before and after the Conquest.

Norman French does not seem to have asserted itself as the language of the farming or fishing industries. Here Anglo-Saxon ruled into the Middle Ages. Nor does it seem to have resulted in a spate of new Norman French place-names. We can point to a few, such as Ashby-de-la-Zouche, Melton Mowbray, Stoke Mandeville and Thorpe Morieux, where French family names were combined with older English names, and a few others, such as Beauchamp, Beaufort, Beauly and Richmond which were estate names. By and large, however, they relate to the new aristocracy, and reflect no change at humble level.

Little or no change took place in the rural scene. Most

Epilogue
The Normans and after

Epilogue
The Normans and after

English villages seem to have late Saxon origins, as has been shown to be the case by excavation at Wharram Percy in Yorkshire and West Whelpington in Northumberland, but there are still too many gaps in our knowledge to speak with confidence about village development in the period between AD 1000 and 1200. From the twelfth century onwards the longhouse, with byre and dwelling quarters under the same alignment, is the dominant house type in England until climatic and other factors led to new house types in the later Middle Ages. There is no doubt that the longhouse is of respectable, even prehistoric, ancestry in Europe, but when it came to England is something of a mystery, for we have no evidence for it before the twelfth century that is in any way conclusive. It is unlikely to be a Norman introduction, for many reasons, and in the absence of other information must be assumed to be late Saxon, like the field systems that went with village life.

But if any proof is needed of the ultimate blending of traditions, Saxon, Norman and even Viking, to form something distinctively English, one need look no further than the little parish church of Kilpeck, Hereford. Built in the twelfth century, the church is a veritable museum of styles. Appropriately enough, part of the very fabric is pre-Conquest – the north-east quoin of the nave. But everything else was put up in the twelfth century, when Norman England was an established reality. The architecture is Norman Romanesque, of the type developed not in England but on the Continent. The fine south porch is a classic example of the Normal ideal, with its round head and carved tympanum. But the rich carving which adorns it and other parts of the church could never be found in France. Some of the twisting animals are in the Viking Urnes style, while other figures echo a Saxon and a Celtic past. Alongside these images native to Britain are others, some Norman, some more exotic still – strange beasts from the East which perhaps made their first appearance on English soil on tapestries and other luxuries brought by Crusaders from far-off lands.

Among the small gargoyle-like sculptures on the outside of Kilpeck, one is famous. The Whore of Kilpeck offers herself to pious visitors, blatantly of the human world. Yet she represents a survival from a more remote past even than that of Anglo-Saxon England, a barbaric past, which runs as a dark stream through British history.

The best of Anglo-Saxon England

Visible remains of the Anglo-Saxons in England are mostly confined to churches and sculptures, with a very few earthworks. A comprehensive survey of the visible remains can be found in L. and J. Laing, *A Guide to the Dark Age Remains of Britain* (London, 1979); here we list fifty of the best arranged geographically.

Site	County	OS Grid Ref	Description
Wareham	Dorset	SY 9287	Town defences and church
Bradford-on-Avon	Wilts	ST 8261	Church and sculpture
Codford St Peter	Wilts	ST 9640	Cross shaft
Worth	Sussex	TQ 3036	Church
Sompting	Sussex	TQ 1605	Church
Bosham	Sussex	SU 8003	Church
Stoughton	Sussex	SU 8011	Church
Romsey	Hants	SU 3521	Church and sculptures
Breamore	Hants	SU 1518	Church
Reculver	Kent	TR 2269	Church
Canterbury	Kent	TR 1557	Churches
Deerhurst	Glos	SO 8729	Church, and Odda's Chapel
Sandbach	Cheshire	SJ 7661	Crosses
Offa's Dyke	English-Welsh	SJ 2558 etc.	Linear earthwork
Wat's Dyke	Border	SJ 2369 etc.	Linear earthwork
Bakewell	Derbys	SK 2168	Sculptures
Wirksworth	Derbys	SK 2854	Sculpture
Repton	Derbys	SK 3026	Church with crypt
Breedon-on-the-Hill	Derbys	SK 4022	Sculptures
Earl's Barton	Northants	SP 8563	Church
Brixworth	Northants	SP 7470	Church
Brigstock	Northants	SP 9485	Church
Barnack	Northants	TF 0705	Church
Peterborough	Cambs	TL 1998	Hedda's Stone, sculpture
Devil's Ditch	Cambs	TL 5864 and Tl 6261	Linear earthwork
Wing	Bucks	SP 8822	Church
North Elmham	Norfolk	TF 9821	Cathedral
Great Dunham	Norfolk	TF 8714	Church
Greensted	Essex	TL 5303	Timber church
Bradwell-on-Sea	Essex	TM 0308	Church
Stow	Lincs	SK 8881	Church
Barton-on-Humber	Lincs	TA 0321	Church
Broughton	Lincs	SE 9608	Church
Ripon	Yorks	SE 3171	Church with crypt
Nunburnholme	Yorks	SE 8548	Sculpture
Brompton	Yorks	SE 3896	Sculptures

The best of Anglo-Saxon England

Site	County	OS Grid Ref	Description
Leeds	Yorks	SE 3033	Cross, parish churchyard
York	Yorks	SE 5951	Tower on town wall
Ilkley	Yorks	SE 1147	Crosses
Kirk Hammerton	Yorks	SE 4655	Church
Escomb	Durham	NZ 1930	Church
St Andrew, Bishop Auckland	Durham	NZ 2228	Church, sculpture
Monkwearmouth	Durham	NZ 4057	Monastic church
Jarrow	Durham	NZ 3365	Monastic church
Durham	Durham	NZ 2743	Sculptures and relics of St Cuthbert in cathedral
Hexham	Northumberland	NY 9364	Crypt and sculptures
Bewcastle	Cumbria	NY 5674	Cross
Irton	Cumbria	SD 1000	Cross
Gosforth	Cumbria	NY 0703	Cross
Ruthwell	Dumfries	NY 1068	Cross

Further reading

General
The best general introduction to Anglo-Saxon England is perhaps G. A. Lester, *The Anglo-Saxons, How they Lived and Worked* (Newton Abbot, 1976). Though now out of date in many respects, D. Whitelock, *The Beginnings of English Society* (Harmondsworth, 1952) in the Pelican History of England, is also a useful general introduction. Slightly less useful are R. I. Page, *Life in Anglo-Saxon England* (London, 1970), which confines itself almost entirely to documentary sources; D. P. Kirby, *The Making of Early England* (London and New York, 1967) and P. Hunter-Blair, *An Introduction to Anglo-Saxon England* (Cambridge, 1959). The last two are similarly document-oriented, and Hunter-Blair's book now seems very old-fashioned. H. R. Loyn, *Anglo-Saxon England and the Norman Conquest* (London, 1962) is a first-rate introduction to the economic and social history of the period, and gives some consideration to archaeological evidence.

For the archaeology, the best introduction is D. M. Wilson, *The Anglo-Saxons* (2nd edn, Harmondsworth, 1971). The new 'standard' text is D. M. Wilson (ed.), *The Archaeology of Anglo-Saxon England* (London and Harmondsworth, 1976), which is a collection of studies of particular topics with linking essays by the editor. The pagan Saxons are dismissed cursorily, as is art and a number of other important topics, and though the individual essays contain much useful information they are very technical and not readily intelligible to the non-specialist.

For the history, the standard text is F. M. Stenton, *Anglo-Saxon England* (2nd edn, Oxford, 1947) in the Oxford History of England, though R. H. Hodgkin, *A History of the Anglo-Saxons* (Oxford, 1933) is very good for the period up to Alfred the Great.

The Continental background
The best study of the continental Germans before the migrations is M. Todd, *The Northern Barbarians, 100 BC – 300 AD* (London, 1975), though M. Todd, *Everyday Life of the Barbarians* (London, 1972) is also very useful. P. Dixon, *Barbarian Europe* (London, 1976) is a first-rate survey of the migration period, lavishly illustrated, and also discusses Anglo-Saxon England.

The pagan Saxons
A highly personal introduction to the history of the period is furnished by J. Morris, *The Age of Arthur* (rev. edn, London, 1975); a more orthodox view of both history and archaeology is to be found in L. Alcock, *Arthur's Britain* (Harmondsworth, 1971). The settlements viewed through pottery evidence are traced in J. N. L. Myres, *Anglo-Saxon Pottery and the Settlement of England* (Oxford, 1969) and J. N. L. Myres, *The Angles, the Saxons and the Jutes* (1970), available as a reprint in *Proceedings of the British Academy*, LVI,

Further reading

145–74. Myres's dating and attribution of particular pot styles to named groups of settlers is not followed by all. The archaeology of pagan Saxon cemeteries is reviewed in G. Baldwin Brown, *The Arts in Early England*, vols II and III, *Saxon Art and Industry in the Pagan Period* (1915), in N. Aberg, *The Anglo-Saxons in England in the early Centuries after the Invasion* (Uppsala, 1926) and in E. T. Leeds, *Early Anglo-Saxon Art and Archaeology* (Oxford, 1936) and his *The Archaeology of the Anglo-Saxon Settlements* (Oxford, 1913, reprinted 1970). All these are very out-of-date in various ways, and should be read in the light of the more recent books. Some discussion of burial practice precedes A. Meaney, *A Gazetteer of Early Anglo-Saxon Burial Sites* (London, 1964), which is otherwise exactly what the title suggests, while V. Evison, *The Fifth-century Invasions South of the Thames* (London, 1965) discusses a lot of interesting material from a standpoint which few accept. The British Museum *Guide to Anglo-Saxon Antiquities* (London, 1923) discusses the main pagan as well as Christian antiquities. All these books, with the exception of the last, are technical and for the enthusiast rather than the general reader.

The general reader, however, will enjoy two studies of Sutton Hoo, C. Green, *Sutton Hoo* (London, 1963) and R. L. S. Bruce-Mitford, *The Sutton Hoo Ship Burial: A Handbook* (London, 1968). The first volume of the final report on Sutton Hoo has been published, but is of little interest to the non-specialist. For pagan religion, B. Branston, *Lost Gods of England* (London, 1974) is a good introduction.

Midde Saxon England
Apart from the general works already listed which cover the history of the period, churches are described in detail alphabetically in H. M. and J. Taylor, *Anglo-Saxon Architecture*, 2 vols (Cambridge, 1965) and vol. 3 (1978), while a slightly old-fashioned historical account of them can be found in A. Clapham, *English Romanesque Architecture*, vol. I (Oxford, 1930). Coinage is outlined in G. C. Brooke, *English Coins* (London, 1950), now somewhat out of date, M. Dolley (ed.), *Anglo-Saxon Coins* (London, 1961) and J. J. North, *English Hammered Coinage*, vol. I: *Early Anglo-Saxon to Henry III* (London, 1963).

Late Saxon England
Apart from the general works, a good account of the history of the Vikings in Britain can be found in H. Loyn, *The Vikings in Britain*, (London, 1977). The background to Viking England can be found in P. H. Sawyer, *The Age of the Vikings* (2nd edn, London, 1971) and D. Wilson, *The Vikings and Their Origins* (London, 1970).

Art
Art is surveyed in two companion volumes, T. D. Kendrick, *Anglo-Saxon Art to AD 900* (London, 1938) and *Late Saxon and Viking Art* (London, 1949). Late Saxon art is also dealt with in D. Talbot Rice, *English Art 871–1100* (London, 1952). For manuscripts, see M. Rickert, *Painting in Britain in the Middle Ages* (Harmondsworth, 1965) and for sculpture, L. Stone, *Sculpture in Britain in the Middle Ages* (Harmondsworth, 1955). For ornamental metalwork, see R. Jessup, *Anglo-Saxon Jewellery* (1950) and his *Anglo-Saxon Jewellery* (Aylesbury, 1974).

Index

A

Abercorn shaft, 114
Aberlady shaft, 114
Acca's Cross, 114
adzes, 120
Aethelbald of Mercia, 94
Aethelbert of Kent, 33
Aethelflaed, 137, 145, 146
Aethelfrith of Bernicia, 93
Aethelred the Unready, 138, 139, 140, pl. 84
Aethelstan, king of Wessex, 137, 138
Aethelwold, St, 132, 161
Akerman, John Yonge, 5, pl. 4
Aidan, St, 99
Alaric, king of the Visigoths, 17
Alcfrith, king of Deira, 114
Alcuin of York, 132, 133, 136, 168
Aldborough, 41
Alfred, king of Wessex, 116, 128, 131, 137, 143–5, 157, 162
Alfred Jewel, 130–1, pl. 83
Alfriston (Sussex), 121
Alkham (Kent), 86
Allamanni, 10, 28
altar, of St Cuthbert, 111–12
amber, 150
Ambrosius, 30
Ambrosius Aurelianus, 30, 32
Amherst Brooch, 69
Ammianus Marcellinus, 11
Anastasius Dish, 50, pl. 21
Ancaster (Lincs), 40
Angles, 10, 23, 25, 26, 79, 97, 137
Anglo-Saxon Chronicle, 22, 133, 136, 138
Antonine Wall, 27, 129
architecture, church, 101–4
armour, 14, 121
army, Roman, 28
Arnegunde, Queen, 72
art: Ada School, 168; Carolingian, 168–9; Fusion Style, 73; Jellinge Style, 177–8, pls 106, 107; Late Antique, 104; Late Saxon, 167–82; Middle Saxon, 104–16; Pagan Saxon, 57–75; Rheims School, 168; Ringerike, 178–9; Style I, 63–5, 69; Style II, 71–3; Urnes, 179; Winchester School, 167 ff; *see also* embroideries, metalwork, sculpture
Arthur, king of the Britons, 32
Asdings, *see* Vandals
Ashmolean Museum (Oxford), 130, 178
Asser, *Life of King Alfred*, 132
Astarte, 86
Athelney (Somerset), 130
Attila the Hun, 16, 17
Aubrey, John, 4
augers, 120
Augustine, St, 94, 95, 98, 100, 101
Augustine of Hippo St, 96
Augustus, 9, 10
axe hammers, 120
axes, 120

B

barrel, 121
Barton-on-Humber (Lincs), 121; church, 162–3
Bassa, 88
Bath (Somerset), 33
Battle of Maldon, 57
Bede, 6, 22, 23, 24, 90, 104, 110
belt fittings, 34, 60, pls 10, 30
Benedict Biscop, 104, 105
Benedictine Rule, 161
Benedictional of St Aethelwold, 172, pl. 102
Benty Grange (Derbys), 50, 131, pl. 22
Beowulf, 48–9, 52, 55, 75, 117
Bernicia, 93
Bertha, queen of Kent, 33, 97, 100, 101
Bewcastle Cross, 112–13, pl. 70
Bifrons (Kent), 60, 65, pls 29, 33
Blacklow Hill (Warwick), 86
boat, 152
bone, 121; boneworking, 127
Book of Cerne, pl. 105
Book of Chad, *see* Lichfield Gospels
Book of Durrow, 75, 106, pl. 65
Bornholm, 15
Boudicca, queen of Iceni, 27
bowl; Sutton Hoo, pl. 59; York, pl. 89
bows, 54
bracteates, 43, 65, 71, 73
Bradford-on-Avon (Wilts), 167
Bradwell-on-Sea (Essex), 101, 102
Breedon-on-the Hill (Leics), 174–5
bretwaldas, 117
Brighthampton (Oxon), 55, pl. 26
British Museum, 21, 115
Brixworth (Northants), 103, pl. 63
brooches: cruciform, 60, pl. 31; disc, 67–9, pls 40, 41, 87; equal-armed, 61; long, pls 38, 39; plate, 61–2; quoit, 59, 60, pl. 28; saucer, 61, 62, pl. 32; square-headed, 64–5, pls 33, 34, 35; *see also* jewellery
Brown, Baldwin, 6
Brunanburh, battle of, 138
Brunswick Casket, 175, 176
buckelurnen, 79, pl. 52
buckets, 121, pl. 56
buckles, pls 11, 29, 42, 43, 58
building techniques, 150, 163–4, pl. 86
Burgh Castle (Norfolk), pl. 14
Burgundians, 10, 28
burghs, 143–6, pl. 85
burial rites, 81–5
burials, 11, 12, 15, 19, 20, 24, 34, 41–2, 49–50, 54, 58, 75–87, 141, pls 15, 16, 53, 54; Cuthbert's tomb, 109–12, pl. 68; Christian graves, 90, 95–6
Butley, 86
Byzantium, 14, 18

C

Cadwallon, 93, 119
Caenby (Lincs), 13, 75
Caistor-by-Norwich (Norfolk), 40, 56, pls 49, 50
Cambridge, 41
Camden, William, 4, 9, 54, pl. 1
Camlann, battle of, 32
camps, Danish, 143
Canterbury (Kent), 38, 88, 95, 97, 100, 101, 123, 124, 126, 140, 161; manuscripts, 108–9
Canterbury Psalter, 108, pl. 67
Caractacus, 27

Carausius, 16
carpentry, 120, 127
Cassian, John, 100
Casterton (Lincs), 40
Catholme (Notts), 47, 118
Catterick (Yorks), 41
Ceawlin, 33, 94
Cedd, St, 102
cemetery, 57, 95 ff, 141; *see also* burials
Ceolfrith, abbot of Jarrow, 107
ceramics, *see* pottery
Cerdic, 56, 94
Chadlington (Oxon), 81
Chalton (Hants), 45, 47, 48, 118
charcoal burning, 120
Charlemagne, 94, 132, 168
Cheddar (Somerset), 159–60, pls 95, 96
Chepstow (Gwent), 129
chisel, 120, 121, 127
Christianity, 88, 129, 141
Church, 85, 135, 160–2; Anglo-Saxon churches, 88–9, 99–104, 162–7, pls 60, 62, 63, 97, 98, 99
churl, 117
Cirencester (Glos), 33
Clapham, Sir Alfred, 103
clothing, 11, pl. 17
Clovis, king of the Franks, 33
Cnut (Canute), king, 136, pl. 84, 139, 140, 153, 158, 177
Codex Ammianus MS, 107
Codex Aureus, 108
Codford St Peter (Wilts), 173
coinage, 157–9; coins, 25, 43, 66, 122–5, 139, 153, pls 1, 8, 9, 76, 77, 78, 79, 80, 84, 93, 94
Constantinople, 17, 18
Colchester (Essex), 146
Colherne (Wilts), 173
combs, 77, 111, 121, pl. 88
Constantine, king of the Scots, 137
Constantine III, 29, 32, pl. 9
Constantius, 97
Coombe (Kent), 55
Council for British Archaeology, 8
Council of Hertford, 99
cowrie shells, 84
Crayke (Yorks), 120
cremations, 76ff
Cricklade (Wilts), 145, pl. 85
Crondall Hoard, pls 4, 77
cross, pectoral, 112, 114, pl. 69
Crundale (Kent), 72, 73, pls 43, 45
'Cumbri', 26
Cuthbert, St, 96, 99, 109–12
Cuthwulf, 33
Cynethryth, 124
Cynewulf, king of Wessex, 55
Cynheard, 55
Cynric, 32, 56, 94

D

Dacia, 16
Dalriada, 27
Danegeld, 139, 158
Danelaw, 136, 137, 140
Danes, 130, 140–3, 176; *see also* Vikings
Danish raids, 160, 162
Deerhurst (Glos), 166
defences, town, 128 ff, 143 ff, pl. 81
Deira, 93
Derby, 133
Devil's Ditch (Suffolk), 128, pl. 61
diet, 11, 149
dinar, 125
dogs, 83
Domesday Book, 146, 183
Dorchester-on-Thames (Oxon), 34, 38, 60
Dorestad, 126
Dover (Kent), 126; brooch, 69
drills, 120
Droitwich (Cheshire), 154
Dublin, 137
duck eggs, 83
Dunham Magna (Norfolk), 166
Dunnichen Moss, 93
Dunstan, St, 132, 161, 169, 170
Durham, 110
Durham Cathedral MS AII, 10, 105, pl. 64
dykes, 128–9
Dyrrham, battle of, 33

E

Eadred, king, 88
ealdorman, 117
Ealdred of Bamburgh, 137
Earl's Barton (Northants), 164, pls 97, 98
East Anglia, 91, 136
Easter, 86
Ecgberht, king of Kent, 124
Ecgfrith, king of Northumbria, 93
Echternack Gospels, 107
Eddius Stephanus, 90
Edgar, king, 146, 158
Edmund, king, 138
Edward the Confessor, 140, 159
Edward the Elder, 137
Edward the Martyr, 138
Edward III, 124
Edwin, king, 93, 98, 118, 119
Egbert, king, 88
Egypt, 85, 106
embroideries, 168–9, pl. 100
Eostre, 86
Eric Bloodaxe, 137, 138
Escomb (Co. Durham), 104

Essex, 91, 98
Ethandun, battle of, 130
Ethelburh, 98

F

farmsteads, 141
Farthingdown (Surrey), 81
Faussett, Rev. Bryan, 5, 19, 57, pls. 2, 3, 5, 6
Faversham (Kent), 55, 60, 72, 73, 75, 121, pls 42, 47
feasting, 57
Fetter Lane sword, 115, pl. 72
file, 121
Finglesham (Kent), 81
flute, 56
folc-gemot, 117, 118
Fordwich (Kent), 126
forts, 29, 30, 38, 39, 88–9, 102, 113, 118, 145, pls 13, 14
Franks, 10, 12, 14, 18, 23, 25, 33, 67, 135
Franks Casket, 52, 115–16, pl. 73
Franks, Sir Wolaston, 115
Fraomar, king, 28
Frig, 86
Frisia, 12, 123
Frisians, 10
Frobury, 86
Froyle, 86
Frydaythorpe, 86
Fuller Brooch, 131, 182, pl. 111
Furfooz, 15
futhorc, 87

G

Gainsborough (Yorks), 139
Gaiseric, 18
gaming pieces, 56–7
Gaul, 10, 15, 17, 97, 104
Gaut, 180
Germani, 10, 15, 28, 34
Germanus, St, 96, 97
gesith, 117
Gildas, 22, 23, 31, 32, 33
Gilton (Kent), 21
glassmakers, 104
glassware, 13, 48, 85, 121, 127, 149, pl. 57
Glastonbury (Somerset), 122
Gloucester, 33, 90, 133
Godwine, earl, 140
gold, 14–15, 19, 20, 71, 114
Gosforth Cross, 179–80, pl. 108
Gospel Book (Corpus Christi MS 286), 98
Gotland, 15
Goths, 10, 14, 16, 17, 69
Grauballe, 11

Graveney Boat, 151–2
graves, graveyards, *see* burials
Greasby (Cheshire), 143
Gregory, Pope, 97, 98, 131
Grendel, 56
Grimsby (Lincs), 133
Grimston End (Suffolk), 48
grubenhäuser, 13, 45, 48
Guthrum, 137
Gwynedd, 98

H

habitation, 12, 13, 24, 36, 40, 44–8, 118–19; *see also* houses, towns
Haddiscoe Thorpe (Norfolk), pl. 99
Hadrian's Wall, 27, 28, 34, 129
hammer, 120, 121
Hamwih, 126–8
Harald of Denmark, 139
Harleian Psalter, 171, pl. 101
Harley 603 MS, 172, pl. 103
Harold I, 140
Harrow-on-the-Hill (Middx), 86
Harthacnut, 140
Hatfield (Herts), 99
Hatfield Chase (Northumberland), 93
Hatton Rock, 119
hazel nuts, 83
Heaberht, king of Kent, 124
helmet, 50–1, 52, pls 22, 23
Hengist, 30, 31, 55
Heraclius, 96
Hereford, 128, pl. 81
heriot, 117
Heswall (Cheshire), 143
Hildesheim, 114
Hinton St Mary (Dorset), 95
Holy Roman Empire, 18
Holywell (Clwyd), 129
hones, 150
Honoratus, 100
Honorius, 29, pl. 9
Horsa, 30, 55
horses, 83
houses, 12, 13, 44–8, 149, 151, pl. 18
Huldremose, 11
Huns, 16, 17
Hurbuck (Co. Durham), 120
Hwicce, 91

I

Ida, 93
Illington–Lackford potter, 48, 80
industry, 127, 151–9
Ine, king of Wessex, 55
inhumation, 80–3

Iona, 98
Ipswich (Suffolk), 126
Irby (Cheshire), 143
iron, 154; iron-working, 121
ivories, 174, pls 104, 107
Ixworth Brooch, 115

J

Jarrow (Co. Durham), 23, 104, 107
jewellery, 15, 19, 20, 21, 24, 42, 43, 49–50, 57 ff, 77, 84–5, 96, 121, 130–1, pls 3, 4, 5, 7, 36, 37; *see also* brooches
Julius Caesar, 10, 14
Justinian, 17
Jutes, 10, 22, 24, 25, 65, 66, 78, 79

K

Kemble, John, 5
Kempston, 85
Kent, 33, 67 ff, 91, 101 ff, 121, 122, 124
keys, 85, 127
kingdoms, English, 91–5
Kingston (Kent), 85
Kingston Brooch, 19, 20, 57, pls 5, 6
Kingston Down (Kent), 81, 96, 121
knives, 77, 84, 127

L

Lammastide, 86
language, 142
lava quarries, 127
lead, 121, 154–5
leather, 15, 149
Leeds, E. T., 6
Leofric of Mercia, 140
Lichfield Gospels, 108
Lindisfarne (Northumberland), 99, 110; Gospels, 107, pl. 66
Lindsey, 91
linen, 121
Little Paxton, 132
Liudhard, 97, 101
Liverpool Museum, 19, 21
Llangollen (Clwyd), 97
Lombard, 10, 69
London, 38, 123, 126, 137, 139, 140, 146
Long Wittenham (Berks), 96
loom, 127
Lovedon Hill (Lincs), 87
lyre, 56, pl. 27

M

Magnus Mazimus, 29, pl. 8
Magonsaetan, 91
manors, 159–60
manuscripts, 104–9, 169–72
Marcomanni, 14, map 1
Marius, 10
Markshall (Norfolk), 79, pl. 51
Maroboduus, 14
Marston (Northants), 81
marten pelts, 152
Martin of Tours, St, 100
Mayer, Joseph, 21, pl. 3
Maxey (Northants), 118
mercenaries, 30, 34
Mercia, 91, 93, 99, 119, 128, 136, 137, 145, 157, 167, 174–5
metalworking, 48, 59–75, 114–15, 120, 127, 180–2
migrations, 16 ff
millstone grit, 127; millstones, 150
mints, 123
Mitcham (Surrey), 81
monasteries, 99–104, 130, 161
Mongols, 16
Monkton Brooch, 21, 69, pl. 7
Monkwearmouth (Co. Durham), 104, 107, 121
Mucking (Essex), 45, 121, pls 30, 36, 48, 53, 56, 57
music, 56

N

Nennius, 22, 23
New Minster (Winchester), 171
New Minster Charter, 171–2, 174
Norman Conquest, 140, 146, 147, 160, 183 ff
Norse, *see* Vikings
North Elmham (Norfolk), 57, 118, pl. 52
North Luffenham (Rutland), pl. 55
Northumbria, 91, 93, 99, 100, 110 ff, 118–19, 125, 136, 138, 167, 174
Norwegians, 140–3
Norwich, 146
Novgorod, 149

O

oak, 121
Odda's Chapel (Glos), 166
Offa of Mercia, 94, 124, 125, 128, 132, 157
Offa's Dyke, 128–9, pl. 82
Oland, 15
Old Minster (Winchester), 161
Old Windsor (Berks), 119

Orkneyinga Saga, 135
Ormside Bowl, 175, 176
Oswald, archbishop of York, 161
Oswy, king, 99
Otley Cross shaft, 178
Oxford, 65, 145, 146
ox sculls, 86
oysters, 48, 83

P

Paeda of Mercia, 99
painting, 104 ff, 169–72
palaces, 159–60
Paulinus, 98, 118
Pelagianism, 96
Pelagius, 96
Penda of Mercia, 93, 99, 119
pendants, *see* jewellery
Persia, 16
pewter, 121, 122
Picts, 28, 29, 97
place-names, 22, 26–7, 43–4, 85–6, 142–3
plane, 120
population, 146
Porchester (Hants), 38, 121, pl. 13
pottery, 13, 15, 25, 35, 41, 48, 77–80, 127, 141, 142, 151, 152, 153, pls 12, 15, 48, 49, 50, 51, 52, 90, 91, 92; Stamford Warae, 156–7, pl. 92; St Neots' Ware, 156–7; Thetford Ware, 156–7, pl. 91
priest, pagan, 85
Procopius, 23
Ptolemy, 10
purse (Sutton Hoo), pl. 19

Q

Quentovic, 126, 135
querns, 15, 127

R

Raedwald, king, 49, 98, pl. 19
Raegnald of York, 137
Reculver (Kent), 88–9, 101, pl. 60
religion, pagan, 75–87
Repton (Derbys), pl. 62
Richborough (Kent), 34, 95
Rickert, Dr Margaret, 109
Robert of Jumièges, 140
Rochester (Kent), 123
Romans, 27 ff
Rome, 17, 18, 132
Rome Gospels, 109
Rothbury Cross, 174
round towers (Norfolk), 166
Royal IE VI (Gospel book), 109

runes, 87, 124
Ruthwell Cross, 112–13

S

Saffron Walden (Essex), 80
Salin, 63–4
salt, 154; salt-making, 120
Sapperton (Yorks), 120
Sarre (Kent), 57, 120, 126; brooch, 69, pl. 28
Saxons, 10, 12, 23, 25, 26, 29, 97, 140–3
Scandinavia, 10 ff
sceattas, 123, 126
Scots, 93, 138
Scotti, 27, 28, 29
Scramasax, 54, pl. 25
sculpture, 112–14, 173–6
Scunthorpe (Lincs), 133
serfdom, 117
settlements, *see* habitation
Sevington (Wilts), 121, 127
Sewerby (Yorks), 81, pl. 54
shaft-furnaces, 121
Shakenoak (Oxon), 40
Shapur I, 16
shears, 48
Sherborne Pontifical, 170
shields, 53, 84, pl. 24
shrine, pagan, 85, 86
Sidonius Apollinarius, 40
silver, 121
silverware, 50
Siward of Northumbria, 140
slaves, 117, 153
Smith, Charles Roach, 5, 20, pl. 3
Snape (Suffolk), 81, 152
soap-making, 120
social structure, 116
Sompting (Sussex), 163
Southampton, 123; *see also* Hamwih
spade, 127
spear, 84; spearheads, 54
spindle whorls, 127
Spong Hill (Norfolk), 87
St Albans (Herts), 97
St Neots (Huntingdon), 132
Stamford (Lincs), 121
Staxton, 133
steatite, 150
Stone-by-Faversham (Kent), 95
stone trade, 155
Stonyhurst Gospels, 111
Strathclyde, 138
Strickland Brooch, 182
Strood (Glos), 96
stylus, 130
Sulgrave (Northants), 160
Sussex, 91, 99
Sutton Courtenay (Berks), 8

Sutton Hoo (Suffolk), 49, 50, 51, 52, 55, 56, 73, 75, 81, 85, 107, 123, 131, 152, pls 23, 24, 27, 59
Swedes, *see* Vikings
Swein Forkbeard, 139
swords, 13, 14, 54, 55, 84, 121, 181, pl. 26
Symeon of Durham, 44, 90, 132
Synod of Whitby, 99

T

Tacitus, 10
Tamworth (Staffs), 121, 128, 146, pl. 75
tanneries, 149
Taplow (Bucks), 57, 72, 81, 85, pl. 44
Tassilio Chalice, 115
temples, pagan, 86
textiles, 121, 127
thane, 117
Theodore of Tarsus, 99
Theodoric, 17, 181, pl. 110
Thetford (Norfolk), 151
Thingwall (Cheshire), 143
Thor, 80
Thoresbjerg, 11
thrymsas, 123
Thundersfield (Essex), 86
Thunor, 86
Thuringians, 10
Thurmaston (Leics), 41
timber, 150
Tiw, 86, 87
Tollund Man, 11
tongs, 121
tools: woodworking, 120; smith's, 121
Tovi the Proud, 140
towns, 122–9, 143–51
trade, 14 ff, 48, 85, 127, 148–50, 151–9
tremisses, 122–3, pl. 76
Treuddyn (Clwyd), 129
tribal organisation, 15ff
Tuesley, 86
tweezers, 77

V

Valerian, 16
Vallhagar, 12
Vandals, 10, 17, 18, 28
Varangian guard, 135
Vermand, 34, 60, 61, 62
Victoria and Albert Museum, 174
Vikings, 95, 133–40, 175, 177, 183
villas, 39–40
Vinland Saga, 135
Visigoths, 17
Vortigern, 29, 30, 31, 34, 35

W

Wakerley (Northants), 121
Wales, 91
Wallingford (Berks), 145
Wansdyke, 86
Wareham (Dorset), 145
warriors, 49–57
watermill, 75, 119, 121
Wat's Dyke, 128–9
weapons, 13, 49–57
weaving, 48, 85, 120
wedges, 120
Wednesbury (Staffs), 86
Wednesfield (Stafs), 86
Weedon Beck (Northants), 86
Weeford, 86
weekdays, 86
Wehden, 80
Weland Smith, 121
well, 121
Welsh, 26, 93
wergild, 116, 117
Wessex, 91, 92, 93, 94–5, 116, 129, 137, 144, 157, 167, 173
Westley Waterless (Cambs), 120
West Dean (Sussex), 47
West Runton (Norfolk), 121
West Stow (Suffolk), 46, 48, pl. 18
Weyhill, 86
Wharram Percy (Yorks), 118
whetstones, 127, 153
Whitby (Yorks), 100
Wilfred, St, 99, 114
William the Conqueror, 140
Wilton (Norfolk), 96
Winchester (Hants), 34, 38, 120, 121, 126, 145, 161
wine, 57
Winnal (Hants), 82
Wirral (Cheshire), 143
Witan, 117
Witham Pins, 115, pl. 71
Woden, 86, 93
wood, 13; woodworking, 120, 149
wool, 152–3
Worthy Park (Hants), 82
Wroxeter (Salop), fig. 1
wyrm, 80

Y

Yeavering (Northumberland), 118–19, 159, pl. 74
York, 38, 41, 123, 126, 136, 137, 138, 147–50, pls 86, 87

For Product Safety Concerns and Information please contact our EU representative GPSR@taylorandfrancis.com
Taylor & Francis Verlag GmbH, Kaufingerstraße 24, 80331 München, Germany

www.ingramcontent.com/pod-product-compliance
Lightning Source LLC
Chambersburg PA
CBHW061446300426
44114CB00014B/1859